The Best of Hack and /

Linux Admin Crash Course

Kyle Rankin

Copyright © 2023 Kyle Rankin

PUBLISHED BY KYLE RANKIN

HTTPS://KYLERANK.IN/WRITING.HTML

All Rights Reserved. No part of this work may be reproduced or transmitted in any form or by any means, electronic or mechanical, including photocopying, recording, or by any information storage or retrieval system, without the prior written permission of the copyright owner and the publisher.

ISBN-13: 978-1-312-74300-7
First edition, April 2023

To Joy, who has supported my writing from the beginning, and who always encourages me by words and example to be a better writer.

Contents

1	Sysadmin 101	1
1.1	The Importance of Learning IT Fundamentals	2
1.2	Leveling Up: A Sysadmin Career Path	3
1.3	Automation	9
1.4	Ticketing	13
1.5	Patch Management	17
1.6	Alerting	19
1.7	Preparing for Vacation	25
1.8	Travel Laptops Tips in Practice	30
2	Sysadmin's Toolbox	35
2.1	Filesystem Hierarchy Standard	36
2.2	Scheduling One-time Jobs with At	40
2.3	Sort and Uniq	43
2.4	Tracking Bandwidth with Iftop	46
2.5	Right Command, Wrong Server	49
2.6	Chopping Logs	52
2.7	Shorter Commands	56
2.8	Add Progress Bars to dd	57

| 2.9 | Lock Files with the flock Command | 59 |

3 Home Servers … 63
3.1	Setting Up Your Network	64
3.2	Setting Up A Home DNS Server	67
3.3	A Local Mail Server	75
3.4	Clustering with Raspberry Pis	78
3.5	Home As Your Backup Data Center	85

4 Server Projects … 91
4.1	Last Minute Secondary Mail Server	92
4.2	Check Exchange from the Command Line	95
4.3	Migrate to a New Hard Drive	98
4.4	Remotely Wipe a Server	101
4.5	Preseeding Full Disk Encryption	105
4.6	Localhost DNS Cache	107
4.7	PXE Magic	110
4.8	More PXE Magic	117

5 When Disaster Strikes … 125
5.1	Stop Killing Your Cattle	125
5.2	Troubleshooting High Load	126
5.3	Troubleshooting the Local Network	133
5.4	Troubleshooting Remote Networks	138
5.5	Troubleshooting with Telnet	143
5.6	Collecting Server Metrics with Sar	146
5.7	Dynamic DNS Disaster	150
5.8	Troubleshoot Full Disks	152
5.9	Hard Drive Crashes	156
5.10	Recover the Master Boot Record	160
5.11	Restoring Deleted Files	165

Appendices … 169

A My Favorite Infrastructure … 169

Index 183

Preface

I wrote for Linux Journal magazine for almost 12 years starting in their January 2008 issue until Linux Journal closed for good on August 7, 2019. I wrote a monthly column titled "Hack and /" that aimed to provide useful tips and tricks on topics ranging from system administration to security to 3D printing to VIM. In addition to the column I also wrote a number of feature and "Deep Dive" articles over the years.

After we published my final farewell article for Linux Journal, one of the most common questions I got was "what's going to happen to the giant archive of articles?" The question made sense, given I find myself routinely returning to my own Linux Journal articles. When you write a monthly column on Linux tips, they ultimately become a brain dump of whatever it is you happen to be working on at the time. As I would discover something useful, the column became a great place to document it. After Linux Journal shut down, I started reviewing my own backlog of articles and discovered so many useful gems–many of which I had forgotten about and many that were just as relevant today as when I originally wrote them. While I covered many topics in my column, since I was a sysadmin throughout most of my time at Linux Journal many of my articles focused on that topic. I realized I had a whole book's worth of material just in sysadmin tips alone.

When I got started in system administration there was a much better opportunity for someone to learn the fundamental skills you need to manage Linux servers. I started out in IT but a major part of that job involved setting up bare-metal Linux servers to host web sites, act as local office file servers, routers or DNS servers, or any number of common tasks. Just using Linux as your desktop OS exposed you to so many networking fundamentals and other skills that directly translated into system administration. Beyond that, as I worked in larger organizations I got a chance to work with other more senior sysadmin who taught me their own shortcuts, tips, and hard lessons learned when production went down.

Today many of these tasks have either been outsourced to cloud services, office appliances, or wrapped in GUI tools so that someone starting out in IT or system administration today has much less of an opportunity to learn these fundamentals. What's more, because of outsourcing and automation, the sysadmin roles that do exist are often added onto an existing "full stack" developer in a company. If a startup grows large enough, it may justify a full-time hire, but even then there's much less of an opportunity to mentor under a senior sysadmin and learn these skills. Many people in these roles today may never actually rack a physical server, or at least not as a junior sysadmin at a startup.

This book doesn't aim to be an exhaustive guide to everything you need to know to be a system administrator. Instead, this book allows me to act as a remote mentor to someone starting out in IT or system administration whether as a full-time job or as a full stack developer. Think of each section in a chapter like sitting down with me over lunch or looking over my shoulder as I show you a tip to save you time, a tool I've found useful, a lesson I learned the hard way, or an explanation of how I'd tackle a project you got assigned. While you can certainly read the book cover to cover, each section in a chapter also stands alone. This means you can also just skip through the book to sections you find interesting or relevant to you at the time. After all, it's not like a mentor would sit you down every morning at work with a curriculum to study–they'd show you tips and lessons as they come up at work or as you have questions.

> **Note:** I've made a conscious choice in this book to use the term system administrator or "sysadmin" to refer to Linux server administration roles. In many cases these same roles now fall under titles like DevOps Engineer, Production Systems Engineer, or Site Reliability Engineer and while in some companies those roles do have distinctions apart from a traditional sysadmin, in many cases they are the same. I am an advocate of the modern DevOps approach and philosophy to server administration. This philosophy encourages administrators to think about automation, reliability, and redundancy. It also aims to break down some of the traditional walls between administrators and developers, and encourages cooperation between those teams. It also encourages administrators to embrace software development practices of their own and become more embedded into development workflows.
>
> That said, some people today who are fans of DevOps philosophy use the

> term sysadmin with a negative connotation and as a way to refer to someone who holds on to outdated, pre-DevOps, anti-developer practices. I'm not one of those people. I've chosen to use the term sysadmin simply because most of the topics in this book fall under more traditional system administrator tasks.

The articles that comprise this book go back over a decade. Obviously technology constantly changes and where necessary, I've made sure to update any outdated information that works differently today then when I first wrote it. There were also articles that I did not include in the book because the tips were too out of date. That said, in many cases commands and projects haven't *needed* much updating because they happen to cover topics that haven't changed much. So if you see an old kernel, a reference to an old Linux distribution, or a log entry with a date stamp from years ago don't be alarmed—it's just a demonstration of how tried-and-true these tips are that they work just as well today as they did when they were first written.

Chapter 1: Sysadmin 101

In Chapter 1, I discuss the philosophy and craft of system administration. Instead of telling you how to configure a particular alerting or automation tool, or how to set up ticketing software, I discuss how to approach those topics at a high level regardless of which tools you use. I also outline a typical system administrator career path and discuss what kinds of skills and abilities you need to master to move to the next level in your career. Finally I talk about something very important to any sysadmin: time off! With production alerts going off all hours of the night and interruptions throughout the day, this line of work is prone to burnout. If you don't have a solid plan in place, a vacation for a sysadmin can be anything but restful, so I discuss how to plan ahead for vacation so that you can get the relaxation you need.

Chapter 2: Sysadmin's Toolbox

One of the most important fundamentals for a sysadmin to master is the command line, and in Chapter 2 I focus on command line tools and time-saving tips. I cover tools like sort, uniq, at, and flock and discuss tips to make sure you know which server you are running commands on so you don't make a mistake that brings down production. Finally I talk about how to parse logs on the command line, how to save keystrokes with shorter versions of common command-line commands, and how to get progress output with the powerful dd imaging command.

Chapter 3: Home Servers

One of the best places to learn new administration skills is at home and in the modern cloud-focused world, home servers are also one of the places you might still put traditional sysadmin skills into practice. Chapter 3 goes through a number of home server projects including DNS and mail servers, and how to use a pair of Raspberry Pis to create a fault-tolerant server cluster.

Chapter 4: Server Projects

Chapter 4 moves past home projects into projects aimed at enterprise environments. Think of this chapter as sitting down with me as I explain how I tackled a particular project at work, with tips you can use and adapt to your own projects. I cover tasks like creating emergency secondary mail servers, migrating to new hard drives, remotely wiping servers, and also how to set up a PXE network boot environment with menus.

Chapter 5: When Disaster Strikes

Disasters are where many sysadmin shine, and also where you often learn the most about Linux. Chapter 5 starts with a section that guides you through how to troubleshoot common server problems including high load and network connectivity issues. Then I dive into a few specific examples of how to recover from disasters including hard drive crashes, missing master boot records, and recovering deleted files.

Appendix A: My Favorite Infrastructure

At the very end of the book I decided to add an appendix where I explain in detail the infrastructure I built that I was the most proud of. While frameworks and approaches to building infrastructure change over time, I still look back on how that particular environment was organized and feel like there are lessons to learn there that you can apply to your own infrastructure even if you are locked into a particular cloud provider's toolset and approach.

Ultimately, I assembled this book because I recognized just how often I was looking up my own articles for tips on how to accomplish something. While I knew where the articles were scattered either on my local system or on the Linux Journal site, most people would have a hard time locating them or even remembering they existed. I hope that this book makes these tips, tricks and advice easier to find and use.

About The Author

Kyle Rankin has over two decades of professional Linux experience, and was a long-time systems administrator with a particular focus on infrastructure security, architecture, automation, and troubleshooting. In addition to this book he is the author of *Linux Hardening in Hostile Networks* (Pearson, 2017), *DevOps Troubleshooting* (Addison-Wesley, 2012), *The Official Ubuntu Server Book, Third Edition* (Prentice Hall, 2013), *Knoppix Hacks, 2nd Edition* (O'Reilly, 2007), and *Ubuntu Hacks* (O'Reilly, 2006), among other books. Rankin was an award-winning columnist and tech editor for Linux Journal, and speaks frequently on Open Source software including at SCALE, FOSDEM, O'Reilly Security Conference, Linux Fest NorthWest, BSidesLV, CactusCon, OSCON, Linux World Expo, and Penguicon.

1. Sysadmin 101

The combination of the DevOps approach to systems administration and the prevalence of cloud computing has fundamentally changed not just the responsibilities of a systems administrator but also the types of people who work in these modern roles and the kinds of teams they work on. DevOps has made the job title "systems administrator" seem a bit archaic much like the "systems analyst" title it replaced. Of course, more has changed than just the job title. DevOps positions are often rather different from sysadmin jobs in the past with a much larger emphasis on software development far beyond basic shell scripting and a focus on cloud automation using third party APIs. As a result where traditional sysadmins started out in IT roles, modern DevOps positions are often filled by people with software development backgrounds and without much prior sysadmin experience.

In modern DevOps positions it can even be challenging to gain traditional sysadmin experience. In the past, a sysadmin would enter the role at a junior level and be mentored by a senior sysadmin on the team who would pass down all of the hard lessons learned over the years. Teams are smaller now and in many cases startups can accomplish quite a lot with cloud outsourcing alone before they have to fill their first DevOps role. Even then, the role might be filled by someone who identifies more as a "full stack developer" than a sysadmin. As a result, the DevOps engineer might be thrust into a role managing production services with no mentor around apart from search engines and Stack Overflow posts.

This chapter aims to act as a kind of mentor so that if you are starting out or by yourself you don't have to learn these lessons the hard way. Where other chapters in the book feature more technical how-tos, this chapter is more philosophical. Each section passes down lessons learned over my many years as a systems administrator in topics ranging from the overall sysadmin career path, automation, ticketing, patch management, managing alerts both when on call and on vacation, and tips for when you work at home.

1.1 The Importance of Learning IT Fundamentals

I was recently discussing the Sysadmin/DevOps/IT industry with a colleague, and we started marveling at just how few of the skills we learned when we were starting out are actually needed today. It seems like every year a tool, abstraction layer or service makes it so you no longer need to know how this or that technology works. Why compile from source when all of the software you could want is prepackaged, tested and ready to install? Why figure out how a database works when you can just point to a pre-configured database service? Why troubleshoot a malfunctioning Linux server when you can nuke it from orbit and spawn a new one and hope the problem goes away?

This is not to say that automation is bad or that abstractions are bad. When you automate repetitive tasks and make complex tasks easier, you end up being able to accomplish more with a smaller and more junior team. I'm perfectly happy to take a tested and validated upstream kernel from my distribution instead of spending hours making the same thing and hoping I remembered to include all of the right modules. Have you ever compiled a modern web browser? It's not fun. It's handy being able to automate myself out of jobs using centralized configuration management tools.

As my colleague and I were discussing the good old days, what worried us wasn't that modern technology made things easier or that past methods were obsolete–learning new things is what drew us to this career in the first place–but that in many ways, modern technology has obscured so much of what's going on under the hood, we found ourselves struggling to think of how we'd advise someone new to the industry to approach a modern career in IT. The kind of opportunities for on-the-job training that taught us the fundamentals of how computers, networks and Linux worked are becoming rarer and rarer, if they exist at all.

My story into IT mirrors many of my colleagues who started their careers somewhere between the mid-1990s and early 2000s. I started out in a kind of hybrid IT and sysadmin jack-of-all-trades position for a small business. I did everything from installing and troubleshooting Windows desktops to setting up Linux file and web servers to running and crimping network wires. I also ran a Linux desktop, and in those days, it hid very little of the underpinnings from you, so you were instantly exposed to networking, software and hardware fundamentals whether you wanted them or not.

Being exposed to and responsible for all of that technology as "the computer guy", you learn pretty quickly that you just have to dive in and figure out how things work to fix them. It was that experience that cemented the Linux sysadmin and networking skills I continued to develop as I transitioned away from the help desk into a full-time Linux sysadmin. Yet small businesses are more likely to farm out most of their IT functions to the cloud, and sysadmins truly may not need to know almost anything about how Linux or networking works to manage Linux servers (and might even manage them from a Mac). So how do they learn what's going on under the hood?

This phenomenon isn't limited to IT. Modern artists, writers and musicians also are often unschooled in the history and unskilled in the fundamentals of their craft. While careers in science still seem to stress a deep understanding of everything that has come before, in so many other fields, it seems we are content to skip that part of the lesson and just focus on what's new. The problem when it comes to IT, however, isn't that you need to understand the fundamentals to get a good job–you don't–but when something goes wrong, without understanding what's happening behind the scenes at least to some degree, it's almost impossible to troubleshoot. When you can't fix the problem yourself, you are left rebooting, respawning or calling your vendor's support line. Without knowing about the technologies of the past and their features and failings, you are more likely to repeat their mistakes when someone new to the industry convinces you they just invented them.

Fortunately the openness of Linux still provides us with one way out of this problem. Although you can use modern Linux desktops and servers without knowing almost anything about how computers, networks or Linux itself works, unlike with other systems, Linux still will show you everything that's going on behind the scenes if you are willing to look. You can set up complex networks of Linux servers running the same services that power the internet–all for free (and with the power of virtualization, all from a single machine). For the budding engineer who is willing to dive deep into Linux, you will have superior knowledge and an edge over all of your peers.

1.2 Leveling Up: A Sysadmin Career Path

In this section, I describe the overall sysadmin career path and what I consider the attributes that might make you a "senior sysadmin" instead of a "sysadmin" or "junior sysadmin", along with some tips on how to level up. Keep in mind that titles are pretty fluid and loose things, and that they mean different things to different people. Also, it will take different people different amounts of time to "level up" depending on their innate sysadmin skills, their work ethic and the opportunities they get to gain more experience. That said, be suspicious of anyone who leveled up to a senior level in any field in only a year or two–it takes time in a career to make the kinds of mistakes and learn the kinds of lessons you need to learn before you can move up to the next level.

Junior Systems Administrator

Junior sysadmins are early on in their sysadmin training. It might be their first sysadmin job where they are learning everything from scratch, or they might have a few years of experience under their belts. Either way, a few attributes are common among junior sysadmins:
- Tasks will require help from other members of the team to complete.
- They will rely heavily on documentation and may not understand what individual steps actually do.
- It may take weeks or even months to be productive at a new job.
- Most of their time will be spent with daily tickets.
- Eventually they might take on a project, but will need quite a bit of help to complete it.

One of the first attributes that defines junior sysadmins is the amount of outside help they will need to do their jobs. Generally speaking, they will need help and direction to perform day-to-day tasks, especially at first. If you document your routine tasks (and you should!), you will find that junior sysadmins will dutifully follow your procedures step by step, but they may not understand exactly what those steps do. If a task deviates from the norm, or if for some reason a step fails, they will escalate up to a more senior member of the team for help–this is a good thing, because this mentoring is one of the main ways that junior sysadmins build their experience besides making mistakes and fixing them.

It might take sysadmins at this level a few weeks or even months at a new organization until they are productive and can start doing daily tasks independently without help. These are great opportunities for a team to audit documentation and for junior members of the team to flag gaps in documentation or places where they are out of date. If you have junior team members add documentation themselves, just make sure that a more senior team member goes over it to make sure it's correct and complete.

A sysadmin's task list is usually divided into two main categories: day-to-day tasks and projects. Junior sysadmins often end up being assigned more of the day-to-day "grunt work", not as a punishment, but just because projects usually require more experience–experience they will get as they master daily tickets.

That said, at some point, it will be important for junior sysadmins to take on their first project. Ideally, this will be a project without a strict deadline, so they can take the time they need to research and get it right. At this level, a more senior team member will need to devote a fair amount of time to act as a mentor and help direct the planning and research for the project and answer any questions.

Both daily tasks and projects are important for junior sysadmins, as it's the mastery of daily tasks and the successful completion of a couple projects that will help prepare junior sysadmins to level up. Each task they master will add a certain level of confidence and proficiency in routine sysadmin work, and projects will help develop their research skills and the ability to complete tasks that fall outside a playbook.

Mid-Level Systems Administrator

It can be difficult to draw the exact line where a sysadmin levels up past the junior level. There isn't an exact number of years' experience needed; instead, it has more to do with sysadmins' competency with their craft and their overall confidence and independence. Here are a few attributes that are common to mid-level sysadmins:

- They generally perform day-to-day tasks independently.
- They understand some of the technology behind their routine tasks and don't just parrot commands they see in documentation.
- It takes a few weeks up to a month to be productive at a new job.
- Their time is pretty equally balanced between daily tickets and longer-term projects.
- They are able to come up with new approaches and improvements to existing tasks.
- They can complete simple projects independently and more complex projects with some help from more senior team members.

The main difference between junior sysadmins and mid-level sysadmins has to do with their independence. As sysadmins become more comfortable with servers in general, and the processes within an organization specifically, they start to be able to perform typical tasks by themselves. Mid-level sysadmins should be able to handle all of the normal tasks that are thrown at them without outside help. It's only when they get an odd "curve ball", such as a one-off task that hasn't been done before or some unique emergency, that mid-level sysadmins may need to reach out to the more senior members of the team for some guidance. As with junior sysadmins, this type of help is very important, and it would be a mistake for mid-level sysadmins not to ask for help with odd requests just to try to be "more senior". Asking questions and getting advice from more experienced sysadmins will help them level up. If they try to go it completely alone, no matter what, it will take much longer.

Mid-level sysadmins also take on more projects than their junior counterparts, and they are able to complete simple projects independently. Junior sysadmins might be able to maintain an existing system, but mid-level sysadmins actually might be able to set it up from scratch. They also can start tackling larger, more complicated projects that may require them to learn new technologies and come up with some approaches independently, although in those cases, they'll still sometimes need to reach out to more experienced team members to make sure they are on the right track.

As sysadmins master all of the day-to-day tasks, they also naturally will start to come up with improvements and efficiencies for those tasks, and they may make some suggestions to the team along those lines. These improvements may become projects for them in their own right. They also should be able to provide some level of mentorship and training for junior members on the team, at least with daily tasks.

One of the most important things for mid-level sysadmins to do if they want to level up is to take on projects and help triage emergencies. Projects and emergencies often provide opportunities to think outside established playbooks. It's this kind of critical thinking, research and problem-solving that builds the experience that's so important for sysadmins. They will start to notice some common patterns the more emergencies and projects they work through, and that realization builds a certain level of confidence and deeper understanding that is vital for moving to the next level.

Senior Systems Administrator

Although some may consider people to be senior sysadmins based on a certain number of years' experience, to me, what makes someone a senior sysadmin versus a mid-level sysadmin isn't years of experience or number of places worked at, it's more a particular state of mind that one can get to via many different means. Many people get the title before they get the state of mind, and often it takes getting the title (or some of the responsibilities associated with it) to make a person level up.

The main difference between senior sysadmins and mid-level sysadmins is that one day, something clicks in senior sysadmins' minds when they realize that basically every emergency they've responded to and every project they've worked on to that point all have a common trait: given enough time and effort, they can track down the cause of just about any problem and complete just about any sysadmin task. This is a matter of true confidence, not false bravado, and it's this kind of real independence that marks senior sysadmins.

Early on in your career, certain tasks or projects just seem over your head, and you absolutely need help to complete them. Later on, you master daily tasks, but weird emergencies or complex projects still may intimidate you. Senior sysadmins have completed so many projects and responded to so many emergencies, that they eventually build the confidence such that they aren't intimidated by the next project, the next emergency or the prospect of being responsible for important mission-critical infrastructure. Like mid-level sysadmins might approach their daily tickets, senior sysadmins approach any task that comes their way.

1.2 Leveling Up: A Sysadmin Career Path

Here are some attributes common to senior sysadmins:
- They can perform both daily tasks and complex projects independently.
- They understand the fundamentals behind the technologies they use and can distill complex tasks down into simple playbooks everyone on the team can follow.
- They can be productive at a new job within a week or two.
- Their time is spent more on large projects and odd requests that fall outside the norm.
- They mentor other team members and have a good sense of best practices.
- They come up with new projects and improvements and can suggest appropriate designs to solve new problems.
- They understand their own fallibility and develop procedures to protect themselves from their own mistakes.

Again, it's the confidence and independence of senior sysadmins that separates them from mid-level sysadmins. That's not to say that senior sysadmins never ask for help. Along with the confidence of being able to tackle any sysadmin task is the humility that comes with a career full of mistakes. In fact, part of their experience will have taught them the wisdom of asking other people on the team for feedback to make sure they haven't missed anything. Often senior sysadmins will come up with multiple ways to tackle a problem, each with pros and cons, and use the rest of the team as a sounding board to help choose which approach would work best in a specific case.

Senior sysadmins' experiences exposes them to many different technologies, systems and architectures through the years. This means they start to notice which approaches work, which don't, and which work at first but cause problems in the long run. In particular, they might track some project they completed themselves through its lifetime and note how their initial solutions worked to a particular point and then either failed as it scaled, or needed to change with the advent of some new technology. The more this happens, the more senior sysadmins start to develop a natural sense of best practices and what I call the "sysadmin sense", which, like Spiderman's "spidey sense", starts to warn them when they see something that is going to result in a problem down the road, like a backup system that's never been tested or a system that has a single point of failure. It's in developing this expertise that they are able to level up to the last major level outside management.

Systems Architect

Although every organization is a bit different, there are two main career paths senior sysadmins might choose from as they gain experience. The most common path is in management. Senior sysadmins over time end up spending more time mentoring their team and often are promoted to team leads and from there into full managers over their teams. The other path continues on with the "individual-contributor" role where they may or may not act as team leads, but they don't have any direct reports and don't spend time doing employee evaluations or things of that sort. Of course, there also are paths that blend those two extremes. In this last section, I describe one of the last levels for an individual-contributor sysadmin to move to: systems architect.

In many organizations, the line between a systems architect and a senior sysadmin can be blurry. Equally blurry are the qualifications that may make someone a systems architect. That said, generally speaking, systems architects have spent a number of years as senior sysadmins. During the course of their careers, they have participated in a large number of projects, both with a team and independently, and they have started to see what works and what doesn't. It's this accumulation of experience with a wide variety of technologies and project designs that starts to build this inherent sense of best practices that makes someone a systems architect.

The following are some attributes common to systems architects:

- They are familiar with many different technologies that solve a particular problem along with their pros and cons.
- When solving a problem, they come up with multiple approaches and can explain and defend their preferred approach.
- They understand the limitations to a solution and where it will fail as it scales.
- They can distill a general problem down to individual tasks as part of a larger project that can be divided among a team.
- They can evaluate new technologies based on their relative merits and not be distracted by hype or popularity.

Systems architects aren't necessarily married to a particular approach, although they may have a set of approaches for tackling certain problems based on what's worked for them in the past. Because they have operated at a senior level for some time, they have developed a deeper understanding of what defines a good architecture versus a bad one and how to choose one technology over the other. Technology moves in trends, and those trends tend to repeat themselves over a long enough timeline. Systems architects have been around long enough that they have seen at least one of those trend cycles for some hyped technology, and they probably have been burned at some point in the past by adopting an immature technology too quickly just because it was popular. Whereas junior administrators are more likely to get caught up in the hype behind a particular new technology and want to use it everywhere, systems architects are more likely to cut through the hype and, for any new technology, be able to identify where it would be useful and where it wouldn't.

1.3 Automation

In this section, I discuss how to automate yourself out of your job. There is a quote that you see from time to time in sysadmin circles that goes something along the lines of "Be careful or I will replace you with a tiny shell script." Good system administrators hate performing mundane tasks and constantly seek to apply that saying to themselves. That said, there are many different approaches to automation, and not all of them result in a time-savings. Here, I discuss my experience with automation and describe what, when, why and how you should (and shouldn't) automate.

Why You Should Automate

There are a number of different reasons why you should take steps to automate your work as a sysadmin:

1. It frees up time spent doing mundane tasks to focus on more important work

With all of the automation that's already built in to servers, it's easy to take for granted just how many mundane tasks sysadmin have had to perform in the past. Logs weren't always rotated automatically; backups usually were home-grown affairs that often were triggered manually. Even now, there still are system administrators who install every single server by hand, log in to a machine manually and install or update software, and configure server configuration files on the host by hand.

Let's take server OS installation as an example–a modern interactive server OS installation may take anywhere from 15 minutes to an hour of sysadmin time to walk through and answer questions. These are the kinds of actions that don't really require a sysadmin's expertise once you've made the initial decisions about how you want a server to be set up. By automating these mundane tasks, you can get back to the more difficult work that does require your expertise.

2. Automation reduces mistakes in routine tasks

The thing about performing the same task over and over by hand is that it is easy to make mistakes, and if it's something you do every day, eventually you even may stop paying attention to whether your task succeeded. Also, the way that you may perform a certain task might be a little bit different from how a different administrator on the team does it. By automating a task, the team can agree on the ideal way to perform it and know that when you run your automation script, it is performed the same way every single time with no skipped steps or commands run in the wrong order.

3. Automation allows everyone on the team to be productive

With automation, you can take even a complex process and reduce it down to a command. That command then becomes something that anyone on the team can run, whereas the complex process may have required more senior members of the team. For instance, if you take production software deployment as an example, often there can be a complex arrangement of triggering load balancer and monitoring maintenance modes, software versions to check, mirrors to sync up, and services to restart and test. Even though these individual steps may be mundane, combined, they become pretty complicated and could overwhelm a junior member of the team–especially when production uptime hangs in the balance. By automating that process, senior administrators can put all of their expertise into creating the right process that performs the right checks, and they can go on vacation knowing that anyone else on the team now can perform the task the right way.

4. Automation reduces documentation workload

Often instead of automating a task, a sysadmin team will spend time documenting a process. There is still an important place for documentation, and in the next section, I discuss when that makes sense and when it doesn't. The fact is though, if you take an entire process and put it into a single automated task, you no longer need a full wiki page of documentation (that inevitably will become out of date), because you've reduced it down to "run this command". Because the process is now automated, you also know the process is kept up to date; otherwise, the script wouldn't work.

What You Should Automate

Not everything is appropriate for automation, and even things that may be good candidates for automation may not be good candidates today (the next section covers when you should automate). Following are a few different types of tasks that make good candidates for automation.

1. Routine tasks

In general, tasks that you perform frequently (at least monthly) are good candidates for automation. The more frequent the task, in theory, the more time-savings you would get from automating it. Tasks that you perform only once a year may not be worth the effort to build automation around, and instead, those are the kinds of tasks that benefit from good documentation.

2. Repeatable tasks

If you could document a process as a series of commands, and then copy and paste them one by one in a terminal and the task would be complete, that's a repeatable task that may be a good candidate for automation. On the other hand, one-off tasks that have custom inputs or are something you may never have to do again aren't worth the time and effort to automate.

3. Complex tasks

The more complex a task, the more opportunities you have for mistakes if you do it manually. If a task has multiple steps, in particular steps that require you to take the output from one step and use it as input for another, or steps that use commands with a complex string of arguments are all great candidates for automation.

4. Time-consuming tasks

The longer the tasks take to complete (especially if there are periods of running a command, waiting for it to complete, and then doing something with that command's output), the better a candidate it is for automation. OS installation and configuration is a great example of this, as when you install an OS, there are periods when you enter installation settings and periods when you wait for the installation to complete. All of that waiting is wasted time. By automating long-running tasks, you can go do some other work and come back to the automation (or better, have it alert you) to see if it is complete.

When You Should Automate

My coworkers know that I enjoy automating myself out of my job, and sometimes in the past they have been surprised to learn that I haven't automated a task that by all measures is a prime candidate for automation. My answer is usually "Oh I plan to, I'm just not ready yet." The fact is that even if you have a task that is a great candidate for automation, it may not necessarily be the right time to automate it.

When I need to perform a new task that's a series of mundane, manual steps, I like to force myself to perform it step by step at least a few times "in the wild" before I start automating it. I find I usually need to perform a task a few times to understand where automation makes the most sense, what areas of the task may require extra attention, and what sorts of variables I might encounter for the task. Otherwise, if I just charge ahead and write a script, I may find myself rewriting it from scratch a few weeks later because I discover the process needs to be adapted to a new variation of the task. If I'm not quite sure about parts of a process, I may automate only the parts I am sure of first and get those right. Later on when the rest of the process starts to gel in my mind, I then go back and incorporate it into the automation I've already completed.

I also avoid automating tasks if I'm not sure I can do so securely. For instance, a number of organizations are big fans of using ChatOps (automating tasks using bots inside a chatroom) for automation. Although I know that many bots can authenticate tasks before they perform them, I still worry about the potential for abuse with a service that's usually shared across the whole company, not to mention the fact that production changes are being triggered by a host outside the production environment. With my current threat model, I have to maintain strict separation between development and production environments, so having a bot accessible to anyone in the company, or having a Jenkins continuous integration server in the development environment performing my production tasks, just doesn't work. In many cases, I have fully automated tasks up to the point that it still requires an administrator with the proper access to go to the production environment (thereby proving that they are authorized to be there) before they push "the button."

How You Should Automate

Since the whole goal of automation is to save time, I don't like to waste time refactoring my automation. If I don't feel like I understand a process and its variables well enough to automate it, I wait until I do or automate only the parts I feel good about. In general, I'm a big fan of building a foundation of finished work that I then build upon. I like to start with automating tasks that will give me the biggest time-savings or encourage the most consistency and then build off them.

I like doing the hard work up front so that it's easier down the road, and that is why I am a big fan of configuration management to automate server configuration. Once something like that is in place, rolling out changes to configuration becomes trivial, and creating new servers that match existing ones should be easy. These big tasks may take time up front, but they provide huge cost savings from then on, so I try to automate first.

I also favor automation tasks that can be used in multiple ways down the road. For instance, I think all administrators should have a simple, automated way to query their environment for whether a package is installed and on what hosts, and then be able to update that package easily on the hosts that have it. Some administrators refer to this as part of orchestration.

Package updates are something that sysadmins do constantly both for in-house software that changes frequently and system software that needs security updates. If a security update is a burden, many sysadmin won't bother. Having automation in place to make package updates easy means administrators save time on a task they have to perform frequently. Sysadmins then can use that automated package update process both for security patches, in-house software deployments and other tasks where package updates are just one component of many.

As you write your automation, be careful to check that your tasks succeeded, and if not, alert the sysadmin to the problem. That means shell scripts should check for exit codes, and error logs should be forwarded somewhere that gets the administrator's attention. It's all too easy to automate something and forget about it, but then check back weeks later and discover it stopped working!

In general, approach automation as a way to free up your brain, time and expertise toward tasks that actually need them. For me, I find that means time spent improving automation and otherwise dealing with exceptions–things that fall outside the normal day. If you keep it up, you eventually will find that when there are no crises or new projects, the day-to-day work should be automated to the point that your task is just to keep an eye on your well-oiled machine to make sure everything's running. That is when you know you have replaced yourself with a shell script.

1.4 Ticketing

In this section, I explore something that on the surface may seem boring or mundane but is absolutely critical to get right if you want to be an effective sysadmin: ticketing.

By ticketing, I'm referring to systems that allow sysadmins to keep track of tasks both internally and those requested by their coworkers or customers. There are many ways to get ticketing wrong so that it becomes a drain on an organization, so many sysadmins avoid or it use it begrudgingly. Also, ticketing approaches that work well for developers may be horrible for sysadmins, and vice versa. If you don't currently use a ticketing system, I hope by the end of this section, I've changed your mind. If you do use tickets, but you wish you didn't, I hope I can share how to structure a ticketing system that makes everything easier, not more difficult.

Why Tickets Are Important

Like documentation, tickets are one of those important things in a mature organization that some administrators think are unnecessary or even a waste of time. A ticketing system is important no matter the size of your organization. In a large organization, you have a large volume of tasks you need to keep track of distributed among a group of people. In a small organization, you often have one person taking on many roles. This leads me to the first reason why tickets are important.

1. Tickets Ensure That Tasks Aren't Forgotten

Sysadmins are asked to do new tasks constantly. There are any number of ways a coworker might ask for your help, from an email, to a phone call, to a message in a chat program, to a tap on the shoulder. If you weren't doing anything else, you immediately could start working on that task, and everything would be fine. Of course, usually sysadmins have to balance needs from many different people at the same time. Even requests that come in through email have a tendency to fall through the cracks and be forgotten. By storing every request in a ticket, no matter how you got the request, it is captured, so that even if you do forget about it, you'll remember it the next time you look at your ticketing system.

2. Tickets Make Sure the Task Is Done Right

Even if you can remember what someone wants you to do, you may not remember on Monday all of the details that someone told you in person on Friday. A ticket lets you capture exactly what people want done in their own words and provides a way for them to confirm that you completed the task the way they wanted before you close the ticket.

3. Tickets Help You Prioritize Tasks

Every request is important to the person who makes it. Every request may not be as urgent to you or your team compared to your other tasks, however. When all of your tasks are captured in tickets, the team lead or manager can go through and re-prioritize tasks so they are worked on in the right order. This ends up being more fair for everyone; otherwise, new tasks have a way of cutting in line, especially when the person asking for something is standing over your shoulder.

With a ticketing system, team leads or managers have a full list of important tasks they can point to when they need to explain why they aren't dropping everything for a new request. At the very least, it will help direct the conversation about why a particular task should be put at the head of the line.

4. Tickets Distribute the Work

If you have only one sysadmin, distributing tickets and projects is easy. Once your team grows though, it's important to distribute the work so no member of the team gets burned out. Coworkers have a tendency of finding that senior member of your team who is most productive and going to them directly when they have any issue. Of course, that team member is probably already working on plenty of other tasks or may be trying to focus on an important project.

When a task is captured in a ticket, the team lead or manager can assign and reassign tickets to different members of the team to make sure no one gets burned out, and also to ensure that everyone learns how to do things. Otherwise, you end up cultivating specialists within the team that always take tickets related to certain systems, which leads to problems later when that team member goes on vacation.

5. Tickets Provide an Audit Trail for Changes

Every time you change a system, you create an opportunity for something to break. If you are lucky, things break immediately after you make the change. More often, you'll find that it takes some time for a change to cause a problem. You'll discover two weeks later that something stopped working, and with a ticketing system, you can pull up all of the tasks that were worked on around

1.4 Ticketing

that time. This makes it much easier to pinpoint potential causes of a problem.

Tickets also provide an audit trail for tasks that require approval or proof of completion, like creating or revoking accounts, granting new privileges or patching software. When someone asks who said it was okay for Bob to get access to production and when it happened, you can answer the question. If you need to prove that you applied a security patch, you can point to command output that you capture and then store in the corresponding ticket.

Qualities of an Effective Ticketing System

Many different ticketing systems exist, and sometimes when you hear people complain about tickets, what they are really complaining about is a bad ticketing system. When choosing between ticketing systems, you should look for a few particular traits.

Some systems that developers use to track code through the development process result in very complicated workflows. For a sysadmin though, the simpler the ticketing system the better. Because you already are asking a sysadmin to take time out of solving a problem to document it in a ticket, it helps if the ticketing process is fast and simple. I prefer very simple ticket workflows for sysadmins where there may be only a few states: open, assigned, in progress, resolved and closed. (I'll talk more about how I treat each of those states in the next section.)

The fewer required fields in a ticket, the better. If you want to add extra fields for tags or other information, that's fine, just don't make those fields mandatory. The goal here is to allow sysadmins to create tickets based on someone walking up and tapping them on the shoulder in less than a minute.

Ideally, the ticketing system would allow you some other way to generate tickets from a script, either from sending an email to a special address or via an exposed API. If it has an API that lets you change ticket state or add comments, all the better, as you potentially can integrate those into your other automation scripts. For instance, I've created a production deployment script that integrates with my ticketing system, so that it reads the manifest of packages it should install from the ticket itself and then outputs all of the results from the deployment as comments in the ticket. It's a great way to enforce a best practice of documenting each of your software releases, but it does it in a way that makes it the path of least resistance.

Favor ticketing systems that allow you to create dependencies or other links between tickets. It's useful to know that task A depends on task B, and so you must complete task B first. These kinds of ticketing systems also make it easier to build a master ticket to track a project and then break that large project down into individual tickets that describe manageable tasks. These kinds of systems often show all of the subordinate tickets in the master ticket, so a quick glance at the master ticket can give you a clue about where you are in a project.

How to Manage and Organize Tickets

Each ticketing system has its own notion of ticket states, but in my opinion, you should, at a minimum, have the following:

- Open: a task that needs to be completed, but hasn't been assigned to anyone.
- Assigned: a task that's in a particular person's queue, but they haven't started work on it yet. Tasks in this state should be safe to reassign to someone else.
- In progress: a task that has been assigned to someone who is currently working on the task. You definitely should communicate with the assignee before you reassign tickets in this state.
- Resolved: the sysadmin believes the task has been completed and is waiting for confirmation from the person who filed the ticket before closing it.
- Closed: the task has been completed to everyone's satisfaction.

A well run ticketing system should provide the team with the answers to a few important questions. The first question is "What should I work on now?" To answer that question, each member of the team should be able to claim tickets, and team leads or managers should be able to assign tickets to individual members of the team. It's important for people to claim tickets and start work only after they are claimed; otherwise, it's easy (and common) for two members of the team to start working on the same task without realizing it. Once claimed, everyone on the team can start working on tickets in their personal queue, starting with the highest-priority tasks.

The next question a good ticketing system should answer is "What should I work on next?" Once sysadmins' personal queues are empty, they should be able to go to the collective queue and see a list of tasks ordered by priority. It should be clear what tasks they should put on their queue, and if there's any question about it, they can go to the team lead or manager for some clarity. Again, ticket priority helps inform everyone on the team about what's next–higher-priority tasks trump lower-priority ones, not necessarily because they are less important (a ticket is always important to the person who filed it), but because they are less urgent.

I approach ticket priority as a way for users to help inform the team about how important the ticket is to them, but not how urgent it is for the team. The fact is, there's no way every employee in the company can know all of the other important tasks the sysadmin has to perform for other people nor can they be expected to weigh the importance of their need against everyone else's needs.

A good manager should reserve the right to weigh the priority assigned to a ticket against the other tickets in the queue and change the priority up or down based on its urgency relative to the other tasks. It also may be the case where a task that was low urgency two weeks ago has become urgent now because of how long it was in the queue, so a good manager would be aware of this and bump the priority. If you are going to start the practice of changing ticket priorities though, be sure to inform everyone of your intentions and how you will determine the urgency of a ticket.

Another key to managing tickets is to make sure all of your requests are captured in the ticketing system. Sometimes a coworker can be guilty of trying to skip ahead in line by messaging you with a request or walking directly to your desk to ask you to do something. Even in those cases where you really are going to drop everything to work on their request, you should insist on capturing the request in a ticket so you can track the work. This isn't just so you can prioritize it based on other tasks or so you don't forget it, it's so in a week when some problem crops up based on this urgent change, you'll see this ticket along with other tasks completed that day and it will help you track down the cause.

Finally, as a manager, be careful to distribute work fairly among your team. Even if one member of the team happens to be an expert on a particular service, don't assign that person every task related to that service; it's important for everyone on the team to cross-train. Pay attention if employees try to get tickets assigned to their favorite member of the team, and don't be afraid to reassign tasks to spread the work around evenly. Finally, every ticket queue has routine, mundane grunt work that must be done. Be sure to distribute those tasks throughout the team so no one gets burnt out.

1.5 Patch Management

Patch management is one of the most important tasks for a sysadmin–in particular when it comes to the security of the system. If you pay attention to security news you find out about breaches all the that that could have been stopped if only the administrators had applied widely-available patches. In this section, I cover some of the fundamentals of patch management under Linux, including what a good patch management system looks like, the tools you will want to put in place and how the overall patching process should work.

What Is Patch Management?

When I say patch management, I'm referring to the systems you have in place to update software already on a server. I'm not just talking about keeping up with the latest-and-greatest bleeding-edge version of a piece of software. Even more conservative distributions like Debian that stick with a particular version of software for its "stable" release still release frequent updates that patch bugs or security holes.

Of course, if your organization decided to roll its own version of a particular piece of software, either because developers demanded the latest and greatest, you needed to fork the software to apply a custom change, or you just like giving yourself extra work, you now have a problem. Ideally you have put in a system that automatically packages up the custom version of the software for you in the same continuous integration system you use to build and package any other software, but many sysadmins still rely on the outdated method of packaging the software on their local machine based on (hopefully up to date) documentation on their wiki. In either case, in the event of a security bug, you will need to confirm that your particular version has the flaw, and if so, make sure that the new patch applies cleanly to your custom version.

What Good Patch Management Looks Like

Patch management starts with knowing that there is a software update to begin with. First, for your core software, you should be subscribed to your Linux distribution's security mailing list, so you're notified immediately when there are security patches. If you use any software that doesn't come from your distribution, you must find out how to be kept up to date on security patches for that software as well. When new security notifications come in, you should review the details so you understand how severe the security flaw is, whether you are affected and gauge a sense of how urgent the patch is.

Some organizations have a purely manual patch management system. With such a system, when a security patch comes along, the sysadmin figures out which servers are running the software, generally by relying on memory and by logging in to servers and checking. Then the sysadmin uses the server's built-in package management tool to update the software with the latest from the distribution. Then the sysadmin moves on to the next server, and the next, until all of the servers are patched.

There are many problems with manual patch management. First is the fact that it makes patching a laborious chore. The more work patching is, the more likely a sysadmin will put it off or skip doing it entirely. The second problem is that manual patch management relies too much on the sysadmin's ability to remember and recall all of the servers they are responsible for and keep track of which are patched and which aren't. This makes it easy for servers to be forgotten and sit unpatched.

The faster and easier patch management is, the more likely you are to do it. You should have a system in place that quickly can tell you which servers are running a particular piece of software at which version. Ideally, that system also can push out updates. Personally, I prefer orchestration tools like MCollective for this task, but Red Hat provides Satellite, and Canonical provides Landscape as central tools that let you view software versions across your fleet of servers and apply patches all from a central place.

Patching should be fault-tolerant as well. You should be able to patch a service and restart it without any overall down time. The same idea goes for kernel patches that require a reboot. My approach is to divide my servers into different high availability groups so that lb1, app1, rabbitmq1 and db1 would all be in one group, and lb2, app2, rabbitmq2 and db2 are in another. Then, I know I can patch one group at a time without it causing downtime anywhere else.

So, how fast is fast? Your system should be able to roll out a patch to a minor piece of software that doesn't have an accompanying service (such as bash in the case of the ShellShock vulnerability) within a few minutes to an hour at most. For something like OpenSSL that requires you to restart services, the careful process of patching and restarting services in a fault-tolerant way probably will take more time, but this is where orchestration tools come in handy. Regardless of the tool you use, you should put a system in place that makes it easy to patch and restart services in a fault-tolerant and automated way.

When patching requires a reboot, such as in the case of kernel patches, it might take a bit more time, but again, automation and orchestration tools can make this go much faster than you might imagine. I can patch and reboot the servers in an environment in a fault-tolerant way within an hour or two, and it would be much faster than that if I didn't need to wait for clusters to sync back up in between reboots.

Unfortunately, many sysadmins still hold on to the outdated notion that uptime is a badge of pride. Given that serious kernel patches tend to come out at least once a year if not more often, to me, it's proof you don't take security seriously.

Many organizations also still have that single point of failure server that can never go down, and as a result, it never gets patched or rebooted. If you want to be secure, you need to remove these outdated liabilities and create systems that at least can be rebooted during a late-night maintenance window.

Ultimately, fast and easy patch management is a sign of a mature and professional sysadmin team. Updating software is something all sysadmins have to do as part of their jobs, and investing time into systems that make that process easy and fast pays dividends far beyond security. For one, it helps identify bad architecture decisions that cause single points of failure. For another, it helps identify stagnant, out-of-date legacy systems in an environment and provides you with an incentive to replace them. Finally, when patching is managed well, it frees up sysadmins' time and turns their attention to the things that truly require their expertise.

1.6 Alerting

In this section, I cover on-call alerting. Like with any job title, the responsibilities given to sysadmins, DevOps and Site Reliability Engineers may differ, and in some cases, they may not involve any kind of 24x7 on-call duties, if you're lucky. For everyone else, though, there are many ways to organize on-call alerting, and there also are many ways to shoot yourself in the foot.

The main enemies of on-call alerting are false positives, with the main risks being ignoring alerts or burnout for members of your team. This section talks about some best practices you can apply to your alerting policies that hopefully will reduce burnout and make sure alerts aren't ignored.

Alert Thresholds

A common pitfall sysadmins run into when setting up monitoring systems is to alert on too many things. It's simple to monitor just about any aspect of a system's health, so it's tempting to overload your monitoring system with all kinds of system checks. One of the main ongoing maintenance tasks for any monitoring system is setting appropriate alert thresholds to reduce false positives. This means the more checks you have in place, the higher the maintenance burden. As a result, I have a few different rules I apply to my monitoring checks when determining thresholds for notifications.

Rule 1: Critical alerts must be something I want to be woken up about at 3am.

A common cause of sysadmin burnout is being woken up with alerts for systems that don't matter. If you don't have a 24x7 international development team, you probably don't care if the build server has a problem at 3am, or even if you do, you probably are going to wait until the morning to fix it. By restricting critical alerts to just those systems that must be online 24x7, you help reduce false positives and make sure that real problems are addressed quickly.

Rule 2: Critical alerts must be actionable.

Some organizations send alerts when just about anything happens on a system. If I'm being woken up at 3am, I want to have a specific action plan associated with that alert so I can fix it. Again, too many false positives will burn out a sysadmin that's on call, and nothing is more frustrating than getting woken up with an alert that you can't do anything about. Every critical alert should have an obvious action plan the sysadmin can follow to fix it.

Rule 3: Warning alerts tell me about problems that will be critical if I don't fix them.

There are many problems on a system that I may want to know about and may want to investigate, but they aren't worth getting out of bed at 3am. Warning alerts don't trigger a pager, but they still send me a quieter notification. For instance, if load, used disk space or RAM grows to a certain point where the system is still healthy but if left unchecked may not be, I get a warning alert so I can investigate when I get a chance. On the other hand, if I got only a warning alert, but the system was no longer responding, that's an indication I may need to change my alert thresholds.

1.6 Alerting

Rule 4: Repeat warning alerts periodically.

I think of warning alerts like this thing nagging at you to look at it and fix it during the work day. If you send warning alerts too frequently, they just spam your inbox and are ignored, so I've found that spacing them out to alert every hour or so is enough to remind me of the problem but not so frequent that I ignore it completely.

Rule 5: Everything else is monitored, but doesn't send an alert.

There are many things in my monitoring system that help provide overall context when I'm investigating a problem, but by themselves, they aren't actionable and aren't anything I want to get alerts about. In other cases, I want to collect metrics from my systems to build trending graphs later. I disable alerts altogether on those kinds of checks. They still show up in my monitoring system and provide a good audit trail when I'm investigating a problem, but they don't page me with useless notifications.

Kyle's rule.

One final note about alert thresholds: I've developed a practice in my years as a sysadmin that I've found is important enough as a way to reduce burnout that I take it with me to every team I'm on. My rule is this:

> *If sysadmins were kept up during the night because of false alarms, they can clear their projects for the next day and spend time tuning alert thresholds so it doesn't happen again.*

There is nothing worse than being kept up all night because of false positive alerts and knowing that the next night will be the same and that there's nothing you can do about it. If that kind of thing continues, it inevitably will lead either to burnout or to sysadmins silencing their pagers. Setting aside time for sysadmins to fix false alarms helps, because they get a chance to improve their night's sleep the next night. As a team lead or manager, sometimes this has meant that I've taken on a sysadmin's tickets for them during the day so they can fix alerts.

Paging

Sending an alert often is referred to as paging or being paged, because in the past, sysadmins, like doctors, carried pagers on them. Their monitoring systems were set to send a basic numerical alert to the pager when there was a problem, so that sysadmins could be alerted even when they weren't at a computer or when they were asleep. Although we still refer to it as paging, and some older-school teams still pass around an actual pager, normally notifications more often are handled by alerts to mobile phones.

The first question you need to answer when you set up alerting is what method you will use for notifications. When you are deciding how to set up pager notifications, look for a few specific qualities.

Something that will alert you wherever you are geographically.

A number of cool office projects on the web exist where a broken software build triggers a big red flashing light in the office. That kind of notification is fine for office-hour alerts for non-critical systems, but it isn't appropriate as a pager notification even during the day, because a sysadmin who is in a meeting room or at lunch would not be notified. This generally means some kind of notification needs to be sent to your phone.

An alert should stand out from other notifications.

False alarms can be a big problem with paging systems, as sysadmins naturally will start ignoring alerts. Likewise, if you use the same ringtone for alerts that you use for any other email, your brain will start to tune alerts out. If you use email for alerts, use filtering rules so that on-call alerts generate a completely different and louder ringtone from regular emails and vibrate the phone as well, so you can be notified even if you silence your phone or are in a loud room. In the past, when BlackBerries were popular, you could set rules such that certain emails generated a "Level One" alert that was different from regular email notifications.

The BlackBerry days are gone now, and currently, many organizations (in particular startups) use Google Apps for their corporate email. The Gmail Android application lets you set per-folder (called labels) notification rules so you can create a filter that moves all on-call alerts to a particular folder and then set that folder so that it generates a unique alert, vibrates and does so for every new email to that folder. If you don't have that option, most email software that supports multiple accounts will let you set different notifications for each account so you may need to resort to a separate email account just for alerts.

Something that will wake you up all hours of the night.

Some sysadmins are deep sleepers, and whatever notification system you choose needs to be something that will wake them up in the middle of the night. After all, servers always seem to misbehave at around 3am. Pick a ringtone that is loud, possibly obnoxious if necessary, and also make sure to enable phone vibrations. Also configure your alert system to re-send notifications if an alert isn't acknowledged within a couple minutes. Sometimes the first alert isn't enough to wake people up completely, but it might move them from deep sleep to a lighter sleep so the follow-up alert will wake them up.

While ChatOps (using chat as a method of getting notifications and performing administration tasks) might be okay for general non-critical daytime

1.6 Alerting

notifications, they are not appropriate for pager alerts. Even if you have an application on your phone set to notify you about unread messages in chat, many chat applications default to a "quiet time" in the middle of the night. If you disable that, you risk being paged in the middle of the night just because someone sent you a message. Also, many third-party ChatOps systems aren't necessarily known for their mission-critical reliability and have had outages that have spanned many hours. You don't want your critical alerts to rely on an unreliable system.

Something that is fast and reliable.

Your notification system needs to be reliable and able to alert you quickly at all times. To me, this means alerting is done in-house, but many organizations opt for third parties to receive and escalate their notifications. Every additional layer you can add to your alerting is another layer of latency and another place where a notification may be dropped. Just make sure whatever method you choose is reliable and that you have some way of discovering when your monitoring system itself is offline.

In the next section, I cover how to set up escalations–meaning, how you alert other members of the team if the person on call isn't responding. Part of setting up escalations is picking a secondary, backup method of notification that relies on a different infrastructure from your primary one. So if you use your corporate Exchange server for primary notifications, you might select a personal Gmail account as a secondary. If you have a Google Apps account as your primary notification, you may pick SMS as your secondary alert.

Email servers have outages like anything else, and the goal here is to make sure that even if your primary method of notifications has an outage, you have some alternate way of finding out about it. I've had a number of occasions where my SMS secondary alert came in before my primary just due to latency with email syncing to my phone.

Create some means of alerting the whole team.

In addition to having individual alerting rules that will page someone who is on call, it's useful to have some way of paging an entire team in the event of an "all hands on deck" crisis. This may be a particular email alias or a particular key word in an email subject. However you set it up, it's important that everyone knows that this is a "pull in case of fire" notification and shouldn't be abused with non-critical messages.

Alert Escalations

Once you have alerts set up, the next step is to configure alert escalations. Even the best-designed notification system alerting the most well-intentioned sysadmin will fail from time to time either because a sysadmin's phone crashed, had no cell signal, or for whatever reason, the sysadmin didn't notice the alert. When that happens, you want to make sure that others on the team (and the on-call person's second notification) is alerted so someone can address the alert.

Alert escalations are one of those areas that some monitoring systems do better than others. Although the configuration can be challenging compared to other systems, I've found Nagios to provide a rich set of escalation schedules. Other organizations may opt to use a third-party notification system specifically because their chosen monitoring solution doesn't have the ability to define strong escalation paths. A simple escalation system might look like the following:

- Initial alert goes to the on-call sysadmin and repeats every five minutes.
- If the on-call sysadmin doesn't acknowledge or fix the alert within 15 minutes, it escalates to the secondary alert and also to the rest of the team.
- These alerts repeat every five minutes until they are acknowledged or fixed.

The idea here is to give the on-call sysadmin time to address the alert so you aren't waking everyone up at 3am, yet also provide the rest of the team with a way to find out about the alert if the first sysadmin can't fix it in time or is unavailable. Depending on your particular SLAs, you may want to shorten or lengthen these time periods between escalations or make them more sophisticated with the addition of an on-call backup who is alerted before the full team. In general, organize your escalations so they strike the right balance between giving the on-call person a chance to respond before paging the entire team, yet not letting too much time pass in the event of an outage in case the person on call can't respond.

If you are part of a larger international team, you even may be able to set up escalations that follow the sun. In that case, you would select on-call administrators for each geographic region and set up the alerts so that they were aware of the different time periods and time of day in those regions, and then alert the appropriate on-call sysadmin first. Then you can have escalations page the rest of the team, regardless of geography, in the event that an alert isn't solved.

On-Call Rotation

During World War One, the horrors of being in the trenches at the front lines were such that they caused a new range of psychological problems (labeled shell shock) that, given time, affected even the most hardened soldiers. The steady barrage of explosions, gun fire, sleep deprivation and fear day in and out took its toll, and eventually both sides in the war realized the importance of rotating troops away from the front line to recuperate.

It's not fair to compare being on call with the horrors of war, but that said, it also takes a kind of psychological toll that if left unchecked, will burn out your team. The responsibility of being on call is a burden even if you aren't alerted during a particular period. It usually means you must carry your laptop with you at all times, and in some organizations, it may affect whether you can go to the movies or on vacation. In some badly run organizations, being on call means a nightmare of alerts where you can expect to have a ruined weekend of firefighting every time. Because being on call can be stressful, in particular if you get a lot of nighttime alerts, it's important to rotate out sysadmins on call so they get a break.

The length of time for being on call will vary depending on the size of your team and how much of a burden being on call is. Generally speaking, a one- to four-week rotation is common, with two-week rotations often hitting the sweet spot. With a large enough team, a two-week rotation is short enough that any individual member of the team doesn't shoulder too much of the burden. But, even if you have only a three-person team, it means a sysadmin gets a full month without worrying about being on call.

Holiday on call

Holidays place a particular challenge on your on-call rotation, because it ends up being unfair for whichever sysadmin it lands on. In particular, being on call in late December can disrupt all kinds of family time. If you have a professional, trustworthy team with good teamwork, what I've found works well is to share the on-call burden across the team during specific known holiday days, such as Thanksgiving, Christmas Eve, Christmas and New Year's Eve. In this model, alerts go out to every member of the team, and everyone responds to the alert and to each other based on their availability. After all, not everyone eats Thanksgiving dinner at the same time, so if one person is sitting down to eat, but another person has two more hours before dinner, when the alert goes out, the first person can reply "at dinner", but the next person can reply "on it", and that way, the burden is shared.

If you are new to on-call alerting, I hope you have found this list of practices useful. You will find a lot of these practices in place in many larger organizations with seasoned sysadmins, because over time, everyone runs into the same kinds of problems with monitoring and alerting. Most of these policies should apply whether you are in a large organization or a small one, and even if you are the only DevOps engineer on staff, all that means is that you have an advantage at creating an alerting policy that will avoid some common pitfalls and overall burnout.

1.7 Preparing for Vacation

Every year or two my family and I like to take a vacation abroad. Normally, vacation is a time to unplug, and if you are a sysadmin who's on an on-call rotation, someone else on the team typically takes over your on-call duties. Yet as you progress in your career, you start to gain more expertise and responsibilities over systems, and even with someone else on-call, there's a certain class of emergency where the team might need to reach out to you for help even when you're on vacation. I recently took a vacation abroad, and before I left, I went through a set of tasks to reduce the chance that I would need to jump on an emergency while I was away. So in this section, I describe some of the steps I take to prepare for a vacation that will help you unplug on your next trip.

Preparing Your Computer

One of the first questions you should answer before going on vacation is whether you will need to take your work laptop with you. Depending on your organization and its security controls, you might be able to perform basic emergency administrative tasks from your personal computer, tablet or phone, or you may be able to connect to production only from your work computer. In other cases, you may not need a computer, because you can just serve an advisory role over the phone or chat with other people on the team and walk them through what to do in the event of an emergency.

If you do need to take your computer, I highly recommend making a full backup before the trip. Your computer is more likely to be lost, stolen or broken while traveling than when sitting safely at the office, so I always take a backup of my work machine before a trip. Even better than taking a backup, leave your expensive work computer behind and use a cheaper more disposable machine for travel and just restore your important files and settings for work on it before you leave and wipe it when you return. If you decide to go the disposable computer route, I recommend working one or two full work days on this computer before the vacation to make sure all of your files and settings are in place.

Why Choose a Different Laptop?

I was faced with the dilemma of choosing a travel laptop when I went on vacation a few months ago. I needed to be reachable while on vacation, just in case, but I knew I didn't want to lug around and cross borders with an expensive company laptop. There are a number of reasons why this is a good idea, and most of the reasons you would want to use a separate, cheap laptop for travel also apply for an on-call laptop.

First, although it's true that your laptop might get lost, stolen or damaged while you commute to work, it's much more likely to happen outside your normal work routine. While you are traveling or on call, you might take your laptop to restaurants, bars, events or a friend's house, and because you are outside your normal routine, it's more likely that it will be stolen or that you might accidentally leave it behind. Also when you are commuting to work, you likely have some kind of backpack or case for your laptop, but outside work, you may be more likely just to throw your laptop in the trunk of your car.

1.7 Preparing for Vacation

While traveling, especially traveling abroad, you are most definitely outside your normal routine, and a laptop is even more likely to get lost, damaged or stolen. The more expensive laptop you have with you, the more enticing of a target, and the more you have to lose. Also, with increased security around airports and customs, laptops are more likely to be inspected, confiscated or forced into checked luggage. Plus, if you do have to put your laptop in checked luggage, you must lock your luggage with keys that security agents can unlock. Unfortunately, there are many stories of unscrupulous airport employees who have taken advantage of this fact to steal high-value items from luggage while it's out of its owner's possession.

Secondly, having a second laptop that's ready at any moment to take over work duties adds an extra backup in case your work laptop itself breaks. Instead of being out of commission while you are waiting for a replacement, you immediately can resume work on your backup. It also provides you with a backup in case you leave your work laptop at the office.

How to Choose Your Laptop

The key to a good on-call or travel laptop is to get something cheap. As computers have continued to get faster, the fact is that many people can get their general work done (especially in a pinch) with laptops that are many years old. This is especially true on a Linux desktop, even if you aren't someone who spends a decent amount of time on a terminal.

Used Thinkpads are a great choice for travel laptops, because they have good Linux compatibility and are rugged and easy to repair with replacement parts that are easy to find. Because so many organizations have used them as company laptops, you almost always can find a used one cheap on an auction site. Keep an eye out for a model that is listed as having no OS. Those laptops tend to be cheaper because people want to avoid having to install an OS, but as Linux users, we would just overwrite the OS anyway! I've consistently found that if I'm patient, I can get a Thinkpad with reasonable specs for less than $50 on auction sites. If you are willing to splurge on extra RAM or an SSD, these old machines can be surprisingly speedy.

Another option, especially if you want a more portable laptop, is a Chromebook. Although these machines normally are designed to run a limited, secured OS that centers on Google services, they also can run Linux well once you switch into developer mode. Some people use cheap Chromebooks as their default travel computers since they just want to check Gmail and browse the web while traveling. Personally, I found a used Acer C710 for $40 and was able to add RAM and an SSD from a spare Thinkpad, and it turned out to be a rather capable Qubes-compatible machine.

Setting Up Your Laptop

I use Qubes both on my work and personal laptops, and I've long used its built-in backup and restore tool whenever I travel to make sure I have a fresh backup in case my laptop is lost or stolen. Now that I rely on a separate laptop for travel, I just restore that fresh backup onto my travel machine and test it by working on it for a day before the trip. This also means I can selectively restore only the files and settings (appVMs in my case) that are relevant for the situation. In the case of its use as an on-call computer, I don't have to worry as much about fresh backups as long as all of my VPN, SSH and other credentials are kept up to date.

Since most people don't use Qubes, just take advantage of whatever tool you prefer to back up your laptop (you do back up your laptop regularly, don't you?) and restore onto your spare computer as regularly as you need to keep important files up to date. Given that you are doing this to protect against the laptop being lost or stolen, be sure to enable full disk encryption when you install the OS to help protect your sensitive files just in case. For those of you who are extra security-conscious, you can take the additional step of wiping and re-installing your OS whenever you return from a long trip, just in case you are worried about any malware that found its way on your computer while you were on untrusted networks.

In general, I highly recommend selecting a cheap laptop for your on-call and travel computer. You will find you have extra peace of mind knowing that not only will it be inexpensive to replace your laptop if it's lost, broken or stolen, but also that you when you return home, you can get on your regular computer and get right back to work.

Documentation

Good documentation is the best way to reduce or eliminate how much you have to step in when you aren't on call, whether you're on vacation or not. Everything from routine procedures to emergency response should be documented and kept up to date. Honestly, this falls under standard best practices as a sysadmin, so it's something you should have whether or not you are about to go on vacation.

First, all routine procedures from how you deploy code and configuration changes, how you manage tickets, how you perform security patches, how you add and remove users, and how the overall environment is structured should be documented in a clear step-by-step way. If you use automation tools for routine procedures, whether it's as simple as a few scripts or as complex as full orchestration tools, you should make sure you document not only how to use the automation tools, but also how to perform the same tasks manually should the automation tools fail.

If you are on call, that means you have a monitoring system in place that scans your infrastructure for problems and pages you when it finds any. Every

1.7 Preparing for Vacation

single system check in your monitoring tool should have a corresponding playbook that a sysadmin can follow to troubleshoot and fix the problem. If your monitoring tool allows you to customize the alerts it sends, create corresponding wiki entries for each alert name, and then customize the alert so that it provides a direct link to the playbook in the wiki.

If you happen to be the subject-matter expert on a particular system, make sure that documentation in particular is well fleshed out and understandable. These are the systems that will pull you out of your vacation, so look through those documents for any assumptions you may have made when writing them that a junior member of the team might not understand. Have other members of the team review the documentation and ask you questions.

One saying about documentation is that if something is documented in two places, one of them will be out of date. Even if you document something only in one place, there's a good chance it is out of date unless you perform routine maintenance. It's a good practice to review your documentation from time to time and update it where necessary and before a vacation is a particularly good time to do it. If you are the only person that knows about the new way to perform a procedure, you should make sure your documentation covers it.

Finally, have your team maintain a page to capture anything that happens while you are gone that they want to tell you about when you get back. If you are the main maintainer of a particular system, but they had to perform some emergency maintenance of it while you were gone, that's the kind of thing you'd like to know about when you get back. If there's a central place for the team to capture these notes, they will be more likely to write things down as they happen and less likely to forget about things when you get back.

Stable State

The more stable your infrastructure is before you leave and the more stable it stays while you are gone, the less likely you'll be disturbed on your vacation. Right before a vacation is a terrible time to make a major change to critical systems. If you can, freeze changes in the weeks leading up to your vacation. Try to encourage other teams to push off any major changes until after you get back.

Before a vacation is also a great time to perform any preventative maintenance on your systems. Check for any systems about to hit a disk warning threshold and clear out space. In general, if you collect trending data, skim through it for any resources that are trending upward that might go past thresholds while you are gone. If you have any tasks that might add extra load to your systems while you are gone, pause or postpone them if you can. Make sure all of your backup scripts are working and all of your backups are up to date.

Emergency Contact Methods

Although it would be great to unplug completely while on vacation, there's a chance that someone from work might want to reach you in an emergency. Depending on where you plan to travel, some contact options may work better than others. For instance, some cell-phone plans that work while traveling might charge high rates for calls, but text messages and data bill at the same rates as at home. If you plan to get a local sim card, text messages sent over the cell network from home might cost more than those sent over the data plan. In the event of a local sim card, you will have to work out some way to communicate that new number to your team.

Discuss with your team what escalation path they should use to contact you in an emergency. For instance, in my case, I knew my cell-phone plan would provide me with unlimited text messages and the same data plan as at home, but I also didn't want work email to distract me. This presented a problem, as email is the primary way I'm paged. In my case, I disabled email syncing while I was on vacation and instructed everyone to contact me via text message in the case of emergency. I also needed to be on the secondary escalation path for any alerts that weren't resolved within a certain amount of time, so I configured my monitoring tool to use an email-to-SMS gateway as my email address for alerts.

If there are certain days when you know you (or your on-call counterpart at home) might be in areas with limited cell coverage, work out those dates ahead of time and put them in your calendar. If nothing else, it might encourage others to wait on making a risky change if they know they absolutely will not be able to reach you for the next two days. In general, set expectations on your availability, and also make sure everyone takes any time zone differences into account.

Overall, a vacation should be a time for you to be completely removed from your work's on-call process. Whether that's possible or not, the more you prepare ahead of time, the less likely your vacation will be interrupted. Finally, when you get back, do a post mortem with your team about anything that went wrong and any documentation that was confusing or incomplete, so you can make improvements for your next vacation.

1.8 Travel Laptops Tips in Practice

So I've written about how to prepare for a vacation or other travel when you're on call, and I just got back from a vacation where I put some of those ideas into practice. In this section I will give some specifics on what I recommended, what I actually did and how it all worked.

1.8 Travel Laptops Tips in Practice

Planning for the Vacation

The first thing to point out is that this was one of the first vacations in a long time where I was not on call, directly or indirectly. In my long career as a sysadmin responsible for production infrastructure, I've almost always been on call (usually indirectly) when on vacation. Even if someone else was officially taking over on-call duties while I was away, there always was the risk that a problem would crop up where they would need to escalate up to me. Often on my vacations something did blow up to the point that I needed to get involved. I've now transitioned into more of a management position, so the kinds of emergencies I face are much different.

I bring up the fact that I wasn't on an on-call rotation not because it factored into how I prepared for the trip, but because, generally speaking, it didn't factor in except that I didn't have to go to as extreme lengths to make sure everyone knew how to contact me in an emergency. Even though I wasn't on call, there still was a chance, however remote, that some emergency could pop up where I needed to help. And, an emergency might require that I access company resources, which meant I needed to have company credentials with me at a minimum. I imagine for most people in senior-enough positions that this would also be true. I could have handled this in a few ways:

1. Hope that I could access all the work resources I might need from my phone.
2. Carry a copy of my password manager database with me.
3. Put a few select work VMs on my travel laptop.

I chose option number 3, just to be safe. Although I'm not superstitious, I still figured that if I were prepared for an emergency, there was a better chance one wouldn't show up (and I was right). At the very least, if I were well prepared for a work emergency, if even a minor problem arose, I could respond to it without a major inconvenience instead of scrambling to build some kind of MacGyver-style work environment out of duct tape and hotel computers.

Selecting the Travel Computer

As I've mentioned previously, I recommend buying a cheap, used computer for travel. That way, if you lose it or it gets damaged, confiscated or stolen, you're not out much money. I personally bought a used Acer Parrot C710 for use as a travel computer, because it's small, cheap and runs QubesOS pretty well once you give it enough RAM.

I originally planned on taking this same small travel computer with me on my vacation. I even prepped the OS and was about to transfer files over when I changed my mind at the last minute. I changed my mind because at my job we are working on integrating a tamper-evident boot firmware called Heads into our laptops that, in combination with our USB security token called the Librem Key, makes it easy to detect tampering. You plug in the key at boot, and if it blinks green, you are fine; if it blinks red, it detected tampering. Normally, I wouldn't recommend taking a work laptop on vacation, but in this case, I wanted to beta-test this firmware protection, so at the last minute, I decided to take my work laptop and try everything out.

Preparing the Travel Computer

Another important part of travel preparation is to make backups of your personal or work laptops. This is important whether you are traveling with your personal laptop, a work laptop or a travel laptop, because in any of those cases, you will want to transfer some files to the laptop you have with you, and you'll also want to be safe in case you lose that machine.

In my case, the backup process has an additional significance because I use QubesOS. QubesOS allows you to separate different workflows, files and applications into individual VMs that all run in a unified desktop. You also can back up and restore those VMs independently. For travel, this means I can perform a full backup of personal and work machines before the trip and then restore just the VMs I need onto my travel laptop. If the laptop is lost, broken or stolen, or if I want to wipe the laptop, I don't have to worry about losing data.

Since I was traveling with my work laptop, this meant that I performed my normal backups of personal and work Qubes VMs, but then I just restored the personal VMs I thought I might need on the trip onto my work laptop. Otherwise, I would have restored both personal and work VMs onto my separate travel laptop. Normally I also recommend that you spend a full day working from your travel laptop after you have set it up, so you can make sure you have all of the access and files you need. Since I was traveling with the work laptop, I could skip this step, of course.

The Results

So what were the results of all this travel preparation? I barely had to open my laptop at all! I had one or two personal obligations that required the laptop at the beginning, but I didn't have to fire up any work VMs. Since I mostly kept my laptop in a bag, I did end up leaving it unattended quite a bit, so it was a good test for that tamper-detection (as you might expect, the laptop wasn't tampered with during the trip). Knowing that I could fire up work VMs if I had to did give me extra peace of mind during the trip, even though I never actually had to try it.

When I returned home, there was some clean up to do. Normally with my travel laptop, this means a complete wipe and re-install of the OS so it's ready for next time. In this case, since I was using my regular work laptop, I just deleted all of the personal VMs I had added.

Telecommuting Tips

I live in the San Francisco Bay Area, known for high-tech companies, horrible traffic and high cost of living. When it came time for me to buy a house, I chose an area that left me with a 90 to 120-minute commute, depending on traffic and the time of day, so through the years, I've negotiated work-from-home days and have experience with telecommuting at companies of various sizes with different proportions of remote workers. Telecommuting is not only more convenient for many employees, it also can get the best work out of people (especially sysadmin), because it can grant better opportunities to focus and lets employees get right to work instead of spending hours getting to and from work. Unfortunately, many places inadvertently sabotage their telecommuters with bad practices, so here are a few tips to help make telecommuting successful.

Invest in Good Teleconference Hardware

I've attended many video conferences where the audio was so horrible, I might as well have not joined. Or worse, there was a time when one speaker was loud and clear, but when the conversation went to the other side of the table, it was inaudible. Although it's nice to have quality cameras, having quality microphones is critical. Make sure each of your meeting rooms has quality microphones that can pick up sounds all around the meeting table, and make sure attendees speak up. Relying on the microphone on someone's laptop just doesn't cut it for meetings involving more than two people. Although it's considered good meeting etiquette to have only one person speak at a time, this protocol is extra important if you have anyone calling in, as cross-talk makes it all but impossible to hear either conversation even over a good microphone.

Add Video Conference Links to Every Meeting

Make it a habit to add a link to your video conference room for each meeting you create, even if all of the attendees are expected to be in the office. This habit ensures that when you realize you forgot to invite a remote worker, you aren't scrambling to figure out how to set up the video conference, plus sometimes even team members in the office need to work from home at the last minute. If your scheduling software can do this automatically, even better (some do this by having each meeting room in a contact list and inviting the relevant meeting room to the meeting). Also make sure you set this up for all-hands company-wide meetings.

Remember Remote Workers in Impromptu Meetings

Companies that rely on a central office often treat telecommuters as second-class citizens. Not only are they left out of impromptu hallway conversations, when those conversations move to a meeting room, the attendees also often forget to invite any remote workers who may be stakeholders in the decision and find out about major decisions only after the fact. Try to keep relevant team discussions in your work chat, so remote workers can participate (this has the added advantage of creating a nice log of your conversation, plus multiple people can participate at once). If you do end up moving a discussion into a meeting room, remember to invite your remote team members.

Take Advantage of Group Chat, Even in the Office

There are many advantages to using group chat for team communication, even if team members are in the same office. The virtual "tap on the shoulder" in a group chat is much less disruptive to someone's focus than the actual in-person tap on the shoulder, which means if someone is deeply focused on a task, your chat notification may not disrupt them, although physically standing behind them forces them to stop anything they are doing. By sticking to group chat for these kinds of communications, you can be sure that remote members of the team aren't left out of any discussions, and every person feels like an equal member of the team.

Be Responsive in Chat

If you work remotely and a lot of your team is in an office, it's more important than ever to stay responsive in chat. In an office, people know you are there by whether you are at your desk, but when telecommuting, it all comes down to whether you respond when someone contacts you in chat. If your chat program provides ways to escalate notifications from your desktop to your phone app, take advantage of them. That way if you step away from your desk for a moment, your phone still can tell you when someone needs you. If you are going to step away from your desk for an extended amount of time to get lunch or run an errand, make sure someone on your team knows (or set a proper away message if your chat supports it). If you are in the office, realize that chat is the main way remote workers will communicate, so try to reward their responsiveness by being responsive yourself.

In summary, the key to telecommuting being a success is to treat remote team members as equals and to take advantage of all of the great collaboration tools that exist to keep teams connected. These small steps can make all the difference in helping remote workers be productive and feel like part of the team.

2. Sysadmin's Toolbox

If a sysadmin were craftsmen, then command-line commands would be their toolbox. No matter how long someone has used the Linux command line, there are always new tools to learn (and new ways to use tools you already know). This is one of the reasons that learning about command-line tools is so rewarding. The other reason is that the more tools in your toolbox (and the better you know how to use them) the easier you will find day-to-day tasks.

Since there is a never-ending supply of command-line tools, this chapter doesn't attempt to describe all of them. Instead it aims to to highlight some specific sysadmin-focused tools and how they can help you perform common sysadmin-focused tasks. These tasks include scheduling one-off tasks, sorting output, parsing through logs, and finding more efficient ways to use commands you already know.

Before I dive into specific commands, though, I figure it's useful to understand how the overall Linux directory structure is organized since you will be throwing commands around in it. So I start with an overview of the Linux Filesystem Hierarchy Standard (FHS)–the conventions behind all those oddly-named directories on your system.

By the end of the chapter, you should have a good sense of some of the ways you can use command-line tools to simplify common tasks and hopefully even seasoned administrators will have learned a few new tricks of their own. Remember, one of the best ways to master command-line tools and to learn new commands and upgraded arguments is to master the most important command-line tool of all: man. If you ever want to know how to use a command and what the available arguments are, type man commandname. For instance, when I heard that recent versions of the dd command included a progress bar, the first thing I did was type:

```
man dd
```

If you want to find out how to get a progress bar from your own dd command, check out the section later in this chapter titled "Add Progress Bars to dd".

2.1 Filesystem Hierarchy Standard

If you are new to the Linux command line, you may find yourself wondering why there are so many unusual directories, what they are there for, and why things are organized the way they are. In fact, if you aren't accustomed to how Linux organizes files, the directories can seem downright arbitrary with odd truncated names and, in many cases, redundant names. It turns out there's a method to this madness based on decades of UNIX convention, and in this section, I provide an introduction to the Linux directory structure.

Although each Linux distribution has its own quirks, the majority conform (for the most part) with the Filesystem Hierarchy Standard (FHS). The FHS project began in 1993, and the goal was to come to a consensus on how directories should be organized and which files should be stored where, so that distributions could have a single reference point from which to work. A lot of decisions about directory structure were based on traditional UNIX directory structures with a focus on servers and with an assumption that disk space was at a premium, so machines likely would have multiple hard drives.

/bin and /sbin

The /bin and /sbin directories are intended for storing binary executable files. Both directories store executables that are considered essential for booting the system (such as the mount command). The main difference between these directories is that the /sbin directory is intended for system binaries, or binaries that administrators will use to manage the system.

/boot

This directory stores all the bootloader files (typically GRUB), kernel files and initrd files. It's often treated as a separate, small partition, so that the bootloader can read it more easily. With /boot on a separate partition, your root filesystem can use more sophisticated features that require kernel support whether that's an exotic filesystem, disk encryption or logical volume management.

2.1 Filesystem Hierarchy Standard

/etc

The /etc directory is intended for storing system configuration files. If you need to configure a service on a Linux system, or change networking or other core settings, this is the first place to look. This is also a small and easy-to-back-up directory that contains most of the customizations you might make to your computer at the system level.

/home

The /home directory is the location on Linux systems where users are given directories for storing their own files. Each directory under /home is named after a particular user's user name and is owned by that user. On a server, these directories might store users' email, their SSH keys, or sometimes even local services users are running on high ports.

On desktop systems, the /home directory is probably the main directory with which users interact. Any desktop settings, pictures, media, documents or other files users need end up being stored in their /home directories. On a desktop, this is the most important directory to back up, and it's often a directory that's given its own partition. By giving /home its own partition, you can experiment with different Linux distributions and re-install the complete system on a separate / partition, and then when you mount this /home partition, all of your files and settings are right there where you left them.

/lib

The /lib directory stores essential shared libraries that the essential binaries in /bin and /sbin need to run. This is also the directory where kernel modules are stored.

/usr, /usr/bin, /usr/lib and /usr/sbin

The /usr directory (which has stood both for UNIX source repository and UNIX system resources) is intended to be a read-only directory that stores files that aren't required to boot the system. In general, when you install additional software from your distribution, its binaries, libraries and supporting files go here in their corresponding /usr/bin, /usr/sbin or /usr/lib directories, among some others. When storage was at a premium, you often would mount this directory separately on its own larger disk, so it could grow independently as you added new software.

These days, there is less of a need to have this kind of logical separation, in particular because systems tend to have everything in a single large root partition, and the initrd file tends to have the tools necessary to mount that filesystem. Some distributions are starting to merge /bin, /sbin and /lib with their corresponding /usr directories via symlinks.

/usr/local

The /usr/local directory is a special version of /usr that has its own internal structure of bin, lib and sbin directories, but /usr/local is designed to be a place where users can install their own software outside the distribution's provided software without worrying about overwriting any distribution files.

/opt

The debates between /usr/local and /opt are legendary, and Bill Childers and I even participated in our own debate in a Linux Journal Point/Counterpoint article. Essentially, both directories serve the same purpose–providing a place for users to install software outside their distributions–but the /opt directory organizes it differently. Instead of storing binaries and libraries for different pieces of software together in a shared directory, like with /usr and /usr/local, the /opt directory grants each piece of software its own subdirectory, and it organizes its files underneath how it pleases. The idea here is that, in theory, you could uninstall software in /opt just by removing that software's directory. For more details on the relative pros and cons of this approach, check out the Point/Counterpoint article.[1]

/root

The /root directory is a special home directory for the root user on the system. It's owned and readable only by the root user, and it's designed otherwise to function much like a /home directory but for files and settings the root user needs. Many systems now disable the root user in favor of using sudo to get superuser privileges, so this directory isn't used nearly as much.

/var

As I've mentioned, classic UNIX servers held disk space at a premium, and the /var directory was designed for storing files that might vary wildly in size or might get written to frequently. Unlike with /usr, which is read-only, the /var directory most definitely needs to be writeable, because within it you will find log files, mail server spools, and other files that might come and go or otherwise might grow in size in unpredictable ways.

Even now, at least on servers, if you had to pick a root-level directory to put on its own large disk, the /var directory would be the first one on the listnot just because it might grow rather large in size, but also because you might want to put /var on a disk that's better-optimized for heavy writes. Also, if you have all of your directories inside one large root partition, and you run out of disk space, the /var directory is a great place to start your search for files to remove.

---

[1] https://www.linuxjournal.com/magazine/pointcounterpoint-opt-vs-usrlocal

/dev

You will find device files here. UNIX systems have an "everything is a file" principle that means even your hardware ends up with a file. This directory contains files for devices on your system from disks and partitions to mice and keyboards.

/proc and /sys

In addition to /dev, two other directories end up with dynamic files that represent something other than a file. The /proc directory stores files that represent information about all of the running processes on the system. You can actually use tools like ls and cat to read about the status of different processes running on your system. This directory also often contains files in /proc/sys that interact with the kernel and allow you to tweak particular kernel parameters and poll settings.

While some kernel state files have shown up in /proc (in particular /proc/sys), they are supposed to be stored in /sys instead. The /sys directory is designed to contain all of these files that let you interact with the kernel, and this directory gets dynamically populated with files that often show up as nested series of recursive symlinks–be careful when running commands like find in here!

/srv

Compared to some of the directories, /srv is a bit of a newcomer. This directory is designed for storing files that a server might share externally. For instance, this is considered the proper place to store web server files (/srv/www is popular).

/mnt and /media

When you add extra filesystems to your computer, whether it's from a USB drive, an NFS mount or other sources, you need some standard place to mount them. This is where /mnt and /media come in. The /mnt directory used to be a catch-all for any mounted disk that didn't have any other place to go, but these days, you should use this directory for various NFS mountpoints and other disks that are intended to be mounted all the time. The /media directory is designed for those disks that are mounted temporarily, such as CD-ROMs and USB disks.

/tmp, /var/tmp and /dev/shm

Even Linux needs a junk drawer, and it provides a number of directories that are designed to store temporary files, based on how long you want to keep them. These directories are ideal for programs that need to store some data in a file temporarily but may not need the data to stick around forever, such as cached data that a process can re-create. What makes these directories ideal for this purpose is that they are created with permissions such that any user can write to them.

The /tmp directory is aimed at storing temporary files that don't need to stick around after a reboot. When a Linux system boots, one of the initial boot processes cleans out all of the files in the /tmp directory. The /var/tmp directory, on the other hand, does not get cleaned out between reboots, so this is a good place to store files, such as caches that you'd appreciate sticking around, even if you don't absolutely need them. Finally, the /dev/shm directory is a small ramdisk, and any files that are stored there reside only in RAM, and after the system is turned off, these files are erased. Hackers love to store files in /dev/shm for this reason. The /dev/shm directory is the best of the three if you have temporary files that store sensitive information like passwords or secrets, as they never will touch the disk–just be sure to give the files appropriate permissions (like 0600) before you put your secrets there so no one else can read them.

This guide covered only some of the directories defined in the standard. If you are curious about some of the other directories on your system–in particular, if you are a developer and want to ensure that you are storing files in the right place–please refer to the official Filesystem Hierarchy Standard[2] for a lot more detail.

2.2 Scheduling One-time Jobs with At

When I first started using Linux, it was like being tossed into the deep end of the UNIX pool. You were expected to use the command-line heavily along with all of the standard utilities and services that came along with your distribution. At lot has changed since then and nowadays you can use a standard Linux desktop without ever having opening a terminal or using old UNIX services. Even as a sysadmin today you are often a few layers of abstraction above some of these core services.

I say all this to point out that for us old-timers, it's easy to take for granted that everyone around us innately knows about all the command line tools we use. Yet even though I've been using Linux for twenty years, I still learn about new (to me) command line tools all the time. In this section I'm going to cover some of the command line tools that those new to Linux may have never used before. First, I'm going to describe how to use the at utility to schedule jobs to run at a later date.

---

[2]https://refspecs.linuxfoundation.org/FHS_3.0/fhs/index.html

2.2 Scheduling One-time Jobs with At

At Versus Cron

At is one of those commands that doesn't get discussed all that much. When people talk about scheduling commands, typically cron gets the most coverage. Cron allows you to schedule commands to be run on a periodic basis. With cron you can run a command as frequently as every minute or as seldom as once a day, week, month, or even year. You can also define more sophisticated rules so commands run, for example, every five minutes, every week day, every other hour, and many other combinations. Sysadmin sometimes will use cron to schedule a local script to collect metrics every minute or schedule backups.

On the other hand, while the at command also allows you to schedule commands, it serves a completely different purpose from cron. While cron lets you schedule commands to run periodically, at lets you schedule commands that run only once at a particular time in the future. This difference means that at fills a different and usually more immediate need than cron.

Using At

At one point the at command came standard on most Linux distributions, but now, even on servers, you may find yourself having to install the at package explicitly. Once installed, the easiest way to use at is to type it on the command line followed by the time you want the command to run:

```
at 18:00
```

The at command can also accept a number of different time formats. For instance, it understands AM and PM as well as words like "tomorrow" so you could replace the above command with the identical:

```
at 6pm
```

If you wanted to run the command at that time tomorrow instead:

```
at 6pm tomorrow
```

Once you press enter, you will drop into an interactive shell:

```
at 6pm tomorrow
warning: commands will be executed using /bin/sh
at>
```

From the interactive shell you can enter the command you would like to run at that time. If you want to run multiple commands, hit Enter after each command and type the new command on the new at> prompt. Once you are done entering your commands, hit Ctrl-D on an empty at> prompt to exit the interactive shell.

For instance, let's say that I've noticed that a particular server has had problems the last two days at 5:10am for around five minutes and so far I'm not seeing anything in the logs. While I could just wake up early and log into the server, instead I could write a short script that collects data from ps, netstat,tcpdump and other command-line tools for a few minutes so when I wake up I can go over the data it collected. Since this is a one-off I don't want to schedule something with cron and risk forgetting about it and having it run every day, so this is how I would set it up with at:

```
at 5:09am tomorrow
warning: commands will be executed using /bin/sh
at>
at> /usr/local/bin/my_monitoring_script
```

Then I would hit Ctrl-D and the shell would exit with this output:

```
at> <EOT>
job 1 at Wed Sep 26 05:09:00 2018
```

Managing At Jobs

Once you have scheduled at jobs, it's useful to be able to pull up a list of all the at jobs in the queue so you know what's running and when. The atq command lists the current at queue:

```
atq
1    Wed Sep 26 05:09:00 2018 a kyle
```

The first column lists the number at assigned to each job and then lists the time the job will be run and the user who it will run as. Let's say that in the above example I realize I made a mistake because my script won't be able to run as a regular user. In that case I would want to use the atrm command to remove job number 1:

```
atrm 1
```

If you were to run atq again you would see that the job no longer exists. Then you could sudo up to root and use the at command to schedule the job again.

At One-Liners

While at supports an interactive mode, you can also pipe commands to it all in one line instead. So for instance I could schedule the above job with:

```
echo /usr/local/bin/my_monitoring_script | at 5:09am tomorrow
```

If you didn't know that at existed, you might find yourself coming up with all sorts of complicated and convoluted ways to schedule a one-off job. Even worse, you might have to set an alarm clock for yourself to wake up early and log into a problem server. Of course if you didn't have an alarm clock, you could use at:

```
echo "aplay /home/kyle/alarm.wav" | at 7am tomorrow
```

2.3 Sort and Uniq

If you've been using the command line for a long time, it's easy to take the commands you use every day for granted. But, if you're new to the Linux command line, there are several commands that make your life easier that you may not stumble upon automatically. In this section, I cover the basics of two commands that are essential in anyone's arsenal: sort and uniq.

The sort command does exactly what it says: it takes text data as input and outputs sorted data. There are many scenarios on the command line when you may need to sort output, such as the output from a command that doesn't offer sorting options of its own (or the sort arguments are obscure enough that you just use the sort command instead). In other cases, you may have a text file full of data (perhaps generated with some other script), and you need a quick way to view it in a sorted form.

Let's start with a file named "test" that contains three lines:

```
Foo
Bar
Baz
```

sort can operate either on STDIN redirection, the input from a pipe, or, in the case of a file, you also can just specify the file on the command. So, the three following commands all accomplish the same thing:

```
cat test | sort
sort < test
sort test
```

And the output that you get from all of these commands is:

```
Bar
Baz
Foo
```

Sorting Numerical Output

Now, let's complicate the file by adding three more lines:

```
Foo
Bar
Baz
1. ZZZ
2. YYY
11. XXX
```

If you run one of the above sort commands again, this time, you'll see different output:

```
11. xxx
1. zzz
2. yyy
Bar
Baz
Foo
```

This is likely not the output you wanted, but it points out an important fact about sort. By default, it sorts alphabetically, not numerically. This means that a line that starts with 11. is sorted above a line that starts with 1., and all of the lines that start with numbers are sorted above lines that start with letters.

To sort numerically, pass sort the -n option:

```
sort -n test

Bar
Baz
Foo
1. zzz
2. yyy
11. xxx
```

Find the Largest Directories on a Filesystem

Numerical sorting comes in handy for a lot of command-line output–in particular, when your command contains a tally of some kind, and you want to see the largest or smallest in the tally. For instance, if you want to find out what files are using the most space in a particular directory and you want to dig down recursively, you would run a command like this:

```
du -ckx
```

This command dives recursively into the current directory and doesn't traverse any other mountpoints inside that directory. It tallies the file sizes and then outputs each directory in the order it found them, preceded by the size of the files underneath it in kilobytes. Of course, if you're running such a command, it's probably because you want to know which directory is using the most space, and this is where sort comes in:

```
du -ckx | sort -n
```

Now you'll get a list of all of the directories underneath the current directory, but this time sorted by file size. If you want to get even fancier, pipe its output to the tail command to see the top ten. On the other hand, if you wanted the largest directories to be at the top of the output, not the bottom, you would add the -r option, which tells sort to reverse the order. So to get the top ten (well, top eight–the first line is the total, and the next line is the size of the current directory):

2.3 Sort and Uniq

```
du -ckx | sort -rn | head
```

This works, but often people using the du command want to see sizes in more readable output than kilobytes. The du command offers the -h argument that provides "human-readable" output. So, you'll see output like 9.6G instead of 10024764 with the -k option. When you pipe that human-readable output to sort though, you won't get the results you expect by default, as it will sort 9.6G above 9.6K, which would be above 9.6M.

The sort command has a -h option of its own, and it acts like -n, but it's able to parse standard human-readable numbers and sort them accordingly. So, to see the top ten largest directories in your current directory with human-readable output, you would type this:

```
du -chx | sort -rh | head
```

Removing Duplicates

The sort command isn't limited to sorting one file. You might pipe multiple files into it or list multiple files as arguments on the command line, and it will combine them all and sort them. Unfortunately though, if those files contain some of the same information, you will end up with duplicates in the sorted output.

To remove duplicates, you need the `uniq` command, which by default removes any duplicate lines that are adjacent to each other from its input and outputs the results. So, let's say you had two files that were different lists of names:

```
cat namelist1.txt
Jones, Bob
Smith, Mary
Babbage, Walter

$ cat namelist2.txt
Jones, Bob
Jones, Shawn
Smith, Cathy
```

You could remove the duplicates by piping to `uniq`:

```
sort namelist1.txt namelist2.txt | uniq
Babbage, Walter
Jones, Bob
Jones, Shawn
Smith, Cathy
Smith, Mary
```

The `uniq` command has more tricks up its sleeve than this. It also can output only the duplicated lines, so you can find duplicates in a set of files quickly by adding the -d option:

```
sort namelist1.txt namelist2.txt | uniq -d
Jones, Bob
```

You even can have uniq provide a tally of how many times it has found each entry with the -c option:

```
sort namelist1.txt namelist2.txt | uniq -c
1 Babbage, Walter
2 Jones, Bob
1 Jones, Shawn
1 Smith, Cathy
1 Smith, Mary
```

As you can see, "Jones, Bob" occurred the most times, but if you had a lot of lines, this sort of tally might be less useful for you, as you'd like the most duplicates to bubble up to the top. Fortunately, you have the sort command:

```
sort namelist1.txt namelist2.txt | uniq -c | sort -nr
2 Jones, Bob
1 Smith, Mary
1 Smith, Cathy
1 Jones, Shawn
1 Babbage, Walter
```

I hope these cases of using sort and uniq with realistic examples show you how powerful these simple command-line tools are. Half the secret with these foundational command-line tools is to discover (and remember) they exist so that they'll be at your command the next time you run into a problem they can solve.

2.4 Tracking Bandwidth with Iftop

Anyone who's had to use a network at a conference has experienced what happens when there just isn't enough network bandwidth to go around. While you are trying to check your e-mail, other people are streaming movies and TV shows, downloading distribution install disks, using p2p networks, upgrading their distributions or watching cat videos on YouTube. Although it's certainly frustrating to try to use one of those networks, imagine how frustrating it would be to be the admin in charge of that network. Whether you run a conference network, a local office network or even a Web server at your house, it can be really nice to know what is using up all of your bandwidth.

iftop is a Linux command-line program designed to give you live statistics about what network connections use the most bandwidth in a nice graphical form. As you may realize from the name, iftop borrows a lot of ideas from the always-useful load troubleshooting tool top. Like top, iftop updates automatically every few seconds, and like top, by default, it sorts the output you see by what's using the most resources. Where top is concerned with processes and how much CPU

2.4 Tracking Bandwidth with Iftop

and RAM they use, iftop is concerned with network connections and how much upload and download bandwidth they use.

Even though iftop is packaged for both Red Hat- and Debian-based distributions, it's probably not installed by default, so you will need to install the package of the same name. In the case of Red Hat-based distributions, you might have to pull it down from a third-party repository. Once it's installed, the simplest way to get started is just to run iftop as the root user. iftop will locate the first interface it can use and start listening in on the traffic and display output similar to what you see in Figure 2.1. To close the program, press q to quit just like with top.

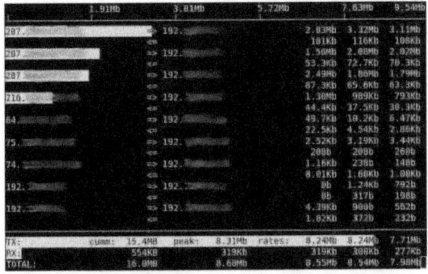

Figure 2.1: iftop output–the IPs have been smudged to protect the innocent.

At the very top of the screen is a scale that goes along with the bar graph iftop might display with each connection. The next rows of output correspond to each network connection between a pair of hosts. In between the two hosts are arrows that let you know the direction the traffic is flowing. The final three columns provide average bandwidth for each connection during the last 2, 10 and 40 seconds, respectively. So for instance, the very top connection in Figure 2.1 has averaged around 2.83Mb during the last 2 seconds, 3.32Mb during the last 10 seconds and 3.11Mb during the last 40 seconds. Underneath all the transmit and receive columns at the bottom of the screen are a series of statistics for overall transmitted and received traffic (TX and RX, respectively) including 2-, 10- and 40-second averages for both those and, finally, the totals for the interface.

> **Note:** If you have a server with multiple interfaces, you may want iftop to monitor a different interface from the default. Just add -i followed by the interface to monitor when you launch iftop. For instance, to monitor eth2, I would type iftop -i eth2.

Disable DNS Lookups

By default, when you run iftop, it will try to translate all of the IP addresses into hostnames. Sometimes this can be useful if you are diagnosing issues on a local network; however, like with a lot of other network diagnostics tools, resolving all of those IPs can slow down the program and also may contribute to the traffic you see in the output. The solution is to run iftop with the -n argument, so it just shows you IP addresses for everything (you always can run a DNS query against an IP you are interested in, in another window). Alternatively, if you already have iftop running, you can press n to disable DNS lookups.

Show Port Data

When you run iftop on a server that might serve multiple purposes, it can be handy to know whether all of that upstream traffic is accessing your Web server, your mail server or something else. Alternatively, if you are trying to figure out what's using up all of your download bandwidth, it can be handy to see whether the top connections are Web connections or some rsync job you have running. To figure all of this out, iftop allows you to toggle the port display on and off. Press the p key while iftop is running, and it will display the ports used for both the source and destination IP for all traffic.

The one big downside to showing both the source and destination ports used for a connection is that you'll find in many cases you are concerned only with one or the other. For instance, if you are running a Web server, you may notice that a lot of traffic is going to your Web port (labeled www in iftop), but all of the ports used by IPs accessing your Web server use all sorts of high ports. In that case, you can press either S or D to toggle the display of either source or destination ports, respectively. Figure 2.2 shows an example of iftop output where I've chosen to display only the source ports.

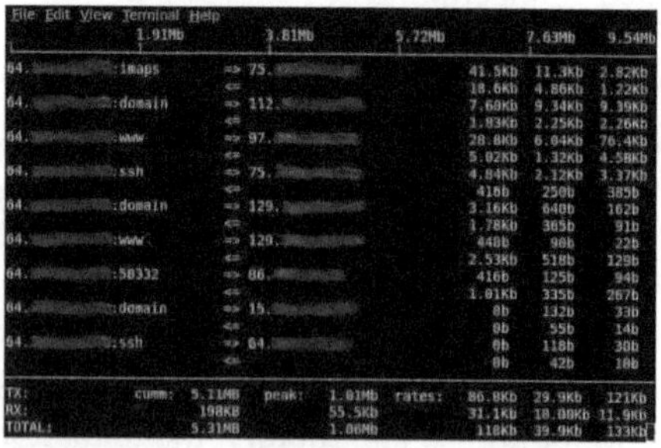

Figure 2.2: iftop with only the source ports displayed.

For me, the really great thing about iftop is that it's a relatively simple command-line tool. It's true that a number of other programs exist that can provide fancy

2.5 Right Command, Wrong Server

Web-based graphs of your network traffic, and I think those are great for trending network data just like they are for trending system load and other metrics. What I like about iftop is the same thing I like about top: when there's a problem, you can get instant real-time data about your system that updates as the situation progresses.

When I first started out in systems administration, I had only a few machines to keep track of. It was relatively easy to remember which servers did which functions (mostly because one or two machines did just about everything). If a server had a problem, I immediately knew everything it would impact.

For better or worse, nowadays my position has become more complicated. When you personally manage tens or hundreds of machines, it can be difficult to keep everything straight. When a server goes down, you might no longer know what services are impacted or who else to notify. Beyond that, there's also the dreaded running-the-right-command-on-the-wrong-server mistake. I think every sysadmin has typed `halt`, `rm -rf` or some other destructive command in the wrong terminal at least once (just ask my old boss Bill).

In this section, I discuss some methods I've found to help you keep track of your servers. Although I can't guarantee you'll never type a command on the wrong server, I can say that as your environment grows to hundreds of servers, these techniques will help you pick up where your brain left off.

Message of the Day

The message of the day (motd) is the message that greets you every time you log in to your system on the command line. For instance, here is the message of the day on one of my old Debian servers:

```
Linux napoleon 2.6.20-1-k7 #1 SMP Tue Apr 24 22:37:29 UTC 2007 i686

The programs included with the Debian GNU/Linux system are free
software; the exact distribution terms for each program are
described in the individual files in /usr/share/doc/*/copyright.

Debian GNU/Linux comes with ABSOLUTELY NO WARRANTY, to the extent
permitted by applicable law.
No mail.
```

Messages like this are pretty generic, so it's easy to take them for granted and leave them alone. After all, in this example, I already know the OS, hostname and kernel version (Linux, napoleon, 2.6.20-1-k7). You can extend this information, however, and list anything you want.

The message of the day is managed in a file called /etc/motd. It's a simple text file, so you can modify it to say anything you want, although you'll want to limit it to what can fit on a standard console screen. Note that on modern

Debian-based systems, the /etc/motd file is somewhat dynamic, so you will want to modify /etc/motd.tail instead.

So, how can you use this file to your advantage? A lot of security-minded administrators add a special terms of use in this file to note that their systems are private and do not allow unauthorized access. In that case, the motd acts like a No Trespassing sign, so if someone hacks in to the system, law enforcement has help demonstrating that the attacker was notified that it was a private system.

Although you may or may not want to add a No Trespassing sign to your motd, there are a number of other things you can add to the motd to make your life as an admin simpler. For instance, you could add a short set of documentation about the server, including what the server does, other groups to contact if there is a problem on the machine and even any special locations where custom files are stored. That way, when you log in, instead of a boring default motd, you could get something more like:

```
Linux napoleon 2.6.20-1-k7 #1 SMP Tue Apr 24 22:37:29 UTC 2007 i686

Welcome to Napoleon.
Local services: DNS, DHCP, Internal Wiki (http://wiki.example.net)

DNS config: /etc/bind, /var/named.
DHCP config: /etc/dhcpd.conf
Wiki files: /var/www/wiki

Support team: root@example.net, wikiadmin@example.net
```

You even might want to use the motd to pass along useful tips to regular users on the system. For instance, let's say your users use vim to view log files. On some systems, vim stores a complete copy of any files you open in /tmp. Although that's fine for a small text file, when you have users opening 1GB+ Apache logs, your /tmp space fills up quickly, and you are paged again and again. One solution might be to add a gentle reminder in your motd to use less, not vim, to read large text files.

Tweaked Shell Prompts

Another great way to help remind you which servers you are on is to tweak your shell prompt. If you are a good security-minded admin and become root only when necessary, a quick tip is to make the root prompt a different color (like red), so it stands out and reminds you that everything you do is with root privileges.

There are many different tastes when it comes to a custom shell prompt, so you might want to tweak this to suit your preferences. Also, I'm assuming you will be using the bash shell that most systems tend to default to, so the file you should edit is /root/.bashrc. What shows up in your prompt is defined by the PS1 environment variable, so if you are curious what it is set to by default, simply type:

2.5 Right Command, Wrong Server

```
root@napoleon:~# echo $PS1
\u@\h:\w\$
```

In this example, you have a very basic prompt that lists the current user (\u), the @ symbol, the hostname (\h), a colon, the current working directory (\w) and a # symbol (if I'm root), or a $ otherwise (\$). On my sample system, it would look like `root@napoleon:~#` when I log in as root.

There are plenty of other ways you can tweak the prompt, and if you are curious, the full list of aliases you can use for it is found in the bash man page–just search for PS1.

Because I'm focused on colorizing the prompt and not necessarily changing the format, I mostly will leave the prompt as is. There are a few ways to colorize the prompt, but the simplest way I've found is to define some of the potential colors you'd like to use in environment variables ahead of time, and then you can assign them to the PS1 variable without going cross-eyed from all the escape characters. Open up /root/.bashrc, and if PS1 already is defined, add these lines above it:

```
NORMAL=`tput sgr0 2> /dev/null`
BOLD=`tput bold 2> /dev/null`
RED="\[\033[31m\]"
GREEN="\[\033[32m\]"
BLUE="\[\033[34m\]"
GREY="\[\033[1;30m\]"
PURPLE="\[\033[0;35m\]"
```

Now that all the colors are defined, I simply can define PS1 with the default settings, only with these color settings around it:

```
PS1 = "$RED\u@\h:\w\$$NORMAL"
```

Once you save the changes to .bashrc, the next time you log in, you will notice your prompt is colorized. Now you can spend the rest of the afternoon tweaking the prompt with different sets of colors and symbols like I did the first time I found out about it. It even might be worthwhile to use a different prompt color scheme for different types of servers.

DNS TXT Records

One of the problems with the previous two methods is that you must log in to a machine to get information on it. That leads me to one of my favorite ways to organize my servers, DNS TXT records. Most people probably are familiar with a DNS A record (it maps a hostname to an IP address) and probably CNAME and PTR records (it maps one hostname to another hostname and an IP address to a hostname, respectively), but many admins aren't aware of (or don't use) TXT records. A TXT record essentially allows you to assign text to a particular hostname. If you have an internal DNS infrastructure for your machines, you probably already have A records for all your servers. If you add a TXT record as well, that gives you a nice centralized place to document what each server does in a way that can be queried from any machine on the network.

To demonstrate how to use TXT records, let's assume I'm using a standard BIND server for DNS, and this is a short section of the file that defines A records for three hosts–napoleon, snowball and major:

```
napoleon    IN    A    192.168.1.6
snowball    IN    A    192.168.1.7
major       IN    A    192.168.1.8
```

All I would do is add a new TXT record below any A records I have that lists what those servers do:

```
napoleon    IN    A    192.168.1.6
napoleon    IN    TXT  "DNS, DHCP, Internal wiki"
snowball    IN    A    192.168.1.7
snowball    IN    TXT  "Primary Internal File Server"
major       IN    A    192.168.1.8
major       IN    TXT  "Failover Internal File Server"
```

Once I save my changes and reload BIND, the TXT records are ready to go. The next time I'm scratching my head trying to figure out what snowball does, I just have to issue a dig query:

```
dig snowball.example.net TXT +short
"Primary Internal File Server"
```

Note that I used the +short option with dig. That way, I get back only the contents of the TXT record instead of the volume of data dig normally gives me. Not only does this make it easy to narrow in on the information I want, it also makes it a handy little one-liner to add to other programs. I even could see some savvy administrators tweaking their shell prompt or motd so that it contained this value.

Again, the beauty of using TXT records to document this is that it puts the information in a central place that you control and that you typically have to modify whenever you add a host anyway. Just be careful if you use this for externally facing DNS hosts–you might not necessarily want to broadcast all of your server info to everyone on the Internet.

2.6 Chopping Logs

If you are a sysadmin, logs can be both a bane and a boon to your existence. On a bad day, a misbehaved program could dump gigabytes of errors into its log file, fill up the disk and light up your pager like a Christmas tree. On a good day, logs show you every clue you need to track down any of a hundred strange system problems. Now, if you manage any Web servers, logs provide even more valuable information in terms of statistics. How many visitors did you get to your main index page today? What spider is hammering your site right now?

2.6 Chopping Logs

Many excellent log-analysis tools exist. Some provide really nifty real-time visualizations of Web traffic, and others run every night and generate manager-friendly reports for you to browse. All of these programs are great, and I suggest you use them, but sometimes you need specific statistics and you need them now. For these on-the-fly statistics, I've developed a common template for a shell one-liner that chops through logs like Paul Bunyan.

What I've found is that although the specific type of information I need might change a little, for the most part, the algorithm remains mostly the same. For any log file, each line contains some bit of unique information I need. Then, I need to run through the log file, identify that information and keep a running tally that increments each time I see the particular pattern. Finally, I need to output that information along with its final tally and sort based on the tally.

There are many ways you can do this type of log parsing. Old-school command-line junkies might prefer a nice sed and awk approach. The whipper-snappers out there might pick a nicely formatted Python script. There's nothing at all wrong with those approaches, but I suppose I fall into the middle-child scripting category—I prefer Perl for this kind of text hacking. Maybe it's the power of Perl regular expressions, or maybe it's how easy it is to use Perl hashes, or maybe it's just what I'm most comfortable with, but I just seem to be able to hack out this kind of script much faster in Perl.

Before I give a sample script though, here's a more specific algorithm. The script parses through each line of input and uses a regular expression to match a particular column or other pattern of data on the line. It then uses that pattern as a key in a hash table and increments the value of that key. When it's done accepting input, the script iterates through each key in the hash and outputs the tally for that key and the key itself.

For the test case, I use a general-purpose problem you can try yourself, as long as you have an Apache Web server. I want to find out how many unique IP addresses visited one of my sites on November 1, 2008, and the top ten IPs in terms of hits.

Here's a sample entry from the log (the IP has been changed to protect the innocent):

```
123.123.12.34 - - [01/Nov/2008:19:34:02 -0700] "GET
↪ /talks/pxe/ui/default/iepngfix.htc HTTP/1.1"
↪ 404 308 "-" "Mozilla/4.0 (compatible; MSIE 7.0;
↪ Windows NT 6.0; SLCC1; .NET CLR 2.0.50727;
↪ Media Center PC 5.0; .NET CLR 3.0.04506; InfoPath.2)"
```

And, here's the one-liner that can parse the file and provide sorted output:

```
perl -e 'while(<>){ if( m|(^\d+\.\d+\.\d+\.\d+).*?
↪ 01/Nov/2008| ){ $v{$1}++; } } foreach( keys
↪ v ){ print "$v{$_}\t$_\n"; }'
↪ /var/log/apache/access.log | sort -n
```

When you run this command, you should see output something like the following only with more lines and IPs that aren't fake:

```
33         99.99.99.99
94         111.111.111.111
138        15.15.15.15
```

For those of you who know and love both Perl and regular expressions, that one-liner probably isn't too difficult to parse, but for the rest of you, let's go step by step. Sometimes it's easier to go through a one-liner if you see it in a formatted way, so here's the Perl part of the one-liner translated as though it were in a regular file:

```perl
#!/usr/bin/perl

while(<>){
   if(m|(^\d+\.\d+\.\d+\.\d+).*?01/Nov/2008|){
      $v{$1}++;
   }
}

foreach( keys %v ){
   print "$v{$_}\t$_\n";
}
```

First, let's discuss the while loop. Basically, while(<>) iterates over every line of input it receives either through a pipe or as a file argument on the command line. Inside this loop, I set up a regular expression to match and pull out an IP address. The regular expression is probably worth looking at in more detail:

```
(^\d+\.\d+\.\d+\.\d+)
```

This section of the regular expression matches the beginning of the line (^), then any amount of numbers (\d+), and then a dot, another series of numbers, another dot, another series of numbers, another dot and finally a fourth series of numbers. This pattern will match, for instance, 123.123.12.34 at the beginning of a line. I surrounded this part of the regular expression in parentheses. Because this is the first set of parentheses, when Perl matches it, it puts the resultant match into the $1 variable so I can pull it out later.

Now, those of you who know regular expressions know that I cheated here. This regular expression is not very explicit at all. For one, it would match completely invalid IP addresses, such as 999.999.999.999. For another, it even would match any series of four numbers with dots in between, such as 12345.6.7.8910. I chose an overly generic regular expression on purpose to make a point. There are explicit regular expressions that match only valid IP addresses, but those expressions are very long, very complex and, in this case, completely unnecessary.

Because I'm dealing with Apache logs, I am pretty confident that the first set of numbers at the beginning of the file is an IP address and not something else, and second, the IP address that Apache logged should be reasonably valid.

2.6 Chopping Logs

In taking the shortcut, I not only saved on typing, but the resulting regular expression also is easier to read and understand even if you aren't a regex wizard.

After I match the IP, I want to match only log entries from November 01, 2008:

```
.*?01/Nov/2008
```

This section performs matches on any number of characters (.*), and with the question mark at the end, it matches only as much as it needs to and no more. Then, it matches the datestamp for November 01, 2008. If I wanted a tally of every day in the log file, I could omit this entire section of the regular expression. Alternatively, if I wanted to match on some other keyword (for instance, when the user performed a GET on a particular file), I could replace or augment the above section with that keyword.

Once I have matched the IP address in a line and have assigned it to $1, I then use it as a key in a hash I call %v here and increment it ($h{$1}++). The power of a hash is that it forces each key to be unique. That means each time I come across a new IP, it will get its own key in the hash and have its value incremented. So, if it's the first time I see the IP, its value will be one. The second time I see the IP, it will increment it to two and so on.

Once I'm done iterating through each line in the file, I then drop to a foreach loop:

```
foreach( keys %v ){
  print "$v{$_}\t$_\n";
}
```

Basically, all this does is increment through every key in the hash and output its value (the number of times I matched that IP in the file) and the IP itself. Note that I didn't sort the values here. I very well could have–Perl has powerful methods to sort output–but to make the code simpler and more flexible, I opted to pipe the output to the command-line sort command. That way, even if you don't know Perl too well but know the command line, you could tweak arguments in sort to reverse the output or even pipe it further to tail, so you could see only the top ten IPs.

If I want to know only the overall number of unique visitors, as each line represents a unique visitor, I just need to count the overall number of lines. To do this, I simply need to pipe the output to wc -l.

And, there you have it, a quick-and-dirty one-liner to chop through your logs and tally results. The beauty of using Perl hashes for this is that you can tweak the regular expression to match all sorts of values in the file–not just IP addressesand tally all sorts of useful information. I've used modified versions of the script to count how many times a particular file was downloaded by unique IPs, and I've even used it to perform statistics on mailq output.

2.7 Shorter Commands

Although a GUI certainly has its place, it's hard to beat the efficiency of the command line. It's not just the efficiency you get with a purely keyboard-driven interface, but the raw power of piping the output of one command into the input of another. This drive toward efficiency influenced the commands themselves. In the age before tab-completion, having a long command, much less a hyphenated command, was something to avoid. That's why we call it "tar" not "tape-archive" and "cp" instead of "copy." I like to think of old UNIX commands like rough stones worn smooth by a river, all their unnecessary letters worn away by the erosion of years of typing.

Tab completion has made long commands more bearable and more common; however, there's still something to be said for the short two- or three-letter commands that pop from our fingers before we even think about them. Although there are great examples of powerful short commands (my favorite has to be dd), in this section, I highlight some short command-line substitutions for longer commands ordered by how many characters you save by typing them.

Save Four Characters with apt

Example:

```
sudo apt install vim
```

I'm a long-time Debian user, but I think I was the last one to get the news that apt-get was being deprecated in favor of the shorter apt command, at least for interactive use. The new apt command isn't just shorter to type, it also provides a new and improved interactive interface to installing Debian packages, including an RPM-like progress bar made from # signs. It even takes the same arguments as apt-get, so it's easy to make the transition to the shorter command. The only downside is that it's not recommended for scripts, so for that, you will need to stick to the trusty apt-get command.

Save Four Characters with dig

Example:

```
dig linuxjournal.com NS
```

The nslookup command is a faithful standby for those of us who have performed DNS lookups on the command line for the past few decades (including on DOS), but it's also been deprecated for almost that long. For accurate and supported DNS searches, dig is the command of choice. It's not only shorter, it's also incredibly powerful. But, with that power comes a completely separate set of command-line options from what nslookup has.

Save Four Characters with nc

Example:

```
nc mail.example.com 25
```

I've long used telnet as my trusty sidekick whenever I wanted to troubleshoot a broken service. I even wrote about how to use it to send email in a Chapter 4. Telnet is great for making simple network connections, but it seems so bloated standing next to the slim nc command (short for netcat). The nc command is not just a simple way to troubleshoot network services, it also is a Swiss-army knife of network features in its own right, and it even can perform basic port-scan style tests in place of nmap via the nc -zv arguments.

Save Five Characters with ss

Example:

```
ss -lnpt
```

When you are troubleshooting a network, it's incredibly valuable to be able to see what network connections are currently present on a system. Traditionally, I would use the netstat tool for this, but I discovered that ss performs the same functions and even accepts similar arguments. The only downside is that it's output isn't formatted quite as nicely, but that's a small price to pay to save an extra five keystrokes.

Save Six Characters with ip

Example:

```
ip addr
```

The final command in this list is a bit controversial among old-timers like me who grew up with the ifconfig command. Sadly ifconfig has been deprecated, so if you want to check network link state, or set IP addresses or routing tables, the ip command is what all the kids are using. The syntax and output formats are dramatically different from what you might be used to with the ifconfig command, but on the plus side, you are saving six keystrokes.

2.8 Add Progress Bars to dd

The dd tool has been a critical component on the Linux (and UNIX) command line for ages. You know a command-line tool is important if it has only two letters, and dd is no exception. What I love about it in particular is that it truly embodies the sense of a powerful tool with no safety features, as described in Neal Stephenson's In the Beginning was the Command Line. The dd command does something simple: it takes input from one file and outputs it to another file, and since in UNIX "everything is a file", that means dd doesn't care if the output file is another file on your disk, a partition or even your active hard drive, it happily will overwrite it! Because of this, dd fits in that immortal category of sysadmin tools that I type out and then pause for five to ten seconds, examining the command, before I press Enter.

Unfortunately, dd has fallen out of favor lately, and some distributions even will advise using tools like cp or a graphical tool to image drives. This is largely out of the concern that dd doesn't wait for the disk to sync before it exits, so even if it thinks it's done writing, that doesn't mean all of the data is on the output file, particularly if it's over slow I/O like in the case of USB flash storage. The other reason people have tended to use other imaging tools is that traditionally dd doesn't output any progress. You type the command, and then if the image is large, you just wait, wait and then wait some more, wondering if dd will ever complete.

But, it turns out that there are quite a few different ways to get progress output from dd, so I cover a few popular ones here, all based on the following dd command to image an ISO file to a disk:

```
sudo dd if=/some/file.iso of=/dev/sdX bs=1M
```

Option 1: Use pv

Like many command-line tools, dd can accept input from a pipe and output to a pipe. This means if you had a tool that could measure the data flowing over a pipe, you could sandwich it in between two different dd commands and get live progress output. The pv (pipe viewer) command-line tool is just such a tool, so one approach is to install pv using your distribution's packaging tool and then create a pv and dd sandwich:

```
sudo dd if=/some/file.iso bs=1M | pv | dd of=/dev/sdX
```

In this command, I'm imaging my ISO image to a disk. Notice that the first dd command lists not only the `if` argument to specify the input file, I also added the `bs` argument to this side. In general, you will want to add all of your dd arguments to the first dd command.

Option 2: Use kill

The dd command has an often-forgotten feature buried within its man pages. If you send a running dd command a `kill -USR1` signal, it will output its current progress. So run the initial dd command in this example, and then in a different terminal, identify its process ID so you can send it the USR1 signal:

```
sudo kill -USR1 <pidofddcommand>
```

You can use a bit of a shell shortcut if you don't want to identify the PID command independently and put this all in one line:

```
sudo kill -USR1 $(pgrep ^dd)
```

Option 3: Use dd's Embedded Progress Bar

Many people are unaware that relatively recently, dd added its own live progress option! For the longest time, I was using the USR1 trick until someone told me about dd's new `status=progress` option added in GNU coreutils 8.24. So now, you just have to type:

```
sudo dd if=/some/file.iso of=/dev/sdX bs=1M status=progress
```

And, dd will output its progress periodically while it's running!

2.9 Lock Files with the flock Command

Cron is an incredibly useful tool, particularly on a server. Cron lets you specify a script to run as frequently as every minute or as infrequently as once per year with powerful syntax that lets you configure just about any kind of frequency in between those two extremes. There are so many different routine tasks a server needs and while you could just login and do them all yourself, it's nice to have cron serve as a timer making sure that routine tasks happen as frequently or infrequently as you need. Backup jobs in particular, whether it's rotating out logs to back them up or backing up local files to a remote location, are particularly ideal to put within a cron job.

Administrators who are starting out, all inevitably hit some form of the following issue: they have a background task that needs to run every few minutes or every hour, so they put it into a cron job. The script runs great and everything is fine for awhile. Then at some point they get paged at 3am because the load on the server is too high. When they login they see multiple instances of their every-five-minute cron job and scratch their head. What happened?

What happened was that their script, at first, only took a couple of minutes to run. At some point the scope of work grew, whether it's a backup job that is now backing up larger files or a server that is getting more loaded overall and causing everything to slow down. Whatever the reason, their every-five-minute cron job now took six minutes to run. That means that a second instance of the cron job started running and took six and a half minutes, because it was competing with the first cron job for the first minute of its run. Ultimately these jobs stack up onto each other until they generate enough of a load to trigger an alert.

The solution to this kind of problem is to make sure only one instance of your script runs at a time and this is typically solved with a lock file. The idea behind a lock file is to have an application create a file in a temporary location before it starts that it deletes after it completes. The script also tests for the existence of that lock file and exits if it exists. That way, as long as the script cleans up after itself, you can only have one instance of it run at a time.

For years when I wrote a cron job that might run this kind of risk, I would write my own lock handler from scratch at the top of the script. It looked something like this:

```
LOCKFILE="/tmp/someuniquename"

if [ -e $LOCKFILE ]; then
  exit 1
fi

touch $LOCKFILE
...
# do some stuff
...
rm -f $LOCKFILE
```

As you can see, managing a lock file is relatively straightforward. You exit first thing if the lock file exists, and otherwise you create the lock file, run your commands, and then remove it when you are done.

Note that I stored my lock file in /tmp. This is intentional as the /tmp directory gets erased at each reboot. One potential risk with a lock file is that you might have a script that gets forcefully killed in such a way that it doesn't have time to clean up after itself. When that happens if your lock file is in a permanent location your script may never run again, at least until you notice it's not running and discover the lock file sitting around. By storing the lock file in /tmp I at least have one form of safety–if the script ever gets in that state it will get cleaned up by a reboot.

An Old Dog Learns a New Trick

So one of the great things about working on teams with other administrators is that no matter how long you've been using Linux, you always learn something new. I had been using the above approach to file locks for many years until one day about five years ago when I added a new cron job script into our shared configuration management. Another administrator saw my code and we had the following exchange on chat:

> OtherAdmin: *Hey Kyle, so I saw your latest commit and I was just wondering, was there a reason you didn't use flock? Security or something?*
>
> Kyle: *flock?*
>
> Kyle: **looks up flock online**
>
> Kyle: *WHY DIDN'T ANYONE TELL ME ABOUT THIS!?*
>
> OtherAdmin: *lol*

2.9 Lock Files with the flock Command

So apparently all of these years I had been doing it wrong! Well, not exactly wrong but I could have saved so much time and lines of code by using flock! For instance, the above code could be replaced with the following flock command:

```
flock -n /tmp/someuniquename somecommand
```

The syntax for flock is to follow the command with any special arguments it needs (more on that next) then the path to the file or directory you want to lock on, and then the command to run. In the above example, I used the -n option which tells flock that in the event that the lock file exists, it should exit with an error. This is probably what you want to do for most cron jobs, however flock supports a number of other modes that could be handy for particular circumstances.

For instance, by default flock creates what's known as an exclusive lock. This means that only one instance of a program is allowed to hold the lock at one time. It's also referred to as a write lock, because typically a file can only be written to by one script at a time. The flock command also supports what's known as a shared or read lock. This can be useful if it's OK if multiple scripts run at the same time, such as in the case they are only reading data but not writing it. If an instance of the script grabs an exclusive lock, then those other versions of the script would fail but otherwise they would be allowed to run.

By default flock also does not enable the -n option that causes a script to exit if the lock file exists. Instead, flock waits indefinitely until the lock file is gone and then runs the command. You can also use the -w option, followed by the number of seconds to wait, to tell flock to only wait a certain amount of time before it gives up.

One big benefit of using flock is that you can wrap your cron commands in it directly so you'd add the above command to your crontab entry instead of calling a script and embedding the flock command inside of it. Another benefit of it is that since it's a standard command line tool, you don't risk introducing some bug into your own shell script implementation of file locking.

For instance, when I set up my own backup jobs that backed up my local documents to my RV, I used flock:

```
flock -n /tmp/rvsync.lock rsync -avxH /mnt/storage/documents/
 ↪ rv:/mnt/storage/documents/ 2>/dev/null 1>>/tmp/rvsync-output
```

I knew that even though this command only ran every three hours, there was a chance that at some point I might have enough changes that it would take longer than three hours to complete. By wrapping the script in flock, I knew I would only have one instance of rsync running at a time.

If you were like me and had never heard of the flock tool, I hope you found this introduction helpful. While you can certainly implement locking many other ways, the flock tool adds many advanced features such as shared locks and waiting that would otherwise take a lot of extra effort to implement yourself.

3. Home Servers

These days, it seems everyone is talking about the cloud. Now, what exactly someone means by "the cloud" seems to vary, but typically, the cloud refers to some sort of service, such as e-mail, Web, DNS, file storage and so on, that is managed for you by a third party. Many people love how easy it can be to outsource their e-mail service, blog or image site to someone else. Like oil changes, home repair and cooking, server administration is yet another task you can pay (either with money or with marketing data) someone else to manage for you.

Alongside this trend to outsource work is a growing movement that values doing things yourself. Some examples include "Makers" involved in designing their own electronics, do-it-yourself home improvement, gardening, amateur cheese making, baking and even home brewing. The fact is, many of these so-called chores actually are rather rewarding and even fun to do yourself. I think we as Linux users should apply this same idea to server management. It turns out it is quite rewarding, educational and not terribly difficult to manage your own services at home instead of outsourcing them to the cloud. This is on top of the fact that when you manage your own server, you are in full control of your server, what's installed on it and who can see it.

In addition to the other reasons why it's valuable to manage some of your own services yourself, having a vibrant home network is the perfect laboratory for sysadmin projects you don't have time or resources to work on during your day job. I developed many of my sysadmin skills first on my home network, especially when I was starting out. It's a great way for junior sysadmin to make up for any gaps in their experience from their day job and it was this experience that got me one of my first full-time sysadmin jobs. During the interview I was asked how to set up a number of different services and it had just so happened I had recently set up the same servers at home for myself. Even though I didn't have much professional experience, my personal experience gave me the confidence (and know-how) to answer the interview questions well and I got the job.

In this chapter, I'm going to discuss how to set up various types of services at home and how to make them available to the Internet at large. In this first section, I discuss some things you should consider about your network before you set up your first server at home. Then I will describe how to set up a DNS server, a personal blog, a local mail server, and a redundant web server hosted on a Raspberry Pi cluster. Finally I will describe how I used my own home servers as an emergency backup when my primary colocated server had a major outage.

3.1 Setting Up Your Network

When it comes to hosting servers at home, all ISPs (Internet Service Providers) are not created equal. Before I even discuss bandwidth, first you should look into your ISP's terms of service. It turns out that some ISPs discourage, disallow or sometimes outright block home users from hosting their own services on the Internet. Take a large dose of caffeine and try to read through your ISP's terms of service (or just call and ask them) to see whether they have any sort of restrictions. At the very least it's common for even server-friendly ISPs to block outbound e-mail traffic (SMTP port 25) by default to prevent spam. Although I'll discuss this more in a future column about e-mail, some ISPs will lift this restriction and some won't. The bottom line is that if hosting your own server is important to you, you will want to make sure you use an ISP that allows it. For me, this policy is more important when choosing an ISP than even speed or price.

Static IPs vs. Dynamic IPs

No matter what type of Internet connection you have, ultimately you are assigned at least one publicly routed IP address. If this address changes each time you connect to the Internet (or each time your DSL or cable modem resets), you have a dynamic IP. If this IP stays the same, it's static. Although people historically have run servers on both static and dynamic IPs, with a dynamic IP, you will have to go through the additional trouble of setting up some sort of dynamic DNS service so that each time your IP changes at home, everyone trying to access your service on the Internet will get the new IP. Unfortunately, due to the nature of how DNS works, you can't always guarantee (even with low TTLs) that everyone will see your changed IP in a timely manner, so if you are serious about running servers at home, I recommend you spring for one or more static IPs.

Connection Speed

Typically when you rate the quality of your Internet connection at home, you first look at your download speed. Average home users rely much more on their download bandwidth than their upload bandwidth as a metric of how "fast" their connection is, and many home Internet connections have much higher download bandwidth than upload. Once you start hosting servers at home, however, you'll find that their performance is governed more by your upload bandwidth. If you want to host bandwidth-hungry services at home, like streaming audio or video or image-heavy Web sites, you might want to upgrade or change your Internet connection to get more upload bandwidth. On the other hand, your personal DNS or e-mail server probably is going to be fine even with somewhat low upload bandwidth. Although upload bandwidth can be slower at home than at a data center, most connections at home (at least in the US) are unmetered so you don't have to worry about bandwidth caps.

Modems and Gateways

Most people who would want to host a server at their homes tend to access the Internet through some sort of DSL or cable modem. This device connects to either a phone line or some other cable on one end and provides a network port (or sometimes a USB port) on the other. More sophisticated modems actually can act as a gateway, and even a DHCP server, and hand out internal IPs to computers in the home while the public IP resides on the modem itself.

If you plan on having multiple computers inside your home network, I recommend getting the modem configured so it acts more like a bridge, so that the publicly routed IP address is assigned to a device that is under your control, whether it's a home router or a computer on your network. Most home routers (including DSL and cable modems, if your ISP gives you the ability to configure them) have the ability to do port forwarding so that incoming traffic intended for your Web server (ports 80 and 443) can be redirected to the internal IP address. The more control you have over your gateway, the more flexibility you will have in how you set up your servers and your network. If you do opt to use a consumer router instead of turning a home computer into the gateway, you might want to choose a router that can be reflashed with custom Linux firmware (like OpenWRT or DD-WRT), so you can have some of the same flexibility you would have if a Linux server acted as the gateway.

Security, Firewalls and Virtual IPs

Of course, any time you open up a service to the Internet, you are opening yourself up to attack. It doesn't matter if you just have a lone server on the Internet; attacks are automated, so your obscurity doesn't ensure security. Be sure that any service and server you make available on the Internet is kept up to date with the latest security patches. If you have the ability to configure a firewall on your gateway router, block all incoming ports by default and allow in only ports you know need to be open. If you are going to open up an SSH server to the public Internet, be sure to audit your passwords, and make sure they are difficult to guess (or better, disable passwords altogether and use key-based authentication). Today, more home (and enterprise) Linux servers are hacked due to bad passwords than just about anything else.

While I'm on the subject of firewalls, here's a quick tip if you happen to use a Linux device as your router with iptables. Even if you are granted multiple public IPs, you may find you prefer to have all Internet traffic come through a central router so it's easier to monitor and secure. To accomplish that, you likely will need to have your gateway device configured to answer on all of the public IPs and assign private IPs to the computers inside your home. Let's assume I have a few static IPs, including 66.123.123.63 and 66.123.123.64, and a gateway router that is configured to answer to both of those IPs on eth0. I have an internal server on my network with an IP address of 192.168.0.7. Because it has an internal IP, I want to forward traffic on my gateway destined for 66.123.123.64 to 192.168.0.7. The first way I could do it is to forward traffic only on specific ports to this host. For instance, if this were a Web server, I might want to forward only ports 80 and 443 to this server. I could use these iptables commands on my gateway router for the port forwarding:

```
iptables -t nat -A PREROUTING -d 66.123.123.64 -i eth0 -p
↪ tcp -m tcp -dport 80 -j DNAT -to-destination 192.168.0.7:80
iptables -t nat -A PREROUTING -d 66.123.123.64 -i eth0 -p
↪ tcp -m tcp -dport 443 -j DNAT -to-destination 192.168.0.7:443
```

This is also a common solution if you have only one public IP but multiple servers in your network, so you can forward Web ports to an internal Web server and e-mail ports to a different e-mail server. This method works; however, I'll have to be sure to add new firewall rules each time I want to forward another port. If I simply want to have the router forward all traffic destined for 66.123.123.64 to 192.168.0.7, I could use these two commands:

```
iptables -t nat -A PREROUTING -d 66.123.123.64 -i eth0 -j
↪ DNAT -to-destination 192.168.0.7
iptables -t nat -A POSTROUTING -s 192.168.0.7 -o eth0 -j
↪ SNAT -to-source 66.123.123.64
```

Note that because these commands forward all traffic to that internal host, regardless of port, I will want to make sure to lock down the firewall rules on that internal server.

This should be enough information to get you started on your network setup at home so that, you'll be ready to set up your first service. In the next section, I'll focus on DNS, including how to register a domain and how to set up your own home DNS server.

3.2 Setting Up A Home DNS Server

I honestly think most people simply are unaware of how much personal data they leak on a daily basis as they use their computers. Even if they have some inkling along those lines, I still imagine many think of the data they leak only in terms of individual facts, such as their name or where they ate lunch. What many people don't realize is how revealing all of those individual, innocent facts are when they are combined, filtered and analyzed.

Cell-phone metadata (who you called, who called you, the length of the call and what time the call happened) falls under this category, as do all of the search queries you enter on the Internet.

For this section, I discuss a common but often overlooked source of data that is far too revealing: your DNS data. You see, although you may give an awful lot of personal marketing data to Google with every search query you type, that still doesn't capture all of the sites you visit outside Google searches either directly, via RSS readers or via links your friends send you. That's why the implementation of Google's free DNS service on 8.8.8.8 and 8.8.4.4 is so genius–search queries are revealing, but when you capture all of someone's DNS traffic, you get the complete picture of every site they visit on the Internet and beyond that, even every non-Web service (e-mail, FTP, P2P traffic and VoIP), provided that the service uses hostnames instead of IP addresses.

Let me back up a bit. DNS is one of the core services that runs on the Internet, and its job is to convert a hostname, like www.linuxjournal.com, into an IP address, such as 76.74.252.198. Without DNS, the Internet as we know it today would cease to function, because basically every site we visit in a Web browser, and indeed, just about every service we use on the Internet, we get to via its hostname and not its IP. That said, the only way we actually can reach a host on the Internet is via its IP address, so when you decide to visit a site, its hostname is converted into an IP address to which your browser then opens up a connection. Note that via DNS caching and TTL (Time To Live) settings, you may not have to send out a DNS query every time you visit a site. All the same, lately TTLs are short enough (often ranging between one minute to an hour or two–www.linuxjournal.com's TTL is 30 minutes) that if I captured all your DNS traffic for a day, I'd be able to tell you every Web site you visited along with the first time that day you visited it. If the TTL is short enough, I probably could tell you every time you went there.

Most people tend to use whatever DNS servers they have been provided. On a corporate network, you are likely to get a set of DNS servers over DHCP when you connect to the network. This is important because many corporate networks have internal resources and internal hostnames that you would be able to resolve only if you talked to an internal name server.

Although many people assume very little privacy at work, home is a different matter. At home, you are most likely to use the DNS servers your ISP provided you, while others use Google's DNS servers because the IPs are easy to remember. This means even if others can't intercept your traffic (maybe you are sending it through a VPN, or maybe that kind of line tapping simply requires more legal standing), if they can get access to your DNS logs (I could see some arguing that this qualifies as metadata), they would have a fairly complete view of all the sites you visit without your ever knowing.

This is not just valuable data from a surveillance standpoint, or a privacy standpoint, but also from a marketing standpoint. Even if you may be fine with the government knowing what porn sites you browse, where you shop, where you get your news and what e-mail provider you use, you may not want a marketing firm to have that data.

Recursive DNS vs. DNS Caching

The key to owning your DNS data and keeping it private is to run your own DNS server and use it for all of your outbound DNS queries. Although many people already run some sort of DNS caching programs, such as dnsmasq to speed up DNS queries, what you want isn't simply a DNS cache, but something that can function as a recursive DNS resolver. In the case of dnsmasq, it is configured to use upstream recursive DNS servers to do all of the DNS heavy lifting (the documentation recommends you use whatever DNS servers you currently have in /etc/resolv.conf). Thus, all of your DNS queries for www.linuxjournal.com go to your DNS caching software and then are directed to, for instance, your ISP's DNS servers before they do the traditional recursive DNS procedure of starting at root name servers, then going to com, then finally to the name servers for linuxjournal.com. So, all of your queries still get logged at the external recursive DNS server.

What you want is a local DNS service that can do the complete recursive DNS query for you. In the case of a request for www.linuxjournal.com, it would communicate with the root, com and linuxjournal.com name servers directly without an intermediary and ultimately cache the results like any other DNS caching server. For outside parties to capture all of your DNS logs, they either would have to compromise your local, personal DNS server on your home network, set up a tap to collect all of your Internet traffic or set up a tap at all the root name servers. All three of these options are either illegal or require substantial court oversight.

Install and Configure A Recursive DNS Server

So, even when you rule out pure DNS caching software, there still are a number of different DNS servers you can choose from, including BIND, djbdns and unbound, among others. I personally have the most experience with BIND, so that's what I prefer, but any of those would do the job. The nice thing about BIND, particularly in the case of the Debian and Ubuntu packages, is that all you need to do is run:

```
sudo apt install bind9
```

and after the software installs, BIND automatically is configured to act as a local recursive DNS server for your internal network. The procedure also would be the same if you were to set this up on a spare Raspberry Pi running the Raspbian distribution. On other Linux distributions, the package may just be called bind.

If BIND isn't automatically configured as a local recursive DNS server on your particular Linux distribution and doesn't appear to work out of the box, just locate the options section of your BIND config (often in /etc/bind/named.conf, /etc/bind/named.conf.options or /etc/named/named.conf, depending on the distribution), and if you can't seem to perform recursive queries, add the following line under the options section:

```
options {
  allow-recursion { 10/8; 172.16/12; 192.168/16; 127.0.0.1; };
  ...
}
```

This change allows any hosts on those networks (internal RFC1918 IP addresses) to perform recursive queries on your name server without allowing the world to do so.

Once you have BIND installed, you'll want to test it. If you installed BIND on your local machine, you could test this out with the dig command:

```
dig @localhost www.linuxjournal.com
; <<>> DiG 9.8.1-P1 <<>> @localhost www.linuxjournal.com
; (1 server found)
;; global options: +cmd
;; Got answer:
;; ->>HEADER<<- opcode: QUERY, status: NOERROR, id: 17485
;; flags: qr rd ra; QUERY: 1, ANSWER: 1, AUTHORITY: 2, ADDITIONAL: 0

;; QUESTION SECTION:
;www.linuxjournal.com.          IN    A

;; ANSWER SECTION:
www.linuxjournal.com.   1800    IN    A     76.74.252.198

;; AUTHORITY SECTION:
linuxjournal.com.       30479   IN    NS    ns66.domaincontrol.com.
linuxjournal.com.       30479   IN    NS    ns65.domaincontrol.com.

;; Query time: 31 msec
;; SERVER: 127.0.0.1#53(127.0.0.1)
;; WHEN: Wed Dec 18 09:37:13 2013
```

```
;; MSG SIZE  rcvd: 106
```

Otherwise, replace localhost with the IP address of your Raspberry Pi or whatever machine on which you installed BIND. To use this name server for all of your requests, update your /etc/resolv.conf file so that it contains:

```
nameserver 127.0.0.1
```

as its only nameserver line. Replace 127.0.0.1 with the IP address of the machine you installed BIND on if it isn't on the same machine. On some modern distributions, there are external tools that tweak /etc/resolv.conf for you, so in those cases, you may have to edit your dhclient.conf or other network configuration files so that you can override the provided list of name servers. Once you do that though, really that's all there is to it. Now you can use DNS knowing that all of your DNS search data sits on a machine under your control.

Install and Configure an Authoritative DNS Server

Recursive DNS servers allow you to resolve other people's domains but what about your own domains? Every server (including your own) that has a presence on the Internet should have a public IP address. In an earlier section I discussed how to set up your home network for a server and to do this you need at least one public IP (hopefully static) you can use. It's true that all you really need to host many services on the Internet is an IP address; however, in practice, there are only so many IP addresses (like phone numbers) that the average person is going to commit to memory. As IPv6 becomes commonplace, this will be even more true. DNS allows you to register a domain name and associate individual host names (like www.example.com and mail.example.com) to IP addresses.

For instance, how many of you (besides you, Katherine) have memorized the IP address for www.linuxjournal.com? If you did want to know the IP address, all you would need to do is perform a simple nslookup command:

```
nslookup www.linuxjournal.com
Server:         192.168.0.1
Address:        192.168.0.1#53

Non-authoritative answer:
Name:    www.linuxjournal.com
Address: 76.74.252.198
```

In this example, the first bit of output tells me that I'm getting this answer from a DNS server at 192.168.0.1 (my own personal DNS server) and that the IP address for www.linuxjournal.com is currently 76.75.252.198. There isn't enough space in this section to describe everything that happened to allow me to get that IP address, but essentially, my DNS server asked other DNS servers on the Internet for this IP address and was subsequently redirected to more and more DNS servers until it finally found the one that knew the answer.

3.2 Setting Up A Home DNS Server

If you are interested in more detail on how this works, books like DNS and BIND do a good job of explaining it, or from the command line, you could run dig www.linuxjournal.com +trace.

Like with the recursive name server example I'm going to use BIND for my DNS server software. When it comes to authoritative name servers, though, you can just rely on the out-of-the-box configuration. Unfortunately, there are slight differences in how each distribution packages BIND. For instance, under Red Hat, you install the bind package, but under Debian-based systems (like Ubuntu), you install bind9. Red Hat stores its core BIND configuration file at /etc/named.conf and all its zone files (files that contain name→IP address mappings for a domain, such as example.org, a subdomain, such as ny.example.org, or possibly both) under /var/named, while Debian-based systems put named.conf and any zone files under the /etc/bind/ directory. Once you get past the differences, however, the syntax inside the files should be similar. Just to simplify things, I'm going to base the rest of this article off a standard Debian server, so we have some sort of baseline. If you use a different distribution, however, it shouldn't be too difficult to adapt these instructions to the different file paths.

Primary DNS Configuration

> **Note:** BIND still uses the outdated terms "master" and "slave" in its configuration files to describe its primary and secondary DNS servers. I will use the terms "primary" and "secondary" instead in this section, except for in the actual configuration files where I will fall back to BIND's terminology.

A DNS primary contains its own zone files that have name→IP address mappings, and it doesn't have to consult any other source to answer queries for those names. By contrast, a DNS secondary is configured to load all of its zone configurations from a DNS primary. Any future changes are made on the primary and propagate to each of the secondary. Any individual BIND instance acts as a DNS primary, a DNS secondary or a caching name server, or all three at the same time (although it can be a primary or a secondary only to any individual zone, not both).

For this example, let's set up a DNS primary for example.org, and this primary will have the following records:

- ns1.example.org, which points to 123.12.34.56 (the public IP of the name server itself).
- example.org, which points to 123.12.34.57.
- www.example.org also points to 123.12.34.57.

To start, I create the zone file at /etc/bind/db.example.org (remember Red Hat stores these zones in a different places) and put the following information in it:

;

```
; BIND data file for example.org
;
$TTL 4h
@   IN   SOA ns1.example.org. root.example.org. (
        2               ; Serial
        604800          ; Refresh
        86400           ; Retry
        2419200         ; Expire
        604800 )        ; Negative Cache TTL
;
@           IN NS    ns1.example.org.
@           IN A     123.12.34.57
www         IN A     123.12.34.57
ns1         IN A     123.12.34.56
```

Make sure this file has similar permissions to the other zone files you find in the /etc/bind directory. The first non-comment line in the file sets the TTL or Time To Live, the default time in which a remote DNS server will cache any answers it gets from your DNS server before it will ask it again. The value you put here will help determine how fast changes you make will propagate. BIND accepts seconds in this field, or you can use shorthand values like 1d for one day, 4h for four hours or 20m for 20 minutes. I set the TTL to four hours here; however, if you make frequent changes to your records (or know you are going to soon), you may want to make the TTL shorter. On the other hand, if you find you hardly ever change these values, you might want to bump up the TTL to a day to reduce load on your DNS server.

Something to note is that zone files use semicolons not hashes at the beginning of a line for comments. A common mistake is to put hashes in a zone file to make a comment, reload BIND and then wonder why your changes didn't take. When BIND sees a mistake like that, it just skips that particular zone.

To keep things simple, I'm going to skip the Retry, Refresh and other values here–just keep them with these defaults unless you know what you are doing. The Serial line is for DNS secondaries, which I discuss later. Below those values, however, you'll see the syntax I used to define the different records:

```
@           IN NS    ns1.example.org.
@           IN A     123.12.34.57
www         IN A     123.12.34.57
ns1         IN A     123.12.34.56
```

The first record starts with @, which means it is a record for example.org itself. In this case, it is an NS record that defines the hostname I'm going to use for my name server. You can use any hostname you control here (including hostnames on a different domain, actually), but one popular convention is to use hostnames like ns1 and ns2 for the first and second name servers. The second record begins with an @ as well, only in this case, it's an A record. An A record is a fundamental DNS record that maps a hostname (like www) to an IP address (like 123.12.34.57). In this case, because the record starts with @, I am setting the IP address for example.org itself. The next two lines define two

3.2 Setting Up A Home DNS Server

more A records, one for www.example.org and one for ns1.example.org. It's important if you used a name within this same domain for your name server (like ns1.example.org) that you be sure to add an A record so that it has an IP address.

Now that I have created my zone, next I need to modify the /etc/bind/named.conf file and add a new section at the end of the file to point to the /etc/bind/db.example.org file I just created:

```
zone "example.org" {
  type master;
  file "/etc/bind/db.example.org";
};
```

After the file is changed, I reload BIND, and I should be able to send DNS requests to my new DNS server:

```
sudo /etc/init.d/bind9 reload
* Reloading domain name server... bind [OK]

nslookup www.example.org localhost
Server:         localhost
Address:        127.0.0.1#53

Name:    www.example.org
Address: 123.12.34.56
```

If there is a problem with the BIND reload, it should tell you on the command line. Otherwise, if it still doesn't work, you may have to look in your syslog file (/var/log/syslog on Debian-based systems and /var/log/messages on Red Hat) for clues.

Secondary DNS Configuration

Many registrars on the Internet require that any domain you register have at least two DNS servers configured with it. It's a good practice to have, because if you have a single DNS server and it goes down, it effectively will make all your servers under that domain inaccessible. This means you need to set up a second DNS server on a different IP, ideally on a different network, or have a friend with a DNS server act as a secondary to your primary DNS server. In either case, it's a relatively simple process. Let's say that my second DNS server is going to be at the IP address 98.76.54.32. First, I would log in to my Master DNS server and add the new NS and A records to my zone file:

```
;
; BIND data file for example.org
;
$TTL 4h
@   IN  SOA ns1.example.org. root.example.org. (
    2            ; Serial
    604800       ; Refresh
    86400        ; Retry
    2419200      ; Expire
    604800 )     ; Negative Cache TTL
```

```
;
@         IN NS     ns1.example.org.
@         IN NS     ns2.example.org.
@         IN A      123.12.34.57
www       IN A      123.12.34.57
ns1       IN A      123.12.34.56
ns2       IN A      98.76.54.32
```

Next, I edit named.conf and add a line to the configuration of example.org so that it will allow zone transfers from my DNS secondary:

```
zone "example.org" {
  type master;
  file "/etc/bind/db.example.org";
  allow-transfer { 98.76.54.32; };
};
```

Finally, I would install BIND on the second server, or if it already exists, all I would have to do is add a new entry at the end of the named.conf file to define the example.org zone and tell this server the IP address of the primary:

```
zone "example.org" {
  type slave;
  file "/var/cache/bind/db.example.org";
  masters { 123.12.34.56; };
};
```

Note that in this case the secondary zone is being stored under /var/cache/bind. That's the default location for secondary zone files under Debian-based systems. Under Red Hat, you would store them under /var/named/. Once I reload BIND on the secondary server, it will pull the new zone information from the primary, and I should be able to perform DNS queries against it.

Once you have set up a secondary, keep in mind that any time you make a change to the primary, you will need to increment the Serial field in the Master's zone file (in my example, it is set to 2, but a lot of administrators like to set it to the current date plus two extra number fields, such as 2010120500). When the secondary needs to know whether its zone information is up to date, it compares its serial number with the serial number on the primary. If the primary's serial number for a zone is higher, it copies down the new zone information; otherwise, it sticks with what it has cached.

Domain Registration

Once you have a functioning DNS server, all that's left is to tell the world to use it. If you haven't already registered your domain with a registrar, find a domain registration service on the Internet (there are too many for me to list here, but a search for domain name registration should turn up plenty). When you register the domain, most registrars will let you use their own DNS servers for your domain, but you don't need them! When you get to the point in the registration process where it asks you about your DNS servers, just give them the public IP address for your own DNS server (in my case, it would be ns1.example.org or

123.12.34.56). Note that many registrars require you to have two DNS servers defined for a domain, so in that case, set up a secondary DNS server and add its IP address as well. Once you complete the registration process and allow the new domain information time to propagate around the Internet, you will have the ability make IP changes for your Web, mail and other servers all from your own machines.

3.3 A Local Mail Server

I've written about the mutt email client a lot over the years. For me, in this day and age of large graphical mail programs and Web-based mail applications, you still can't beat the speed, power and customization of mutt. Let's also not forget the vi-style keybindings—I love those.

One thing that was true for the longest time about mutt, was that it is strictly a MUA (Mail User Agent) and not an MTA (Mail Transfer Agent). This means mutt was concerned only with acting as an e-mail client and didn't actually contain any code to communicate with remote mail servers. That job is done by an MTA. Although many mail clients also include code so they can relay mail through an MTA (including mutt), originally mutt opted to use the system's own local mail server. Traditionally, this hasn't been an issue on Linux, as most Linux servers have had some mail server installed and set up. Now, however, you might not have a fully configured mail server on your desktop install. That's okay though, because in this section, you'll see how simple it is to set up your own local mail server, thanks to Postfix.

Even if you don't use mutt, there are many advantages to having your own local mail server, if only to relay mail for you. For one, it can handle spooling all of your e-mail and will retry delivery automatically if it fails for some reason or another (such as if your wireless connection drops or you close your laptop) without having to leave your mail program open. For another, once you have your mail server set up how you want it, any other mail client on your computer can take advantage of it: simply point your client to localhost.

The Mail Server Holy War

A number of different mail servers are available for Linux, each with its own set of advantages and disadvantages. Many holy wars have been fought over Sendmail vs. Postfix vs. Exim vs. using Telnet to connect directly to port 25 on a mail server and type in raw SMTP commands. I've tried them all over the years (yes, even Telnet), and for me, Postfix has the best balance between stable performance, security and most important, simple configuration files. So for this column, I discuss the specific steps for setting up Postfix as a mail relay.

The first step is to install the Postfix server itself. On most distributions, you'll find this package is split up into a main Postfix package plus a few extra packages that provide specific features, such as MySQL or LDAP integration. Because we are just setting up a basic mail relay here, all we really need is the main Postfix package. Now, if you install this package on a Debian-based system, you will be prompted by the post-install script that acts as a wizard to set up Postfix for you. If you want, you simply can walk through the wizard and pick "Internet Site" to send e-mail out directly to the rest of the Internet or choose "Internet with smarthost" to relay all of your mail through a second mail server (perhaps provided by your ISP) first. Either way, you will be asked a few simple questions, and at the end, you'll have a basic Postfix configuration ready to use.

On other systems (or if you choose "No configuration" on a Debian-based system), you might end up with an empty or very heavily commented Postfix configuration file at /etc/postfix/main.cf. What you'll find is that for a basic mail server, you really need only a few lines in your config. Postfix picks pretty sane and secure defaults, so if you want it to deliver mail on your behalf, you need only a few lines:

```
mynetworks = 127.0.0.0/8
inet_interfaces = loopback-only
```

Yes, that's basically it. Now, restart Postfix with /etc/init.d/postfix restart, and your mail server will be up and running. With the sane defaults in Postfix, you just need to hard-code those two settings to ensure that Postfix accepts mail only on localhost. The `inet_interfaces` line tells Postfix to listen only on the localhost address for e-mail so no clients can connect to your server from the outside. The `mynetworks` line adds to that security and tells Postfix to allow only mail from localhost to be relayed through the server.

The Pesky Port 25 Problem

It used to be that the above was all you needed for a functioning mail server on the Internet. With the rise of spam measures and countermeasures, however, fewer and fewer ISPs are willing to allow port 25 traffic from clients through to the outside world. Even if they do, many mail servers on the Net won't accept traffic from hosts inside ISP networks. If you find yourself on such a network, you likely will need to add a relay host to your main.cf. The relay host is a mail server usually provided by your ISP through which your mail server can send e-mail. If you were setting up a client like Thunderbird, for instance, this would be the SMTP server you would configure for it.

To set up a generic relay host in Postfix, just add:

```
relayhost = mail.somedomain.net
```

to your /etc/postfix/main.cf. Replace mail.somedomain.net with the hostname of your ISP's relay host. Once you modify the file, type `sudo postfix reload` to enable the new settings.

3.3 A Local Mail Server

SMTP AUTH

Of course, some mail servers won't just let anyone on their network relay through them (and rightly so). In that case, usually they require that everyone authenticate with them first. This takes a few extra steps with Postfix, but like with everything else, it's still not very difficult. First, add the following lines to the /etc/postfix/main.cf:

```
smtp_sasl_auth_enable = yes
smtp_sasl_password_maps = hash:/etc/postfix/sasl_passwd
smtp_sasl_security_options = noanonymous
```

This tells postfix to enable SMTP authentication and tells it to look in /etc/postfix/sasl_passwd for logins and passwords to use for hosts. The next step is to create the /etc/postfix/sasl_passwd file. If I wanted to log in to mail.somedomain.net with the user name kyle and the password muttrules, I would put the following line in the file:

```
mail.somedomain.net kyle:muttrules
```

There is a downside to this in that the password for the account is now in clear text. That's less than ideal, but you can at least make sure that only root can read the file. As the root user, type:

```
chown root:root /etc/postfix/sasl_password
chmod 600 /etc/postfix/sasl_passwd
```

Postfix actually doesn't read this file directly; instead, it reads a hash database created from this file. To create the file, run:

```
postmap /etc/postfix/sasl_passwd
```

And, you will see that a new file, /etc/postfix/sasl_passwd.db, has been created. You'll need to run the postmap command any time you modify the /etc/postfix/sasl_passwd file. Now, reload Postfix one final time, and mutt should be able to relay mail through your local host. If you want to perform a quick test without mutt, you can type:

```
echo test | mail -s "test" user@remotehost
```

and it will send an e-mail message with a subject and body of "test" to the user you specify.

Postfix's logfile might vary a bit, depending on your system, but you should be able to find it in /var/log/mail.log or /var/log/maillog. That's the first place you should look if you find that some mail is not being delivered. The second place to look is the mailq command. That command will give you a quick status of all e-mail that is currently in the local spool along with its status. If all of your mail has been delivered successfully to other hosts, the output will look something like this:

```
mailq
Mail queue is empty
```

It's truly that simple. Of course, mail server administration definitely can become more complex than this when you want to do more than relay your own personal e-mail. But, it's good to know that simple configurations like the above are possible. If you are like me, saving time on the Postfix configuration just gives you extra time to tweak your mutt config.

3.4 Clustering with Raspberry Pis

Although many people are excited about the hardware-hacking possibilities with the Raspberry Pi, one of the things that interests me most is the fact that it is essentially a small low-power Linux server I can use to replace other Linux servers I already have around the house. In past Linux Journal columns, I've talked about using the Raspberry Pi to replace the server that controls my beer fridge[1] and colocating a Raspberry Pi in Austria[2]. After I colocated a Raspberry Pi in Austria, I started thinking about the advantages and disadvantages of using something with so many single points of failure as a server I relied on, so I started thinking about ways to handle that single point of failure.

So, in this section, I'm building the foundation for setting up redundant services with a pair of Raspberry Pis. I start with setting up a basic clustered network filesystem using GlusterFS. In later articles, I'll follow up with how to take advantage of this shared storage to set up other redundant services. Of course, although I'm using a Raspberry Pi for this article, these same steps should work with other hardware as well.

Configure the Raspberry Pis

To begin, I got two SD cards and loaded them with the latest version of the default Raspberry Pi distribution from the official Raspberry Pi downloads page, the Debian-based Raspbian. I followed the documentation to set up the image and then booted in to both Raspberry Pis while they were connected to a TV to make sure that the OS booted and that SSH was set to start by default (it should be). You probably also will want to use the raspi-config tool to expand the root partition to fill the SD card, since you will want all that extra space for your redundant storage. After I confirmed I could access the Raspberry Pis remotely, I moved them away from the TV and over to a switch and rebooted them without a display connected.

By default, Raspbian will get its network information via DHCP; however, if you want to set up redundant services, you will want your Raspberry Pis to

---

[1]https://www.linuxjournal.com/content/temper-pi
[2]https://www.linuxjournal.com/content/raspberry-strudel-my-raspberry-pi-austria

3.4 Clustering with Raspberry Pis

keep the same IP every time they boot. In my case, I updated my DHCP server so that it handed out the same IP to my Raspberry Pis every time they booted, but you also could edit the /etc/network/interfaces file on your Raspberry Pi and change:

```
iface eth0 inet dhcp
```

to:

```
auto eth0
iface eth0 inet static
    address 192.168.0.121
    netmask 255.255.255.0
    gateway 192.168.0.1
```

Of course, modify the networking information to match your personal network, and make sure that each Raspberry Pi uses a different IP. I also changed the hostnames of each Raspberry Pi, so I could tell them apart when I logged in. To do this, just edit /etc/hostname as root and change the hostname to what you want. Then, reboot to make sure that each Raspberry Pi comes up with the proper network settings and hostname.

Configure the GlusterFS Server

GlusterFS is a userspace clustered filesystem that I chose for this project because of how simple it makes configuring shared network filesystems. To start, choose a Raspberry Pi that will act as your primary. What little initial setup you need to do will be done from the primary node, even though once things are set up, nodes should fail over automatically. Here is the information about my environment:

```
Primary hostname: pi1
Primary IP: 192.168.0.121
Primary brick path: /srv/gv0
Secondary hostname: pi2
Secondary IP: 192.168.0.122
Secondary brick path: /srv/gv0
```

Before you do anything else, log in to each Raspberry Pi, and install the glusterfs-server package:

```
sudo apt install glusterfs-server
```

GlusterFS stores its files in what it calls bricks. A brick is a directory path on the server that you set aside for gluster to use. GlusterFS then combines bricks to create volumes that are accessible to clients. GlusterFS potentially can stripe data for a volume across bricks, so although a brick may look like a standard directory full of files, once you start using it with GlusterFS, you will want to modify it only via clients, not directly on the filesystem itself. In the case of the Raspberry Pi, I decided just to create a new directory called /srv/gv0 for my first brick on both Raspberry Pis:

```
sudo mkdir /srv/gv0
```

In this case, I will be sharing my standard SD card root filesystem, but in your case, you may want more storage. In that situation, connect a USB hard drive to each Raspberry Pi, make sure the disks are formatted, and then mount them under /srv/gv0. Just make sure that you update /etc/fstab so that it mounts your external drive at boot time. It's not required that the bricks are on the same directory path or have the same name, but the consistency doesn't hurt.

After the brick directory is available on each Raspberry Pi and the glusterfs-server package has been installed, make sure both Raspberry Pis are powered on. Then, log in to whatever node you consider the primary, and use the gluster peer probe command to tell the primary to trust the IP or hostname that you pass it as a member of the cluster. In this case, I will use the IP of my secondary node, but if you are fancy and have DNS set up you also could use its hostname instead:

```
pi@pi1 ~ $ sudo gluster peer probe 192.168.0.122
Probe successful
```

Now that my pi1 server (192.168.0.121) trusts pi2 (192.168.0.122), I can create my first volume, which I will call gv0. To do this, I run the gluster volume create command from the primary node:

```
pi@pi1 ~ $ sudo gluster volume create gv0 replica 2
↳ 192.168.0.121:/srv/gv0 192.168.0.122:/srv/gv0
Creation of volume gv0 has been successful. Please start
the volume to access data.
```

Let's break this command down a bit. The first part, gluster volume create, tells the gluster command I'm going to create a new volume. The next argument, gv0 is the name I want to assign the volume. That name is what clients will use to refer to the volume later on. After that, the replica 2 argument configures this volume to use replication instead of striping data between bricks. In this case, it will make sure any data is replicated across two bricks. Finally, I define the two individual bricks I want to use for this volume: the /srv/gv0 directory on 192.168.0.121 and the /srv/gv0 directory on 192.168.0.122.

Now that the volume has been created, I just need to start it:

```
pi@pi1 ~ $ sudo gluster volume start gv0
Starting volume gv0 has been successful
```

Once the volume has been started, I can use the volume info command on either node to see its status:

```
sudo gluster volume info

Volume Name: gv0
Type: Replicate
Status: Started
Number of Bricks: 2
Transport-type: tcp
```

3.4 Clustering with Raspberry Pis

```
Bricks:
Brick1: 192.168.0.121:/srv/gv0
Brick2: 192.168.0.122:/srv/gv0
```

Configure the GlusterFS Client

Now that the volume is started, I can mount it as a GlusterFS type filesystem from any client that has GlusterFS support. First though, I will want to mount it from my two Raspberry Pis as I want them to be able to write to the volume themselves. To do this, I will create a new mountpoint on my filesystem on each Raspberry Pi and use the mount command to mount the volume on it:

```
sudo mkdir -p /mnt/gluster1
sudo mount -t glusterfs 192.168.0.121:/gv0 /mnt/gluster1
df
Filesystem           1K-blocks     Used Available Use% Mounted on
rootfs                 1804128  1496464    216016  88% /
/dev/root              1804128  1496464    216016  88% /
devtmpfs                 86184        0     86184   0% /dev
tmpfs                    18888      216     18672   2% /run
tmpfs                     5120        0      5120   0% /run/lock
tmpfs                    37760        0     37760   0% /run/shm
/dev/mmcblk0p1           57288    18960     38328  34% /boot
192.168.0.121:/gv0     1804032  1496448    215936  88% /mnt/gluster1
```

The more pedantic readers among you may be saying to yourselves, "Wait a minute, if I am specifying a specific IP address here, what happens when 192.168.0.121 goes down?" It turns out that this IP address is used only to pull down the complete list of bricks used in the volume, and from that point on, the redundant list of bricks is what will be used when accessing the volume.

Once you mount the filesystem, play around with creating files and then looking into /srv/gv0. You should be able to see (but again, don't touch) files that you've created from /mnt/gluster1 on the /srv/gv0 bricks on both nodes in your cluster:

```
pi@pi1 ~ $ sudo touch /mnt/gluster1/test1
pi@pi1 ~ $ ls /mnt/gluster1/test1
/mnt/gluster1/test1
pi@pi1 ~ $ ls /srv/gv0
test1
pi@pi2 ~ $ ls /srv/gv0
test1
```

After you are satisfied that you can mount the volume, make it permanent by adding an entry like the following to the /etc/fstab file on your Raspberry Pis:

```
192.168.0.121:/gv0   /mnt/gluster1   glusterfs   defaults,_netdev  0  0
```

Note that if you also want to access this GlusterFS volume from other clients on your network, just install the GlusterFS client package for your distribution (for Debian-based distributions, it's called glusterfs-client), and then create a mountpoint and perform the same mount command as I listed above.

Test Redundancy

Now that I have a redundant filesystem in place, let's test it. Since I want to make sure that I could take down either of the two nodes and still have access to the files, I configured a separate client to mount this GlusterFS volume. Then I created a simple script called glustertest inside the volume:

```
#!/bin/bash

while [ 1 ]
do
  date > /mnt/gluster1/test1
  cat /mnt/gluster1/test1
  sleep 1
done
```

This script runs in an infinite loop and just copies the current date into a file inside the GlusterFS volume and then cats it back to the screen. Once I make the file executable and run it, I should see a new date pop up about every second:

```
chmod a+x /mnt/gluster1/glustertest
/mnt/gluster1/glustertest
Sat Mar  9 13:19:02 PST 2013
Sat Mar  9 13:19:04 PST 2013
Sat Mar  9 13:19:05 PST 2013
Sat Mar  9 13:19:06 PST 2013
Sat Mar  9 13:19:07 PST 2013
Sat Mar  9 13:19:08 PST 2013
```

I noticed every now and then that the output would skip a second, but in this case, I think it was just a function of the date command not being executed exactly one second apart every time, so every now and then that extra sub-second it would take to run a loop would add up.

After I started the script, I then logged in to the first Raspberry Pi and typed sudo reboot to reboot it. The script kept on running just fine, and if there were any hiccups along the way, I couldn't tell it apart from the occasional skipping of a second that I saw beforehand. Once the first Raspberry Pi came back up, I repeated the reboot on the second one, just to confirm that I could lose either node and still be fine. This kind of redundancy is not bad considering this took only a couple commands.

There you have it. Now you have the foundation set with a redundant file store across two Raspberry Pis. Next, I will build on top of the foundation by adding a new redundant service that takes advantage of the shared storage.

Web Servers Across a Raspberry Pi Cluster

Now that I have the storage up and tested, I'd like to set up these Raspberry Pis as a fault-tolerant Web cluster. Granted, Raspberry Pis don't have speedy processors or a lot of RAM, but they still have more than enough resources to act as a Web server for static files. Although the example I'm going to give is

3.4 Clustering with Raspberry Pis

very simplistic, that's intentional—the idea is that once you have validated that a simple static site can be hosted on redundant Raspberry Pis, you can expand that with some more sophisticated content yourself.

Install Nginx

Although I like Apache just fine, for a limited-resource Web server serving static files, something like nginx has the right blend of features, speed and low resource consumption that make it ideal for this site. Nginx is available in the default Raspbian package repository, so I log in to the first Raspberry Pi in the cluster and run:

```
sudo apt update
sudo apt install nginx
```

Once nginx installed, I created a new basic nginx configuration at /mnt/gluster1/cluster that contains the following config:

```
server {
  root /mnt/gluster1/www;
  index index.html index.htm;
  server_name twopir twopir.example.com;

  location / {
    try_files $uri $uri/ /index.html;
  }
}
```

> **Note:** I decided to name the service twopir, but you would change this to whatever hostname you want to use for the site. Also notice that I set the document root to /mnt/gluster1/www. This way, I can put all of my static files onto shared storage so they are available from either host.

Now that I have an nginx config, I need to move the default nginx config out of the way and set up this config to be the default. Under Debian, nginx organizes its files a lot like Apache with sites-available and sites-enabled directories. Virtual host configs are stored in sites-available, and sites-enabled contains symlinks to those configs that you want to enable. Here are the steps I performed on the first Raspberry Pi:

```
cd /etc/nginx/sites-available
sudo ln -s /mnt/gluster1/cluster .
cd /etc/nginx/sites-enabled
sudo rm default
sudo ln -s /etc/nginx/sites-available/cluster .
```

Now I have a configuration in place but no document root to serve. The next step is to create a /mnt/gluster1/www directory and copy over the default nginx index.html file to it. Of course, you probably would want to create your own custom index.html file here instead, but copying a file is a good start:

```
sudo mkdir /mnt/gluster1/www
cp /usr/share/nginx/www/index.html /mnt/gluster1/www
```

With the document root in place, I can restart the nginx service:

```
sudo /etc/init.d/nginx restart
```

Now I can go to my DNS server and make sure I have an A record for twopir that points to my first Raspberry Pi at 192.168.0.121. In your case, of course, you would update your DNS server with your hostname and IP. Now I would open up http://twopir/ in a browser and confirm that I see the default nginx page. If I look at the /var/log/nginx/access.log file, I should see evidence that I hit the page.

Once I've validated that the Web server works on the first Raspberry Pi, it's time to duplicate some of the work on the second Raspberry Pi. Because I'm storing configurations on the shared GlusterFS storage, really all I need to do is install nginx, create the proper symlinks to enable my custom nginx config and restart nginx:

```
sudo apt-get update
sudo apt-get install nginx
cd /etc/nginx/sites-available
sudo ln -s /mnt/gluster1/cluster .
cd /etc/nginx/sites-enabled
sudo rm default
sudo ln -s /etc/nginx/sites-available/cluster .
sudo /etc/init.d/nginx restart
```

Two DNS A Records

So, now I have two Web hosts that can host the same content, but the next step in this process is an important part of what makes this setup redundant. Although you definitely could set up a service like heartbeat with some sort of floating IP address that changed from one Raspberry Pi to the next depending on what was up, an even better approach is to use two DNS A records for the same hostname that point to each of the Raspberry Pi IPs. Some people refer to this as DNS load balancing, because by default, DNS lookups for a hostname that has multiple A records will return the results in random order each time you make the request:

```
dig twopir.example.com A +short
192.168.0.121
192.168.0.122
dig twopir.example.com A +short
192.168.0.122
192.168.0.121
```

Because the results are returned in random order, clients should get sent evenly between the different hosts, and in effect, multiple A records do result in a form of load balancing. What interests me about a host having multiple A records though isn't as much the load balancing as how a Web browser handles failure. When a browser gets two A records for a Web host, and the first host is unavailable, the browser almost immediately will fail over to the next A record in the list. This failover is fast enough that in many cases it's imperceptible to the user and definitely is much faster than the kind of failover you might see in a traditional heartbeat cluster.

So, go to the same DNS server you used to add the first A record and add a second record that references the same hostname but a different IP address–the IP address of the second host in the cluster. Once you save your changes, perform a dig query like I performed above and you should get two IP addresses back.

Once you have two A records set up, the cluster is basically ready for use and is fault-tolerant. Open two terminals and log in to each Raspberry Pi, and run `tail -f /var/log/nginx/access.log` so you can watch the Web server access then load your page in a Web browser. You should see activity on the access logs on one of the servers but not the other. Now refresh a few times, and you'll notice that your browser should be sticking to a single Web server. After you feel satisfied that your requests are going to that server successfully, reboot it while refreshing the Web page multiple times. If you see a blip at all, it should be a short one, because the moment the Web server drops, you should be redirected to the second Raspberry Pi and be able to see the same index page. You also should see activity in the access logs. Once the first Raspberry Pi comes back from the reboot, you probably will not even be able to notice from the perspective of the Web browser.

Experiment with rebooting one Raspberry Pi at a time, and you should see that as long as you have one server available, the site stays up. Although this is a simplistic example, all you have to do now is copy over any other static Web content you want to serve into /mnt/gluster1/www, and enjoy your new low-cost fault-tolerant Web cluster.

3.5 Home As Your Backup Data Center

New Linux users often ask me "what is the best way to learn about Linux?" My advice always comes down to this: install and use Linux (any distribution will do but something stable works better), and play around with it. Inevitably, you will break something, and then instead of re-installing, force yourself to fix what you broke. That's my advice, because I've personally learned more about Linux by fixing my own problems than just about any other way. After years of doing this, you start to build confidence in your Linux troubleshooting skills, so that no matter what problem comes your way, you figure if you work at it long enough, you can solve it.

That confidence was put to the test recently when I had a problem with a

KVM host. After a power outage, it refused to boot a virtual machine that was my primary personal server for just about everything. In this section, I walk through a problem that almost had me stumped and show how I was able to find a solution in an unorthodox place (at least for me).

The Setup

Before I dive too deep into my problem, it would help to understand my setup. Although I do have servers at home, my primary server is colocated in a data center. I share the server with a friend, so the physical server simply acts as a secured KVM host, and I split the server's RAM and CPU across two virtual machines 50/50. All of my most important services from my primary DNS server and e-mail for me and my immediate family, a number of different Web sites and blogs, and even my main Irssi session sits on one of those two VMs. I end up hosting secondary DNS and e-mail from a server on my home connection, but due to a one-megabit upstream connection, I don't host much else at home for the outside world.

One day (while a relative happened to be visiting from out of town), I noticed that both my main server and the physical server that was hosting it were unavailable. I notified my contact at the data center, and it ended up being an accidental power outage that affected my cabinet. I was taking my relative out to the coast for the day, far away from decent cell-phone reception. So, since there wasn't much I could do, I assumed that long before I got back into town that afternoon, power would be restored, and other than losing over a year's uptime, I would be back up and running.

Everything but the Sync

The first time I knew there was a real problem was when I got back into town and my main server still was down. I could log in to the physical host, however; so at first I wasn't too worried. After all, I had seen KVM instances not recover from a physical host reboot before. In the past, it was either from not setting a VM to start at boot or sometimes even a wayward libvirt apparmor profile that got in the way. Usually once I logged in to the physical host, I could change any bad settings, disable any troublesome apparmor module, then manually launch my VM with virsh. This time was different.

When my VM wouldn't boot manually, I was ready to blame AppArmor. It had blocked VMs from booting in the past, but this time, neither setting the libvirtd AppArmor module to complain mode, disabling all AppArmor modules nor even forcefully stopping AppArmor seemed to help. I even resorted to rebooting the physical host to heed AppArmor's warning that forcibly stopping it after it was running may cause some modules to misbehave. Nothing helped. When I connected a console to the VM as it booted, I started seeing initial kernel

3.5 Home As Your Backup Data Center

errors as though it was having trouble mounting the root filesystem. Great. Did the power outage corrupt my data?

The next step in the troubleshooting process was to attempt to boot from a rescue disk. With KVM, it's relatively easy to add a local ISO image as though it were a CD-ROM. So after not much effort, I discovered I could, in fact, boot a rescue disk and confirmed from the rescue disk I could mount my VM's drives, and the data did not seem corrupted. So then why wouldn't it boot? After I ran a manual fsck from the rescue disk, I attempted to reload GRUB, and that was when I got my first strange clue about the nature of the problem–even from the rescue disk, I wasn't able to write to the filesystem reliably. I would get virtual ATA resets, even though I seemed to be able to read fine.

So, I assumed I had some level of corruption with that particular VM, but because my data wasn't affected, I figured in the worst case, I could spawn a fresh VM and migrate the data over. So, that's what I tried next using the ubuntu-vm-builder wrapper script I used previously to build my VM. The VM seemed to spawn fine; however, once again, even this brand-new VM refused to boot properly and had the same strange disk errors.

It was at this point that my troubleshooting steps start to get a bit hazy, because I started trying more desperate things. I booted different kernel versions in GRUB (after all, the kernel had been updated a few times in the year the server had been up). I audited all of the filesystem permissions on my VM disk images, and I tried to launch the VMs as root just in case. I even tried converting one VM's disks from qcow2 to raw with no results. Even Web searches came up empty. This server had been down longer than it ever had before, and I was starting to run out of options.

The Sync

My first break came when I decided to copy the VM I had just spawned over to almost identical hardware I had at home with the same distribution and see if I could reproduce the problem there. I picked the new host simply because since qcow2 filesystems grow on demand, it happened to have the smallest disks and was the fastest to sync over. The process was pretty straightforward. First I exported that KVM instance's configuration XML file with virsh on the colocated host:

```
virsh dumpxml test1.example.net > test1.example.net.xml
```

Then I copied that XML file to my home server, created a local directory named after this VM to store its disk images and synced them over from the physical host:

```
mkdir test1.example.net
rsync -avx -progress remotehost:/var/lib/libvirt/
    ↪ images/test1.example.net/test1.example.net/
```

Once the disk images were copied, I had to edit the test1.example.net.xml file, because the disk images now were stored in a new location. After I did that, I used virsh again to import this XML configuration file and start the VM:

```
virsh define test1.example.net.xml
virsh start test1.example.net
```

The VM actually started! Although I still had no idea what the problem was on the colocated server, I felt pretty confident that if I could sync over my main server, it would run on this home machine. Of course, with a 12Mb-down, 1Mb-up connection at home, it was going to take a bit longer to copy the 45GB disk images for this VM. Other than the time it took, the process was essentially the same as with the test machine, except once the host booted, I had to change its network configuration to reflect its new public IP.

With my server back up and running, I just had to change a number of DNS entries and firewall rules to reflect the new IP, and even with my slower upstream connection at home, I at least had some breathing room to troubleshoot the problem on the colocated server.

The Last Resort

Now that my VM and its data were safe and services were restored (if a bit slow), I felt free to perform more drastic steps on my colocated server. The first step was trying to figure out what was so different about it compared to my home server. They had the same Ubuntu 10.04 server install and most of the same packages. Luckily, I had a number of old cached libvirt and KVM packages on my home server, so at first I iterated through all of those packages to see if the problem was due to some upgrade. Once I exhausted that, I tried different kernel versions on the physical host and still no results.

Believe me when I tell you that during that week I tried every troubleshooting measure I could think of before I finally went to the second-to-last resort. The fact that I was even considering this should tell you how desperate I was getting. The last resort would be to do a complete re-install from scratch something I wasn't ready to do yet. I was desperate enough though that I went with the second-to-last resort: an in-place distribution upgrade from 10.04 to 12.04. Once the dust settled, I tried my small test image, and it actually worked. We were back in business.

The Sync Back

Well, we were almost back in business. See, I had been using that server at home for a number of days now, and between the e-mail, blogs and other services, it had a lot of new data on it. This meant I couldn't just start up the image that was already on the colocated server. I had to sync up the changes from my home server.

3.5 Home As Your Backup Data Center

The real trick to this was that I couldn't just sync the server hot. For one, the disk would be changing all the time, and two, I didn't want to risk having the same server running in weird states on two different physical hosts. This meant syncing the actual disk images. The problem was that while the 45GB disk images synced to my house relatively quickly over my 12Mb-downstream (plus the server was already down at the time, so downtime wasn't a consideration), syncing the same data up with my 1Mb upstream was going to take a long time–too long for a pure cold sync to be a solution, as I just couldn't have that much downtime.

The solution here was going to be two-fold, and it was based on a few assumptions I could make:

- Although a fair number of files had changed on my local VM instance, the actual size of the change was relatively small compared to the size of the disk images.
- rsync has an excellent mechanism for syncing over only the parts of large files that have changed.
- A lot of the changes in my qcow2 files were likely going to be at the end of those files anyway.
- If I use rsync with the `--inplace` option, it will modify the existing disk image on the remote machine directly and save disk space and time.

So my plan for phase 1 was to run rsync from physical host to physical host and sync over the qcow2 disk images hot while the VM was running and tell rsync to sync the disk images in place. Because I could assume the remote images would be somewhat corrupted anyway (that's the downside of syncing a disk image while the disk is being used), I didn't have to care about `--inplace` leaving behind a potentially corrupted file if it were stopped midway through the sync. I could clean it up later.

The advantage of doing the phase 1 rsync hot was that I could get all of the main differences between the home and colocated images sorted out while the server was still running at home. I even could potentially run that rsync multiple times leading up to phase 2 just to make sure it was as up to date as it could be. Here are the rsync commands I used to perform the phase 1 hot sync:

```
rsync -avz -progress -inplace disk0.qcow2
    ↪ remotehost:/var/lib/libvirt/images/www.example.net/disk0.qcow2
rsync -avz -progress -inplace disk1.qcow2
    ↪ remotehost:/var/lib/libvirt/images/www.example.net/disk1.qcow2
```

Between rsync's syncing only the bits that changed and the fact that I used -z to compress the data before it was transferred, I was able to sync these files way faster than you would think possible on a 1Mb connection. Of course, these commands ended up saturating my bandwidth at home, so since I wasn't under time pressure for the hot sync to complete, I ended up setting a bandwidth limit of 10 kilobytes per second for the larger disk1.qcow2 image:

```
rsync -avz -progress -inplace -bwlimit=10 disk1.qcow2
    remotehost:/var/lib/libvirt/images/www.example.net/disk1.qcow2
```

Once phase 1 was complete, I could start with phase 2. I needed the phase 2 rsync to run while the VM was powered off so I could make sure the disk wasn't being written to during the sync. Otherwise, I would risk corruption on the filesystem. Because this required downtime, I picked a proper maintenance window for my server when it would be less busy, finished a final phase 1 hot sync a few hours before, then halted the VM cleanly before I performed the final syncs:

```
rsync -avz -progress -inplace disk0.qcow2
    remotehost:/var/lib/libvirt/images/www.example.net/disk0.qcow2
rsync -avz -progress -inplace disk1.qcow2
    remotehost:/var/lib/libvirt/images/www.example.net/disk1.qcow2
```

Because of the previous work of syncing up the disk images, the final cold sync took only an hour or two with most of the time being spent with rsync seeking between the local and remote image to confirm they were in sync. Once the commands completed, I was able to power up the server again on my colocated host, change its IPs back, and I was back in business.

4. Server Projects

A sysadmin's time is split between daily tasks and long-term projects. When you are mapping out projects on your own, it can be useful to see how others have tackled a project in the past. This chapter collects a number of stand-alone sysadmin projects that I've found particularly useful in the past.

First I discuss how to set up a last-minute secondary mail server, in case you ever discover you forgot to set up a backup mail server right after the primary goes down. Of course the same approach also works to set up a permanent secondary mail server. I follow that up with another mail-centric project: how to query an Exchange IMAPS server from the command line.

The next part of the chapter covers disk-related projects. First I explain my tried-and-true approach for migrating data to a new hard drive. Then I go the other way and describe how to wipe all of the data off of a remote server when all you have is SSH access. Finally I talk about a pretty unique problem I faced one day: how to preseed full disk encryption without overwriting the disk ahead of time for an OEM Debian install I was working on.

The last part of the chapter deals with network-based projects. First I describe how to reduce the load on your central DNS servers in an environment by setting up a simple DNS cache on localhost that's also easy to troubleshoot. The rest of the chapter is devoted to setting up a PXE boot server so you can boot hardware over the network and install new operating systems remotely. I discuss both the initial setup along with rudimentary menus and finish up with describing how to take advantage of Ubuntu and Debian's graphical PXE menus in your own environment.

While each of these projects was aimed to solve a specific problem I had, hopefully you will be able to find ways to adapt the projects to something that would help your environment. If not, at the very least you should find reading through my approach helpful as you consider how to tackle your own projects.

4.1 Last Minute Secondary Mail Server

It's easy to build redundant systems when time and money are limitless. When you have neither, or you are designing a personal system, often backups and redundancy are parts of the project you plan to get to on a rainy day. Of course inevitably, you put those tasks off until the main system fails, and then you scramble to pick up the pieces. Setting up RAID and doing backups, in fact, are probably the most common examples of these do-it-on-a-rainy-day tasks (and if you haven't heard yet, they are not the same thing). We all know we should back up important data, and we should set up a RAID on that important file server, and by now, enough of us have been bitten by that mistake that I'm not going to talk about either today. Instead, I'm going to talk about one of those services that gets less attention: your mail server.

It is important to have a backup mail server, but whether you work for a small company, or you administer your own personal mail server, you might not have gotten around to a secondary mail relay. Then, disaster strikes. It could be that the primary mail server's hardware failed, or maybe it was hacked and, in either case, it is going to be down for a few days. In the meantime, you still would like to be able to send and receive e-mail. In this section, I cover a few easy, and more important, quick steps to create a secondary mail relay to tide you over until the primary can come back on-line.

Now, my original method for an emergency mail server uses a Knoppix disc. I always had one around somewhere, and because I can install just about any software I need on the live CD, it is ideal when I need a basic Linux system fast. I can just locate a spare machine, boot Knoppix on it, and set up my server. When the emergency is over, I can shut it off with no commitment.

Then again, you might want to make this secondary mail server a bit more permanent. These same steps will work just fine on any ordinary Linux system that has postfix available.

While originally Knoppix was one of the few live discs that offered the ability to install software in a ramdisk, now most distribution live discs that let you try out the system before you install, and let you install software on the live system, should work. These steps should work on any live disk that is based on Debian.

Before you perform any steps, be sure to choose a server that has enough storage to store your mail. This number varies based on your e-mail traffic and the number of clients on the server, but the machine will need to store

4.1 Last Minute Secondary Mail Server

all incoming mail locally until the primary server comes back up. So, if you get 50MB of mail each day and plan for the primary to be down for three days, you should have at least 150MB of spare storage for the mail spool in /var/spool/postfix plus extra, just in case. If you don't have enough spare storage or you use a live disc for this, mount an extra partition, create a postfix directory on it and symlink /var/spool/postfix to it.

Now that you have chosen a server, the first step is to install postfix. Postfix is a common package and should be available for any major Linux distribution you use. On Debian-based systems, the installation process automatically runs a configuration script to set up a reasonable default config. If you do run into this script, choose the "Internet Site" configuration type and accept the rest of the defaults in the script. Alternatively, you can copy a default configuration that ships with your postfix package or run it through a configuration script your distribution includes.

Once postfix is installed, you need to tweak the default configuration so that it can act as your mail relay. Postfix makes this pretty simple, and you need to worry about only a few configuration options. Edit the /etc/postfix/main.cf file, and locate a line called mynetworks. This option tells postfix for which networks to relay mail. Ideally, you should set this only for internal networks or specific external hosts you trust will not relay spam through your system. If you allow all networks, you have just turned your system into an open relay and will likely find yourself on a spam black-hole list in no time. If your local network is 192.168.1.x, for instance, you would add an entry for that and for localhost:

```
mynetworks = 127.0.0.0/8, 192.168.1.0/24
```

Next, you need to tell postfix for which incoming domains it will accept mail for relay. This variable will be set to any domains for which you accept incoming mail. So, if you own example.com and example.org, for instance, you would add:

```
relay_domains = example.com, example.org
```

You even can act as a secondary mail server for friends. Simply add their domains here as well, and your mail server will accept incoming mail to those domains and then forward it to the appropriate primary mail server. How does it know which server to use? It relies on DNS, which I discuss shortly.

The final postfix options to change tell postfix how long to spool and attempt to deliver mail before it bounces it. By default, postfix queues mail for three days, and during that time, it continuously attempts delivery. After three days, postfix bounces the mail and sends an e-mail notification to the sender that the e-mail could not be delivered. If your primary server is going to be down for a few days, you probably will want to extend this default. Locate the following values (or add them if they aren't defined) in /etc/postfix/main.cf, and edit them so they look like the following:

```
bounce_queue_lifetime = 14d
maximal_queue_lifetime = 14d
```

Here I increased the maximum time to 14 days, but you can change it to a value that makes sense for you. Generally, you don't want to hold on to e-mail for too long, as senders likely will want to know eventually if their e-mail could not be delivered. Once these options are changed, type

```
sudo systemctl restart postfix
```

to start the service, or type

```
sudo systemctl reload postfix
```

if postfix already is running.

Next, test the server. Either configure your mail client to use this server as its SMTP gateway and then send an e-mail to your domain, or if you feel fancy, connect to port 25 on the server using Telnet, and type the raw SMTP commands. Check /var/log/mail.log or /var/log/maillog to confirm that postfix accepted and spooled your mail.

The last step is to configure your DNS server so that it lists your new machine as a secondary mail server for your domain. Your DNS server should have at least one MX record defined that looks something like this:

```
example.com.    IN MX    100    mail1.example.com.
```

If I created a new mail server and added its IP to DNS so that mail2.example.com pointed to it, I then would add the following line to my DNS zone:

```
example.com.    IN MX    200    mail2.example.com.
```

Because I assigned mail2 a higher value (200) than mail1 (100), other mail servers know that mail1 is my primary and that mail ultimately will land there. However, if mail1 is unavailable, they know that they can attempt delivery on mail2 (and some mail servers attempt mail delivery on secondary servers first anyway). Once my DNS zone is reloaded, mail that has been queued up on remote servers ever since mail1 went down should start being delivered to mail2. Be sure to add this DNS entry for any domains you added in the `relay_domains` option. It also may go without saying, but be sure that mail2.example.com points to an external IP address that lands on your mail server.

As this server runs, monitor its storage to make sure you have plenty for new incoming mail. You also can run the mailq command to see all the queued messages. Once your primary server comes back up, postfix will start delivering its queued messages automatically (it actually will have been attempting it the entire time). By default, postfix will throttle this delivery so it doesn't flood the primary mail server, but if you want all of the queued e-mail delivered immediately, type `sudo postqueue -f`.

With the primary machine back up, you might want to take down this temporary machine or at least work on a more permanent solution. If you do take it down, be sure to remove its MX record from all your DNS servers. You do have redundant DNS servers, right?

4.2 Check Exchange from the Command Line

Through the years, you tend to accumulate a suite of tools, practices and settings as you use Linux. In my case, this has meant a Mutt configuration that fits me like a tailored suit and a screen session that at home reconnects me to my IRC session and at work provides me with quick access to e-mail with notifications along the bottom of the terminal for Nagios alerts and incoming e-mail. I've written about all of these different tools through years, but in this section, I talk about how I adapted when one of my scripts no longer worked.

My e-mail notification script is relatively straightforward. I configure fetchmail on my local machine, but instead of actually grabbing e-mail, I just run `fetchmail -c`, which returns each mailbox along with how many messages are unseen. I parse that, and if I have any unread mail, I display it in the notification area in screen. I wrote about that in my February 2011 Hack and / column "Status Messages in Screen"[1], and up until now, it has worked well for me. Whenever I set up my computer for a new job, I just configure fetchmail and reuse the same script.

Recently, however, we switched our mail servers at work to a central Exchange setup, which by itself wouldn't be too much of an issue–in the past I just configured Mutt and fetchmail to treat it like any other IMAP host–but in this case, the Exchange server was configured with security in mind. So in addition to using IMAPS, each client was given a client certificate to present to the server during authentication. Mutt was able to handle this just fine with a few configuration tweaks, but fetchmail didn't fare so well. It turns out that fetchmail has what some would call a configuration quirk and others would call a bug. When you configure fetchmail to use a client certificate, it overrides whatever user name you have configured in favor of the user specified inside the client certificate. In my case, the two didn't match, so fetchmail wasn't able to log in to the Exchange server, and I no longer got new mail notifications inside my screen session.

I put up with this for a week or so, until I realized I really missed knowing when I had new e-mail while I was working. I decided there must be some other way to get a count of unread messages from the command line, so I started doing research. In the end, what worked for me was to use OpenSSL's `s_client` mode to handle the SSL session between me and the Exchange server (including the client certificate), and then once that session was established, I was able to

---

[1] https://www.linuxjournal.com/article/10950

send raw IMAP commands to authenticate and then check for unread messages.

OpenSSL s_client

The first step was to set up an OpenSSL `s_client` connection. Most people probably interact with OpenSSL on the command line only when they need to generate new self-signed certificates or read data from inside a certificate, but the tool also provides an `s_client` mode that you can use to troubleshoot SSL-enabled services like HTTPS. With `s_client`, you initiate an SSL connection and after it outputs relevant information about that SSL connection, you are presented with a prompt just as though you used Telnet or Netcat to connect to a remote port. From there, you can type in raw HTTP, SMTP or IMAP commands depending on your service.

The syntax for `s_client` is relatively straightforward, and here is how I connected to my Exchange server over IMAPS:

```
openssl s_client -cert /home/kyle/.mutt/imaps_cert.pem
    ↪ -crlf -connect imaps.example.com:993
```

The `-cert` argument takes a full path to my client certificate file, which I store with the rest of my Mutt configuration. The `-crlf` option makes sure that I send the right line feed characters each time I press enter–important for some touchy IMAPS servers. Finally the `-connect` argument lets me specify the hostname and port to which to connect.

Once you connect, you will see a lot of SSL output, including the certificate the server presents, and finally, you will see a prompt like the following:

```
* OK The Microsoft Exchange IMAP4 service is ready.
```

From here, you use the `tag login` IMAP command followed by your user name and password to log in, and you should get back some sort of confirmation if login succeeded:

```
tag login kyle.rankin supersecretpassword
tag OK LOGIN completed.
```

Now that you're logged in, you can send whatever other IMAP commands you want, including some that would show you a list of mailboxes, e-mail headers or even the full contents of messages. In my case though, I just want to see the number of unseen messages in my INBOX, so I use the `tag STATUS` command followed by the mailbox and then (UNSEEN) to tell it to return the number of unseen messages:

```
tag STATUS INBOX (UNSEEN)
* STATUS INBOX (UNSEEN 1)
tag OK STATUS completed.
```

In this example, I have one unread message in my INBOX. Now that I have that information, I can type `tag LOGOUT` to log out.

expect script

Now this is great, except I'm not going to go through all of those steps every time I want to check for new mail. What I need to do is automate this. Unfortunately, my attempts just to pass the commands I wanted as input didn't work so well, because I needed to pause between commands for the remote server to accept the previous command. When you are in a situation like this, a tool like expect is one of the common ways to handle it. expect allows you to construct incredibly complicated programs that look for certain output and then send your input. In my case, I just needed a few simple commands:

1. confirm Exchange was ready
2. send my login
3. once I was authenticated, send the `tag STATUS` command
4. log out

The expect script turned into the following:

```
set timeout 10
spawn openssl s_client -cert /home/kyle/.mutt/imaps_cert.pem
↪ -crlf -connect imaps.example.com:993
expect "* OK"
send "tag login kyle.rankin supersecretpassword\n"
expect "tag OK LOGIN completed."
sleep 1
send "tag STATUS INBOX (UNSEEN)\n"
expect "tag OK"
send "tag LOGOUT\n"
```

I saved that to a local file (and made sure only my user could read it) and then called it as the sole argument to expect:

```
expect .imapsexpectscript
```

Of course, since this script runs through the whole IMAPS session, it also outputs my authentication information to the screen. I need only the INBOX status output anyway, so I just grep for that:

```
expect /.imapsexpectscript | egrep '\(UNSEEN [0-9]'
* STATUS INBOX (UNSEEN 1)
```

For my screen session, I just want the name of the mailbox and the number of read messages (and no output if there are no unread messages), so I modify my egrep slightly and pipe the whole thing to a quick Perl one-liner to strip output I don't want. The final script looks like this:

```
#!/bin/bash

MAILCOUNT=`expect ~/.imapsexpectscript | egrep '\(UNSEEN [1-9]'
↪ | perl -pe 's/.*STATUS \w+.*?(\d+)\).*?$/$1/'`
if [ "$MAILCOUNT" != "" ]; then
  echo INBOX:${MAILCOUNT}
fi
```

Now I can just update my .screenrc to load the output of that script into one of my backtick fields instead of fetchmail (more on that in a Linux Journal column about screen[2]), and I'm back in business.

4.3 Migrate to a New Hard Drive

In my article "My Move to Solid State" published in the July 2008 issue of Linux Journal[3], I talk about my experiences with the new solid state drive (SSD) I installed on my laptop. One of the things I didn't mention in the article was how I transferred all my data and settings to the new drive. There are a number of ways to solve this problem. For instance, you could image the old drive onto the new one and then grow the last partition to fill up the presumably larger disk (which wouldn't work for me, as my new SSD actually was substantially smaller than the old drive). Other people just re-install their OS every time they get a new drive and then transfer their /home directory and other settings, but I've always had just enough custom programs and settings on my laptop for that method to be a pain. You also could use rsync with certain flags to migrate the files, and although I do like that method for network transfers, for local transfers, it can be a hassle, because it first must scan through the entire drive before it begins.

I've done many hard drive migrations during the years with a tried-and-true combination of find piped to cpio. I like this method because it uses common tools that are sure to be installed, it starts immediately and doesn't need to scan the drive, and with the right flags, it correctly can handle (and avoid) special filesystems, such as /proc, /sys and so on. So far, it hasn't failed me, and this migration was no exception. However, this time, I did run into a few gotchas that I will talk about shortly. First, onto the basic steps.

Move to a Safe State

You don't want files to be changed as you are copying them, so you don't want to do this migration from your normal desktop environment. Traditionally, I would boot in to a rescue disk like Knoppix (but any modern live disc with rescue features would work), so that the filesystem stays frozen. Other times, I simply switch to single-user mode, so most files won't change. For desktop systems, I generally just connect both drives directly to the system, and for laptops, I use a USB hard drive adapter, so that both can be connected at the same time. For my last migration, I didn't happen to have a USB adapter for a 1.8" drive, so I transferred the data to an intermediate drive first, then installed the new drive and transferred again.

---

[2]https://www.linuxjournal.com/article/10950
[3]https://www.linuxjournal.com/magazine/my-move-solid-state

4.3 Migrate to a New Hard Drive

Partition Your New Drive and Format the Filesystems

You can use any partitioning tool that works for you, from fdisk to qtparted. This may sound obvious, but make sure that you allocate plenty of room to fit your existing data, and if you move to a larger hard drive, plenty of room to grow. Once you partition the drive, use mkfs or your preferred formatting tool to write a filesystem to each partition (or mkswap for the swap partition).

Mount the New Partitions

Create mountpoints under /mnt for the new partitions you have created. For my example, I have a root partition at /dev/sdb1 and a home partition at /dev/sdb3, so I would type as root:

```
mkdir /mnt/sdb1
mkdir /mnt/sdb3
mount /dev/sdb1 /mnt/sdb1
mount /dev/sdb3 /mnt/sdb3
```

If you run this from a rescue disk, you also need to make sure your source partitions are mounted as well.

Run the find | cpio Spell

Now this spell doesn't have a lot to it, but it's funny how you memorize scripts like this over the years after using them and passing them along to friends. First, change to the root level of the partition you want to copy and then execute the command as root. So, to migrate my root partition from single-user mode, I did the following:

```
cd /
find ./ -xdev -print0 | cpio -pa0V /mnt/sdb1
```

To migrate from a rescue disk, the command is almost identical, but you change to the mountpoint of the source partition instead (I mounted it at /dev/sda1):

```
cd /mnt/sda1
find ./ -xdev -print0 | cpio -pa0V /mnt/sdb1
```

The find command searches through the entire root partition for files and directories. The -xdev flag tells find to stay within the current mounted filesystem. Otherwise, when find gets to /home, it would copy the contents of that directory as well and potentially fill up the new partition. It then passes the files to cpio, which places them under my new mountpoint while preserving permissions, symlinks and other settings. The cpio command also outputs one dot for each file it copies, so you can have some sense of its progress. However, what I typically do is go to another terminal and monitor the output of df so I can watch it grow:

```
watch df
```

Once the first `find | cpio` command completes, repeat it for each of your other partitions. In my example, if I were in single-user mode, I'd do the following:

```
cd /home
find ./ -xdev -print0 | cpio -pa0V /mnt/sdb3
```

If I were using a rescue disk, I'd do this:

```
cd /mnt/sda3
find ./ -xdev -print0 | cpio -pa0V /mnt/sdb3
```

Update fstab

What you do during this step will vary a bit, depending on how you set up your partitions. If you moved your partition layout around, you need to edit the /etc/fstab file on your new root partition so that it reflects the new drives you have set up.

Traditionally, this has been a simple step for me, because I try to order the partitions the same and generally don't have to touch fstab, but on this last migration, I had to add an extra step due to Ubuntu's use of UUIDs to reference partitions. A lot of modern distributions don't refer to partitions by their device name. Instead, a unique identifier called the UUID is assigned to each partition. If you see UUID=longstringofhex in your /etc/fstab, this means you.

Now, you have two choices here. The first choice is to change all these UUID lines to reference the actual device. This will work, and is less prone to typos that will make the system not boot, but you will lose the advantage of UUIDs. The other method is to reference the UUIDs for your new partitions and put them in place of the old UUIDs. You can find the list of disk-to-UUID mappings under /dev/disk/by-uuid:

```
ls -l /dev/disk/by-uuid/
total 0
lrwxrwxrwx 1 root root 10 2008-04-06 16:00
    ↪ 634719fd-a6da-4fee-8646-0d485d7681db -> ../../sda2
lrwxrwxrwx 1 root root 10 2008-04-06 16:00
    ↪ 665d7008-fde9-4055-8af9-483697acb005 -> ../../sda1
lrwxrwxrwx 1 root root 10 2008-04-06 16:00
    ↪ cf3892fd-e3d8-446f-8552-4c633be9c382 -> ../../sda3
```

Of course, you always could choose a hybrid of the two approaches, and set the hard device names in the fstab for the first boot, and then once you have confirmed the system boots, you then can update fstab with UUIDs.

Update GRUB

As with fstab, if you changed your partition layout, you need to update your GRUB configuration under /boot/grub/menu.lst (or on some systems, in /boot/grub/grub.conf) to reflect your changes. Also, GRUB can reference drives by

UUID, so if you see references to UUID in the GRUB configuration file, be sure to update it to reflect the new values. Once the file has been updated, chroot into your new root partition's mountpoint and then run grub-install:

```
chroot /mnt/sdb1 /usr/sbin/grub-install -recheck /dev/sdb
```

Change /mnt/sdb1 and /dev/sdb to reflect your new mounted root partition and its disk device, respectively. If the chrooted grub-install doesn't work, you typically can use your rescue disk (or single user) grub-install with the --root-directory option:

```
/usr/sbin/grub-install -recheck -root-directory /mnt/sdb1 /dev/sdb
```

(Optionally) Update the Initial Ramdisk

After I used my new system for some time, I noticed it wouldn't resume correctly from hibernation. It seemed like each time the swap partition would get corrupted. After some troubleshooting, I found that the root cause was a hard-coded resume device based on UUID that is put in the initial ramdisk for the machine. You may or may not run into this issue, depending on your Linux distribution, as each distribution manages its initrd differently. But, here is the fix for my Ubuntu system. I was able to find the offending reference to the old UUID in /etc/initramfs-tools/conf.d/resume. All I needed to do was update that file on the new drive to point to the new UUID for my swap partition, then run `update-initramfs` from the new system, and reboot.

4.4 Remotely Wipe a Server

In many ways, I feel sorry for people stuck with proprietary operating systems. When something goes wrong or if they have a problem to solve, the solution either is obvious, requires buying special software or is impossible. With Linux, I've always felt that I was limited only by my own programming and problem-solving abilities, no matter what problem presented itself. Throughout the years that Linux has been my primary OS, I've run into quite a few challenging and strange problems, such as how to hot-migrate from a two-disk RAID 1 to a three-disk RAID 5, or more often, how to somehow repair a system I had horribly broken.

The Problem

Recently, I ran into an interesting challenge when I had to decommission an old server. The server had quite a bit of sensitive data on it, so I also had to erase everything on the machine securely. Finally, when I was done completely wiping away all traces of data, I had to power off the machine. This is a relatively simple request when the server is under your desk: boot a rescue disk, use a tool like shred to wipe the data on all the hard drives, then press the power button. When the server is in a remote data center, it's a little more challenging: use a remote console to reboot into a rescue disk, wipe the server, then remotely pull the power using some networked PDU. When, like me, you have to wipe a server thousands of miles away with no remote console, no remote power, no remote help and only an SSH connection, you start scratching your head.

Why Would You Ever Do This?

At this point, some of you might be asking: "Why would you ever need to do this?" It turns out there are a few different reasons both legitimate and shady:

- You have broken hardware. This could be a server with a broken video card, a malfunctioning KVM or remote serial console, or some other problem where physical hardware access just doesn't work.
- You are locked out from your server. This could happen, for instance, if you colocate your server in a data center but stop paying your bills or somehow have a falling out with the provider. They revoke your physical access to your server, but you need to remove all the sensitive files while the machine is still available over the network.
- You have a bad consulting client. Perhaps you are a responsible and talented sysadmin who sets up a server for a client in good faith only to have that client refuse to pay you once the server is on-line. You want to remove your work securely, the client won't return your calls, yet you still have SSH access to the machine.
- You bought a cloud server with inadequate tools. It is very popular to host your server environment in the cloud; however, one downside is that many cloud providers cut costs by giving you limited access to management of your cloud instance. Do you really trust that when you terminate a server instance it is securely erased? Do you get access to tools that would let you boot a rescue disk on your cloud instance? In some cases, about the only remote management you have for a cloud server might be your SSH connection.
- You are an evil, malicious hacker who wants to cover his tracks. Yes, this is the least legitimate and most shady reason to wipe a server remotely, but I figured I should mention it in the interest of completeness.
- It's a challenge. Some people climb mountains, others run marathons, still others try to wipe servers remotely over SSH. You could just be a person who likes to push things to the limit, and this sounds like an interesting challenge.

4.4 Remotely Wipe a Server

How Would You Ever Do This?

Now that you have worked through the reasons you might need to know how to wipe a server remotely, let's talk about how you actually would do it. First, and most important, there are no redos! When you write random bits to a raw disk device, especially over SSH, you have only one shot to get it right. When I was preparing this process, I tested my procedure multiple times on virtual machines to make sure my steps were sound. I'm glad I did, as it took a few times to get all the steps right, confirm my assumptions and get the commands in the correct order.

What makes this challenge tricky is the fact that you will write randomly over the very filesystem you are logged in to. What happens if you overwrite the sshd and shred files while you are running shred and logged in over SSH? More important, what happens when you overwrite the kernel? The main principle that will make this procedure work is the fact that Linux likes to cache files to RAM whenever it can. As long as you can make sure everything you need is stored in RAM, you can overwrite the filesystem as much as you want. The trick is just identifying everything you need to store in RAM.

Always Have a Plan B

So, I mentioned there was no redo to this procedure, but that doesn't mean you can't set up some sort of safety net for yourself. Although I knew that once I launched the shred command it would run completely from RAM, what I had to figure out was what commands I would need to run after shred. Even commands like ls won't work if there's no filesystem to read. So that I would have some sort of backup plan, I took advantage of the /dev/shm ramdisk that all modern Linux systems make available. This is a directory that any user on the system can write to, and all files will be stored completely in RAM.

Because I wasn't sure whether commands like echo (which I would need later) would work after I had shredded the hard drive, I copied it to /dev/shm along with any other files I thought I would need. If you have the space, why not copy all of /bin, /sbin and /lib if you can. Finally, I knew I would need access to the /proc filesystem to power off the server. I assumed I still would have access to /proc even if I had overwritten the root filesystem, but I wasn't 100% certain, so just to be safe, I became root (you can't assume sudo will work later) and mounted an extra copy of /proc under /dev/shm as the root user:

```
$ sudo -s
# mkdir /dev/shm/proc
# mount -t proc proc /dev/shm/proc
```

It turns out I ultimately didn't need any of these precautions, but it doesn't hurt to be prepared.

It's Clobbering Time

Now is the point of no return. Just to be safe, I changed to the /dev/shm directory so my current working directory would be on a ramdisk. Then, I unmounted any unnecessary mountpoints (like /home) and ran the shred command below on every nonroot drive on the system. In my case, I used software RAID, so I also took the extra step of hot-removing all but one drive from any RAID array and shredded them separately. Finally, I was left with just my root filesystem stored on /dev/sda, so I took a deep breath and typed the following command:

```
shred -n2 -z -v /dev/sda
```

This command writes random bits to /dev/sda for two complete passes (-n2) then does a final pass with zeros so the drive looks perfectly clean (-z) with verbose output so I can see what's going on (-v\). Of course, adjust the -n argument to your particular level of paranoia–two passes was fine for me. I have to admit, there's something satisfying and strange about overwriting the root filesystem while you are still logged in.

Once the shred process completed, I had a completely empty filesystem. It was weird–commands like ls gave odd errors, and I knew I was isolated in my /dev/shm jail. All that was left was to shut down the server, but how do you do that when /sbin/shutdown is erased? No problem, you might say, just kill PID 1, since if you kill init, it will halt the system. That would work if, say, the kill program still were around. In this case, the only way I had left to shut down the system was via the /proc interface. The /proc directory is a special filesystem that allows you access to processes and kernel information, and it resides entirely in RAM, so my little shred stunt didn't wipe it out. To halt the machine, just enable the sysrq interface in the kernel, and then send the right command to sysrq:

```
echo 1 > /proc/sys/kernel/sysrq
echo o > /proc/sysrq-trigger
```

If the halt command doesn't work, or if you just want to reboot the machine instead, you would type:

```
echo b > /proc/sysrq-trigger
```

Now you might be asking yourself, didn't I overwrite the echo command? After all, /bin/echo is on the root filesystem. It turns out I didn't even have to rely on my copy of the command under /dev/shm–echo is one of the programs that are built in to the bash shell. When you execute echo, bash executes the version that is built in to itself, and because I already was inside a bash shell, the executable ran from RAM. Once you run the last echo command, the kernel instantly will halt. Any remote pings or other commands will stop, and the system will be powered off.

As a final note, I want to say that even if you don't think you'll ever need to go to such lengths to wipe a server, I think this procedure is such fun that you should at least try it in a disposable virtual machine. Shred the system and see which commands still work and which ones don't. As an extra challenge, see if you can get commands to run within /dev/shm.

4.5 Preseeding Full Disk Encryption

Usually I try to write articles that are not aimed at a particular distribution. Although I may give examples assuming a Debian-based distribution, whenever possible, I try to make my instructions applicable to everyone. This is not going to be one of those articles. Here, I document a process I went through recently with Debian preseeding (a method of automating a Debian install, like kickstart on Red Hat-based systems) that I found much more difficult than it needed to be, mostly because documentation was so sparse. In fact, I really found only two solid examples to work from in my research, one of which referred to the other.

In this section, I describe how to preseed full-disk encryption in a Debian install. This problem came up as I was trying to create a fully automated "OEM" install for a laptop. The goal was to have an automated boot mode that would guide users through their OS install and use full-disk encryption by default, but would make the process as simple as possible for users. Normally, unless you are going to encrypt the entire disk as one big partition, the Debian installer makes you jump through a few hoops to set up disk encryption during an install.

In my case, I couldn't just use the full disk, because I needed to carve off a small section of the disk as a rescue partition to store the OEM install image itself. My end goal was to make it so users just had to enter their passphrase, and it would set up an unencrypted /boot and rescue disk partition and an encrypted / and swap. As an additional challenge, I also wanted to skip the time-consuming disk-erasing process that typically happens when you enable disk encryption with Debian, since the disk was going to be blank to start with anyway.

Unfortunately, although there is a lot of documentation on how to automate ordinary partitioning and LVM with preseeding (I actually wrote a whole section on the topic myself in one of my books), I had a hard time finding much documentation on how to add encryption to the mix. After a lot of research, I finally found two posts (and as I mentioned, one of them referenced the other) that described the magic incantation that would enable this. Unfortunately, the only supported mode for encrypted disks in Debian preseed requires the use of LVM (something I confirmed later when I read the source code responsible for this part of the install). That's not the end of the world, but it would have been simpler in my mind if it didn't have that requirement.

Since you need a basic unencrypted /boot partition to load a kernel and prompt the user for a passphrase, I had to account for both and preserve a small

2GB rescue disk partition that already was present on the disk. After that, the remaining / and swap partitions were encrypted. Here is the partition section of the preseed config:

```
d-i partman-auto/method string crypto
d-i partman-lvm/device_remove_lvm boolean true
d-i partman-lvm/confirm boolean true
d-i partman-auto-lvm/guided_size string max
d-i partman-auto-lvm/new_vg_name string crypt
d-i partman-auto/disk string /dev/sda
d-i partman-auto/choose_recipe select root-encrypted
d-i partman-auto/expert_recipe string                    \
      root-encrypted ::                                   \
            500 500 500 ext3                              \
                  $primary{ } $bootable{ }                \
                  method{ format } format{ }              \
                  use_filesystem{ } filesystem{ ext4 }    \
                  mountpoint{ /boot }                     \
            .                                             \
            2000 2000 2000 linux-swap                     \
                  $lvmok{ } lv_name{ swap }               \
                  in_vg { crypt }                         \
                  $primary{ }                             \
                  method{ swap } format{ }                \
            .                                             \
            500 10000 1000000000 ext4                     \
                  $lvmok{ } lv_name{ root }               \
                  in_vg { crypt }                         \
                  $primary{ }                             \
                  method{ format } format{ }              \
                  use_filesystem{ } filesystem{ ext4 }    \
                  mountpoint{ / }                         \
            .                                             \
            2000 2000 2000 ext4                           \
                  $primary{ }                             \
                  method{ keep }                          \
                  use_filesystem{ } filesystem{ ext4 }    \
                  label{ rescuedisk }                     \

d-i partman-md/device_remove_md boolean true
d-i partman-basicfilesystems/no_mount_point boolean false
d-i partman-partitioning/confirm_write_new_label boolean true
d-i partman/choose_partition select finish
d-i partman/confirm boolean true
d-i partman/confirm_nooverwrite boolean true
```

If you've never worked with preseeding, this entire section of code probably looks incredibly foreign. As preseeding in general is documented well in a number of other places, I'm not going to bother breaking down every setting here. Instead, let me highlight the settings that matter for disk encryption. The most important one tells partman (the preseed partition manager) to use encryption:

```
d-i partman-auto/method string crypto
```

Next, because preseeded encrypted partitions need to use LVM, I must add LVM-specific preseed settings:

```
d-i partman-lvm/device_remove_lvm boolean true
d-i partman-lvm/confirm boolean true
d-i partman-auto-lvm/guided_size string max
d-i partman-auto-lvm/new_vg_name string crypt
```

In the last of these settings, I told partman to create a new LVM volume group named crypt that I will use to store my encrypted partitions. Further down when I define my swap and root partitions, you can see where I defined the logical volumes by name and set what volume group they are in:

```
2000 2000 2000 linux-swap                      \
        $lvmok{ } lv_name{ swap }              \
        in_vg { crypt }                        \
. . .
500 10000 1000000000 ext4                      \
        $lvmok{ } lv_name{ root }              \
        in_vg { crypt }                        \
```

Once these settings were in place, I was able to preseed an install and have disk encryption be almost fully automated, except that the installer prompted me for a passphrase, which I wanted.

The only missing piece to this automation was that the installer started overwriting the existing disk with random information. Now, there are good reasons why you may want to do this before setting up disk encryption, but in this case, the disk was blank beforehand, and I didn't want to wait the many hours it might take. Try as I might, no options to preseed this feature away seemed to work. After poring through the partman code to find the magic option, I finally resorted to patching the partman-crypto script on the fly in the middle of the install so that it skipped the erase process:

```
d-i partman/early_command \
        string sed -i.bak 's/-f $id\/skip_erase/-d $id/g'
    ↪ /lib/partman/lib/crypto-base.sh
```

This is an ugly hack indeed, but it was the only way I was able to find that worked. With that in place, I was able have an automated partitioning recipe with full-disk encryption that skipped the disk-erasing section. My hope is that the next time other people need to do this and do a search on-line, they at least can find my article and the two other examples and won't have to burn so much time.

4.6 Localhost DNS Cache

Is it weird to say that DNS is my favorite protocol? Because DNS is my favorite protocol. There's something about the simplicity of UDP packets combined with the power of a service that the entire Internet relies on that grabs my interest. Through the years, I've been impressed with just how few resources you need to run a modest DNS infrastructure for an internal network.

Recently, as one of my environments started to grow, I noticed that even though the DNS servers were keeping up with the load, the query logs were full of queries for the same hosts over and over within seconds of each other. You see, often a default Linux installation does not come with any sort of local DNS caching. That means that every time a hostname needs to be resolved to an IP, the external DNS server is hit no matter what TTL you set for that record.

This section explains how simple it is to set up a lightweight local DNS cache that does nothing more than forward DNS requests to your normal resolvers and honor the TTL of the records it gets back.

There are a number of different ways to implement DNS caching. In the past, I've used systems like nscd that intercept DNS queries before they would go to name servers in /etc/resolv.conf and see if they already are present in the cache. Although it works, I always found nscd more difficult to troubleshoot than DNS when something went wrong. What I really wanted was just a local DNS server that honored TTL but would forward all requests to my real name servers. That way, I would get the speed and load benefits of a local cache, while also being able to troubleshoot any errors with standard DNS tools.

The solution I found was dnsmasq. Normally I am not a big advocate for dnsmasq, because it's often touted as an easy-to-configure full DNS and DHCP server solution, and I prefer going with standalone services for that. Dnsmasq often will be configured to read /etc/resolv.conf for a list of upstream name servers to forward to and use /etc/hosts for zone configuration. I wanted something completely different. I had full-featured DNS servers already in place, and if I liked relying on /etc/hosts instead of DNS for hostname resolution, I'd hop in my DeLorean and go back to the early 1980s. Instead, the bulk of my dnsmasq configuration will be focused on disabling a lot of the default features.

The first step is to install dnsmasq. This software is widely available for most distributions, so just use your standard package manager to install the dnsmasq package. In my case, I'm installing this on Debian, so there are a few Debianisms to deal with that you might not have to consider if you use a different distribution. First is the fact that there are some rather important settings placed in /etc/default/dnsmasq. The file is fully commented, so I won't paste it here. Instead, I list two variables I made sure to set:

```
ENABLED=1
IGNORE_RESOLVCONF=yes
```

The first variable makes sure the service starts, and the second will tell dnsmasq to ignore any input from the resolvconf service (if it's installed) when determining what name servers to use. I will be specifying those manually anyway.

The next step is to configure dnsmasq itself. The default configuration file can be found at /etc/dnsmasq.conf, and you can edit it directly if you want, but in my case, Debian automatically sets up an /etc/dnsmasq.d directory and will

4.6 Localhost DNS Cache

load the configuration from any file you find in there. As a heavy user of configuration management systems, I prefer the servicename.d configuration model, as it makes it easy to push different configurations for different uses. If your distribution doesn't set up this directory for you, you can just edit /etc/dnsmasq.conf directly or look into adding an option like this to dnsmasq.conf:

```
conf-dir=/etc/dnsmasq.d
```

In my case, I created a new file called /etc/dnsmasq.d/dnscache.conf with the following settings:

```
no-hosts
no-resolv
listen-address=127.0.0.1
bind-interfaces
server=/dev.example.com/10.0.0.5
server=/10.in-addr.arpa/10.0.0.5
server=/dev.example.com/10.0.0.6
server=/10.in-addr.arpa/10.0.0.6
server=/dev.example.com/10.0.0.7
server=/10.in-addr.arpa/10.0.0.7
```

Let's go over each setting. The first, `no-hosts`, tells dnsmasq to ignore /etc/hosts and not use it as a source of DNS records. You want dnsmasq to use your upstream name servers only. The `no-resolv` setting tells dnsmasq not to use /etc/resolv.conf for the list of name servers to use. This is important, as later on, you will add dnsmasq's own IP to the top of /etc/resolv.conf, and you don't want it to end up in some loop. The next two settings, `listen-address` and `bind-interfaces` ensure that dnsmasq binds to and listens on only the localhost interface (127.0.0.1). You don't want to risk outsiders using your service as an open DNS relay.

The server configuration lines are where you add the upstream name servers you want dnsmasq to use. In my case, I added three different upstream name servers in my preferred order. The syntax for this line is:

```
server=/domain_to_use/nameserver_ip
```

So in the above example, it would use those name servers for dev.example.com resolution. In my case, I also wanted dnsmasq to use those name servers for IP-to-name resolution (PTR records), so since all the internal IPs are in the 10.x.x.x network, I added 10.in-addr.arpa as the domain.

Once this configuration file is in place, restart dnsmasq so the settings take effect. Then you can use dig pointed to localhost to test whether dnsmasq works:

```
dig ns1.dev.example.com @localhost

; <<>> DiG 9.8.4-rpz2+rl005.12-P1 <<>> ns1.dev.example.com @localhost
;; global options: +cmd
;; Got answer:
;; ->>HEADER<<- opcode: QUERY, status: NOERROR, id: 4208
;; flags: qr rd ra; QUERY: 1, ANSWER: 1, AUTHORITY: 0, ADDITIONAL: 0
```

```
;; QUESTION SECTION:
;ns1.dev.example.com.          IN      A

;; ANSWER SECTION:
ns1.dev.example.com.    265    IN      A       10.0.0.5

;; Query time: 0 msec
;; SERVER: 127.0.0.1#53(127.0.0.1)
;; WHEN: Thu Sep 18 00:59:18 2014
;; MSG SIZE  rcvd: 56
```

Here, I tested ns1.dev.example.com and saw that it correctly resolved to 10.0.0.5. If you inspect the dig output, you can see near the bottom of the output that

```
SERVER: 127.0.0.1#53(127.0.0.1)
```

confirms that I was indeed talking to 127.0.0.1 to get my answer. If you run this command again shortly afterward, you should notice that the TTL setting in the output (in the above example it was set to 265) will decrement. Dnsmasq is caching the response, and once the TTL gets to 0, dnsmasq will query a remote name server again.

After you have validated that dnsmasq functions, the final step is to edit /etc/resolv.conf and make sure that you have nameserver 127.0.0.1 listed above all other nameserver lines. Note that you can leave all of the existing name servers in place. In fact, that provides a means of safety in case dnsmasq ever were to crash. If you use DHCP to get an IP or otherwise have these values set from a different file (such as is the case when resolvconf is installed), you'll need to track down what files to modify instead; otherwise, the next time you get a DHCP lease, it will overwrite this with your new settings.

I deployed this simple change to around 100 servers in a particular environment, and it was amazing to see the dramatic drop in DNS traffic, load and log entries on my internal name servers. What's more, with this in place, the environment is even more tolerant in the case there ever were a real problem with downstream DNS servers–existing cached entries still would resolve for the host until TTL expired. So if you find your internal name servers are getting hammered with traffic, an internal DNS cache is something you definitely should consider.

4.7 PXE Magic

It's funny how automation evolves as system administrators manage larger numbers of servers. When you manage only a few servers, it's fine to pop in an install CD and set options manually. As the number of servers grows, you might realize it makes sense to set up a kickstart or FAI (Debian's Fully Automated Installer) environment to automate all that manual configuration at install time. Now, you boot the install CD, type in a few boot arguments to point the machine to the kickstart server, and go get a cup of coffee as the machine installs.

4.7 PXE Magic

When the day comes that you have to install three or four machines at once, you either can burn extra CDs or investigate PXE boot. The Preboot eXecution Environment is an open standard developed by Intel to allow machines to boot over a network instead of from local media, such as a floppy, CD or hard drive. Modern servers and newer laptops and desktops with integrated NICs should support PXE booting in the BIOS. In some cases, it's enabled by default, and in other cases, you need to go into your BIOS settings to enable it.

Because many modern servers offer built-in remote power and remote terminals or otherwise are remotely accessible via serial console servers or networked KVM, if you have a PXE boot environment set up, you can power on remotely, then boot and install a machine from miles away.

If you have never set up a PXE boot server before, the first part of this section covers the steps to get your first PXE server up and running. If PXE booting is old hat to you, skip ahead to the section called PXE Menu Magic. There, I cover how to configure boot menus when you PXE boot, so instead of hunting down MAC addresses and doing a lot of setup before an install, you simply can boot, select your OS, and you are off and running. After that, I discuss how to integrate rescue tools, such as Knoppix and memtest86+, into your PXE environment, so they are available to any machine that can boot from the network.

PXE Setup

You need three main pieces of infrastructure for a PXE setup: a DHCP server, a TFTP server and the syslinux software. Both DHCP and TFTP can reside on the same server. When a system attempts to boot from the network, the DHCP server gives it an IP address and then tells it the address for the TFTP server and the name of the bootstrap program to run. The TFTP server then serves that file, which in our case is a PXE-enabled syslinux binary. That program runs on the booted machine and then can load Linux kernels or other OS files that also are shared on the TFTP server over the network. Once the kernel is loaded, the OS starts as normal, and if you have configured a kickstart install correctly, the install begins.

Configure DHCP

Any relatively new DHCP server will support PXE booting, so if you don't already have a DHCP server set up, just use your distribution's DHCP server package (possibly named dhcpd, dhcp3-server or something similar). Configuring DHCP to suit your network is somewhat beyond the scope of this section, but many distributions ship a default configuration file that should provide a good place to start. Once the DHCP server is installed, edit the configuration file (often in /etc/dhcpd.conf), and locate the subnet section (or each host section if you configured static IP assignment via DHCP and want these hosts to PXE boot), and add two lines:

```
next-server ip_of_pxe_server;
filename "pxelinux.0";
```

The `next-server` directive tells the host the IP address of the TFTP server, and the filename directive tells it which file to download and execute from that server. Change the next-server argument to match the IP address of your TFTP server, and keep filename set to pxelinux.0, as that is the name of the syslinux PXE-enabled executable.

In the subnet section, you also need to add `dynamic-bootp` to the `range` directive. Here is an example subnet section after the changes:

```
subnet 10.0.0.0 netmask 255.255.255.0 {
    range dynamic-bootp 10.0.0.200 10.0.0.220;
    next-server 10.0.0.1;
    filename "pxelinux.0";
}
```

Install TFTP

After the DHCP server is configured and running, you are ready to install TFTP. The pxelinux executable requires a TFTP server that supports the tsize option, and two good choices are either tftpd-hpa or atftp. In many distributions, these options already are packaged under these names, so just install your distribution's package or otherwise follow the installation instructions from the project's official site.

Depending on your TFTP package, you might need to add an entry to /etc/inetd.conf if it wasn't already added for you:

```
tftp         dgram   udp     wait    root    /usr/sbin/in.tftpd
↪ /usr/sbin/in.tftpd -s /var/lib/tftpboot
```

As you can see in this example, the `-s` option (used for tftpd-hpa) specified /var/lib/tftpboot as the directory to contain my files, but on some systems, these files are commonly stored in /tftpboot, so see your /etc/inetd.conf file and your tftpd man page and check on its conventions if you are unsure. If your distribution uses xinetd and doesn't create a file in /etc/xinetd.d for you, create a file called /etc/xinetd.d/tftp that contains the following:

```
# default: off
# description: The tftp server serves files using
#       the trivial file transfer protocol.
#       The tftp protocol is often used to boot diskless
#       workstations, download configuration files to network-aware
#       printers, and to start the installation process for
#       some operating systems.
service tftp
{
        disable = no
```

4.7 PXE Magic

```
        socket_type             = dgram
        protocol                = udp
        wait                    = yes
        user                    = root
        server                  = /usr/sbin/in.tftpd
        server_args             = -s /var/lib/tftpboot
        per_source              = 11
        cps                     = 100 2
        flags                   = IPv4
}
```

As tftpd is part of inetd or xinetd, you will not need to start any service. At most, you might need to reload inetd or xinetd; however, make sure that any software firewall you have running allows the TFTP port (port 69 udp) as input.

Add Syslinux

Now that TFTP is set up, all that is left to do is to install the syslinux package (available for most distributions, or you can follow the installation instructions from the project's main Web page), copy the supplied pxelinux.0 file to /var/lib/tftpboot (or your TFTP directory), and then create a /var/lib/tftpboot/pxelinux.cfg directory to hold pxelinux configuration files.

PXE Menu Magic

You can configure pxelinux with or without menus, and many administrators use pxelinux without them. There are compelling reasons to use pxelinux menus, which I discuss below, but first, here's how some pxelinux setups are configured.

When many people configure pxelinux, they create configuration files for a machine or class of machines based on the fact that when pxelinux loads it searches the pxelinux.cfg directory on the TFTP server for configuration files in the following order:

1. Files named 01-MACADDRESS with hyphens in between each hex pair. So, for a server with a MAC address of 88:99:AA:BB:CC:DD, a configuration file that would target only that machine would be named 01-88-99-aa-bb-cc-dd (and I've noticed it does matter that it is lowercase).
2. Files named after the host's IP address in hex. Here, pxelinux will drop a digit from the end of the hex IP and try again as each file search fails. This is often used when an administrator buys a lot of the same brand of machine, which often will have very similar MAC addresses. The administrator then can configure DHCP to assign a certain IP range to those MAC addresses. Then, a boot option can be applied to all of that group.
3. Finally, if no specific files can be found, pxelinux will look for a file named default and use it.

One nice feature of pxelinux is that it uses the same syntax as syslinux, so porting over a configuration from a CD, for instance, can start with the syslinux options and follow with your custom network options. Here is an example configuration for an old CentOS 3.6 kickstart:

```
default linux
label linux
    kernel vmlinuz-centos-3.6
    append text nofb load_ramdisk=1 initrd=initrd-centos-3.6.img
 ↪ network ks=http://10.0.0.1/kickstart/centos3.cfg
```

Why Use Menus?

The standard sort of pxelinux setup works fine, and many administrators use it, but one of the annoying aspects of it is that even if you know you want to install, say, CentOS 3.6 on a server, you first have to get the MAC address. So, you either go to the machine and find a sticker that lists the MAC address, boot the machine into the BIOS to read the MAC, or let it get a lease on the network. Then, you need to create either a custom configuration file for that host's MAC or make sure its MAC is part of a group you already have configured. Depending on your infrastructure, this step can add substantial time to each server. Even if you buy servers in batches and group in IP ranges, what happens if you want to install a different OS on one of the servers? You then have to go through the additional work of tracking down the MAC to set up an exclusion.

With pxelinux menus, I can preconfigure any of the different network boot scenarios I need and assign a number to them. Then, when a machine boots, I get an ASCII menu I can customize that lists all of these options and their number. Then, I can select the option I want, press Enter, and the install is off and running. Beyond that, now I have the option of adding non-kickstart images and can make them available to all of my servers, not just certain groups. With this feature, you can make rescue tools like Knoppix and memtest86+ available to any machine on the network that can PXE boot. You even can set a timeout, like with boot CDs, that will select a default option. I use this to select my standard Knoppix rescue mode after 30 seconds.

Configure PXE Menus

Because pxelinux shares the syntax of syslinux, if you have any CDs that have fancy syslinux menus, you can refer to them for examples. Because you want to make this available to all hosts, move any more specific configuration files out of pxelinux.cfg, and create a file named default. When the pxelinux program fails to find any more specific files, it then will load this configuration. Here is a sample menu configuration with two options: the first boots Knoppix over the network, and the second boots a CentOS 4.5 kickstart:

```
default 1
timeout 300
prompt 1
display f1.msg
F1 f1.msg
```

4.7 PXE Magic

```
F2 f2.msg
label 1
    kernel vmlinuz-knx5.1.1
    append secure nfsdir=10.0.0.1:/mnt/knoppix/5.1.1
↪ nodhcp lang=us ramdisk_size=100000 init=/etc/init
↪ 2 apm=power-off nomce vga=normal
↪ initrd=miniroot-knx5.1.1.gz quiet BOOT_IMAGE=knoppix
label 2
    kernel vmlinuz-centos-4.5-64
    append text nofb ksdevice=eth0 load_ramdisk=1
↪ initrd=initrd-centos-4.5-64.img network
↪ ks=http://10.0.0.1/kickstart/centos4-64.cfg
```

Each of these options is documented in the syslinux man page, but I highlight a few here. The default option sets which label to boot when the timeout expires. The timeout is in tenths of a second, so in this example, the timeout is 30 seconds, after which it will boot using the options set under label 1. The display option lists a message if there are any to display by default, so if you want to display a fancy menu for these two options, you could create a file called f1.msg in /var/lib/tftpboot/ that contains something like:

```
----| Boot Options |-----
|                        |
| 1. Knoppix 5.1.1       |
| 2. CentOS 4.5 64 bit   |
|                        |
--------------------------

<F1> Main | <F2> Help
Default image will boot in 30 seconds...
```

Notice that I listed F1 and F2 in the menu. You can create multiple files that will be output to the screen when the user presses the function keys. This can be useful if you have more menu options than can fit on a single screen, or if you want to provide extra documentation at boot time (this is handy if you are like me and create custom boot arguments for your kickstart servers). In this example, I could create a /var/lib/tftpboot/f2.msg file and add a short help file.

Although this menu is rather basic, check out the syslinux configuration file and project page for examples of how to jazz it up with color and even custom graphics.

Extra Features: PXE Rescue Disk

> **Note:** This example with embedding Knoppix into a PXE environment no longer works with modern versions of Knoppix. I decided to keep this example in place in case it is helpful for people who do want to adapt it to work with a different modern rescue disk.

One of my favorite features of a PXE server is the addition of a Knoppix rescue disk. Now, whenever I need to recover a machine, I don't need to hunt around for a disk, I can just boot the server off the network.

First, get a Knoppix disk. I use a Knoppix 5.1.1 CD for this example, but I've been successful with much older Knoppix CDs. Mount the CD-ROM, and then go to the boot/isolinux directory on the CD. Copy the miniroot.gz and vmlinuz files to your /var/lib/tftpboot directory, except rename them something distinct, such as miniroot-knx5.1.1.gz and vmlinuz-knx5.1.1, respectively. Now, edit your pxelinux.cfg/default file, and add lines like the one I used above in my example:

```
label 1
    kernel vmlinuz-knx5.1.1
    append secure nfsdir=10.0.0.1:/mnt/knoppix/5.1.1 nodhcp
 ↪ lang=us ramdisk_size=100000 init=/etc/init 2
 ↪ apm=power-off nomce vga=normal
 ↪ initrd=miniroot-knx5.1.1.gz quiet BOOT_IMAGE=knoppix
```

Notice here that I labeled it 1, so if you already have a label with that name, you need to decide which of the two to rename. Also notice that this example references the renamed vmlinuz-knx5.1.1 and miniroot-knx5.1.1.gz files. If you named your files something else, be sure to change the names here as well. Because I am mostly dealing with servers, I added 2 after `init=/etc/init` on the append line, so it would boot into runlevel 2 (console-only mode). If you want to boot to a full graphical environment, remove 2 from the append line.

The final step might be the largest for you if you don't have an NFS server set up. For Knoppix to boot over the network, you have to have its CD contents shared on an NFS server. NFS server configuration is beyond the scope of this section, but in my example, I set up an NFS share on 10.0.0.1 at /mnt/knoppix/5.1.1. I then mounted my Knoppix CD and copied the full contents to that directory. Alternatively, you could mount a Knoppix CD or ISO directly to that directory. When the Knoppix kernel boots, it will then mount that NFS share and access the rest of the files it needs directly over the network.

Extra Features: Memtest86+

Another nice addition to a PXE environment is the memtest86+ program. This program does a thorough scan of a system's RAM and reports any errors. Some distributions even install it by default and make it available during the boot process because it is so useful. Compared to Knoppix, it is very simple to add memtest86+ to your PXE server, because it runs from a single bootable file. First, install your distribution's memtest86+ package (most make it available), or otherwise download it from the memtest86+ site. Then, copy the program binary to /var/lib/tftpboot/memtest. Finally, add a new label to your pxelinux.cfg/default file:

```
label 3
    kernel memtest
```

That's it. When you type 3 at the boot prompt, the memtest86+ program loads over the network and starts the scan. Conclusion

There are a number of extra features beyond the ones I give here. For instance, a number of DOS boot floppy images, such as Peter Nordahl's NT Password and Registry Editor Boot Disk, can be added to a PXE environment. My own use of the pxelinux menu helps me streamline server kickstarts and makes it simple to kickstart many servers all at the same time. At boot time, I can not only indicate which OS to load, but also more specific options, such as the type of server (Web, database and so forth) to install, what hostname to use, and other very specific tweaks. Besides the benefit of no longer tracking down MAC addresses, you also can create a nice colorful user-friendly boot menu that can be documented, so it's simpler for new administrators to pick up. Finally, I've been able to customize Knoppix disks so that they do very specific things at boot, such as perform load tests or even set up a Webcam server—all from the network.

4.8 More PXE Magic

> **Note:** While the examples in this section reference ancient Ubuntu releases, you should be able to adapt the files they reference to modern Ubuntu and Debian releases.

In this section, I've decided to follow up on a topic I wrote about not in my Linux Journal column directly, but as a feature article called "PXE Magic" in the April 2008 issue[4] (and in the previous section). In that section, I talk about how to set up a PXE server from scratch, including how to install and configure DHCP and TFTP. Ultimately, I even provide a basic pxelinux configuration to get you started. Since then, PXE menus with pxelinux have become more sophisticated and graphical and could seem a bit intimidating if you are new to it.

Here, I explain how to piggyback off of the work the Debian and Ubuntu projects have done with their PXE configuration to make your own fancy PXE menu without much additional work. I know not everyone uses Debian or Ubuntu, so if you use a different distribution, hold off on the angry e-mail messages; you still can use the PXE configuration I'm showing here for your distro, provided it gives some basic examples of how to PXE boot its installer. Just use these steps as a launching off point and tweak the PXE config to work for you.

---

[4] https://www.linuxjournal.com/magazine/pxe-magic-flexible-network-booting-menus

Simple Ubuntu PXE Menu

If this is your first time configuring a PXE server, for the first step, I recommend following my steps in the "PXE Magic" section to install and configure DHCP and TFTP. Otherwise, if you have existing servers in place, just make sure that DHCP is configured to point to your TFTP server (if it's on the same machine, that's fine). And, if you already have any sort of pxelinux configuration in your tftpboot directory, I recommend that you back it up and move it out of the way. I'm going to assume that your entire /var/lib/tftpboot (or /tftpboot on some systems) directory is empty to start with. For the rest of this section, I reference /var/lib/tftpboot as the location to store your PXE configuration files, so if you use /tftpboot, adjust the commands accordingly.

Both Debian and Ubuntu provide a nice all-in-one netboot configuration for each of their releases that makes it simple to PXE boot a particular release yourself. The file is called netboot.tar.gz and is located in a netboot directory along with the rest of the different install images. For instance, the netboot.tar.gz for the i386 Ubuntu 12.04 release (named Precise) can be found here[5].

To get started, cd to your tftpboot directory, and then use wget to pull down the netboot.tar.gz file (I'm assuming you'll need root permissions for all of these steps, so I'm putting sudo in front of all of my commands), and then extract the tarball:

```
cd /var/lib/tftpboot
sudo wget http://us.archive.ubuntu.com/ubuntu/dists/precise/
↪ main/installer-i386/current/images/netboot/netboot.tar.gz
sudo tar xzf netboot.tar.gz
ls
netboot.tar.gz   pxelinux.0   pxelinux.cfg
↪ ubuntu-installer   version.info
```

As the ls command shows, an ubuntu-installer directory was created along with pxelinux.0 and pxelinux.cfg symlinks that point inside that ubuntu-installer directory to the real files. Without performing any additional configuration, provided your DHCP and TFTP servers were functioning, you could PXE boot a server with this configuration and get a boot menu like the one shown in Figure 4.1.

---

[5]http://us.archive.ubuntu.com/ubuntu/dists/precise/main/installer-i386/current/images/netboot/netboot.tar.gz

4.8 More PXE Magic

Figure 4.1: Ubuntu Precise PXE Boot Menu

Ubuntu has taken the extra steps of theming its PXE menu with its color scheme and even provided a logo. Unlike the PXE menu I demoed in my previous "PXE Magic" section, this menu functions more like a GUI program. You can use the arrow keys to navigate it, the Enter key to select a menu item and the Tab key to edit a menu entry.

Multi-OS PXE Menu

If all you were interested in was PXE booting a single version of Ubuntu or Debian, you would be done. Of course, what if you wanted the choice of either the 32- or 64-bit versions of a particular release, or what if you wanted to choose between a few different releases? Although you could just overwrite your tftpboot directory every time you wanted to change it up, with only a few extra tweaks to the config, you easily can host multiple releases with the same menu.

Move Precise to a Submenu

To get started, let's clean out any existing files in the /var/lib/tftpboot directory. Let's use the i386 Precise netboot.tar.gz to begin, but let's tweak how the files are organized by isolating precise in its own directory:

```
cd /var/lib/tftpboot
sudo mkdir precise
cd precise
sudo wget http://us.archive.ubuntu.com/ubuntu/dists/precise/
 ↪ main/installer-i386/current/images/netboot/netboot.tar.gz
sudo tar xzf netboot.tar.gz
```

All of the interesting PXE configuration can be found inside the ubuntu-installer/i386 directory, so make a copy of those files back in the root tftpboot directory so you can edit them:

```
cd /var/lib/tftpboot
sudo cp -a precise/ubuntu-installer/i386/boot-screens
```

```
↳ precise/ubuntu-installer/i386/pxelinux.0
↳ precise/ubuntu-installer/i386/pxelinux.cfg .
```

Unfortunately, all of the configuration files under the boot-screens directory you copied reference ubuntu-installer/i386/boot-screens, when you want them to reference just boot-screens, so the next step is to run a quick Perl one-liner to search and remove any instance of ubuntu-installer/i386/ found in the config file:

```
cd /var/lib/tftpboot/boot-screens
sudo perl -pi -e 's|ubuntu-installer/i386/||' *
```

The specific pxelinux configuration that points to the Ubuntu Precise kernel and initrd can be found under precise/ubuntu-installer/i386/boot-screens/txt.cfg. If you were to look at that file, it would look something like this:

```
default install
label install
        menu label ^Install
        menu default
        kernel ubuntu-installer/i386/linux
        append vga=788 initrd=ubuntu-installer/i386/
↳ initrd.gz -- quiet
label cli
        menu label ^Command-line install
        kernel ubuntu-installer/i386/linux
        append tasks=standard pkgsel/language-pack-patterns=
↳ pkgsel/install-language-support=false vga=788
↳ initrd=ubuntu-installer/i386/initrd.gz -- quiet
```

What you want to do is make a copy of this config file under your root-level boot-screens directory, but because you extracted the tarball into a directory named precise (instead of the root directory), you need to do another search and replace, and add precise in front of any reference to the ubuntu-installer directory. Otherwise, the paths to the kernel and initrd will be wrong:

```
cd /var/lib/tftpboot/boot-screens
sudo cp ../precise/ubuntu-installer/i386/boot-screens/txt.cfg
↳ precise-i386.cfg
sudo perl -pi -e 's|ubuntu-installer|precise/ubuntu-installer|g'
↳ precise-i386.cfg
```

When you are done, the /var/lib/tftpboot/boot-screens/precise-i386.cfg file should look something like this:

```
default install
label install
        menu label ^Install
        menu default
        kernel precise/ubuntu-installer/i386/linux
        append vga=788 initrd=precise/ubuntu-installer/i386/initrd.gz
↳ -- quiet
label cli
        menu label ^Command-line install
        kernel precise/ubuntu-installer/i386/linux
        append tasks=standard pkgsel/language-pack-patterns=
```

4.8 More PXE Magic

```
↪ pkgsel/install-language-support=false vga=788
↪ initrd=precise/ubuntu-installer/i386/initrd.gz -- quiet
```

Finally, open up /var/lib/tftpboot/boot-screens/menu.cfg in your favorite text editor. This file contains the bulk of the configuration that has to do with the PXE menu system, and the file should look something like this:

```
menu hshift 13
menu width 49
menu margin 8

menu title Installer boot menu^G
include boot-screens/stdmenu.cfg
include boot-screens/txt.cfg
include boot-screens/gtk.cfg
menu begin advanced
        menu title Advanced options
        include boot-screens/stdmenu.cfg
        label mainmenu
                menu label ^Back..
                menu exit
        include boot-screens/adtxt.cfg
        include boot-screens/adgtk.cfg
menu end
label help
        menu label ^Help
        text help
   Display help screens; type 'menu' at boot prompt to
↪ return to this menu
        endtext
        config boot-screens/prompt.cfg
```

What you want to do is replace the include boot-screens/txt.cfg line with a submenu that points to the new precise-i386.cfg file you created. I used the existing advanced submenu as an example to start from. The resulting file should look like this:

```
menu hshift 13
menu width 49
menu margin 8

menu title Installer boot menu^G
include boot-screens/stdmenu.cfg
menu begin precise-i386
        menu title Precise 12.04 i386
        include boot-screens/stdmenu.cfg
        label mainmenu
                menu label ^Back..
                menu exit
        include boot-screens/precise-i386.cfg
menu end
include boot-screens/gtk.cfg
menu begin advanced
        menu title Advanced options
        include boot-screens/stdmenu.cfg
        label mainmenu
                menu label ^Back..
                menu exit
        include boot-screens/adtxt.cfg
        include boot-screens/adgtk.cfg
```

```
menu end
label help
        menu label ^Help
        text help
  Display help screens; type 'menu' at boot prompt to
↪ return to this menu
        endtext
        config boot-screens/prompt.cfg
```

When you PXE boot now, you should see a menu option labeled Precise 12.04 i386, as shown in Figure 4.2. When you select that option and press Enter, you then can access the standard install options like before.

Figure 4.2: Precise in a Submenu

Add Precise 64-Bit

Now that you have the 32-bit Precise install working, let's add the 64-bit release as well. You'll basically perform the same initial steps as before, after you remove any existing netboot.tar.gz files. The netboot.tar.gz file is structured so that it will be safe to extract it in the same precise directory:

```
cd /var/lib/tftpboot/precise
sudo rm netboot.tar.gz
sudo wget http://us.archive.ubuntu.com/ubuntu/dists/precise/
  ↪ main/installer-amd64/current/images/netboot/netboot.tar.gz
sudo tar xzf netboot.tar.gz
```

Since you already copied over the boot-screens directory, you can skip ahead to copying and modifying the 64-bit txt.cfg, so it gets pointed to the right directory:

```
cd /var/lib/tftpboot/boot-screens
sudo cp ../precise/ubuntu-installer/amd64/boot-screens/txt.cfg
  ↪ precise-amd64.cfg
sudo perl -pi -e 's|ubuntu-installer|precise/ubuntu-installer|g'
  ↪ precise-amd64.cfg
```

Now, open up /var/lib/tftpboot/boot-screens/menu.cfg again, and add an additional menu entry that points to the precise-amd64.cfg file you created. The file ends up looking like this:

4.8 More PXE Magic

```
menu hshift 13
menu width 49
menu margin 8

menu title Installer boot menu^G
include boot-screens/stdmenu.cfg
menu begin precise-i386
        menu title Precise 12.04 i386
        include boot-screens/stdmenu.cfg
        label mainmenu
                menu label ^Back..
                menu exit
        include boot-screens/precise-i386.cfg
menu end
menu begin precise-amd64
        menu title Precise 12.04 amd64
        include boot-screens/stdmenu.cfg
        label mainmenu
                menu label ^Back..
                menu exit
        include boot-screens/precise-amd64.cfg
menu end
include boot-screens/gtk.cfg
menu begin advanced
        menu title Advanced options
        include boot-screens/stdmenu.cfg
        label mainmenu
                menu label ^Back..
                menu exit
        include boot-screens/adtxt.cfg
        include boot-screens/adgtk.cfg
menu end
label help
        menu label ^Help
        text help
   Display help screens; type 'menu' at boot prompt to
 ↪ return to this menu
        endtext
        config boot-screens/prompt.cfg
```

Add a New Ubuntu Release

So, you were happy with your 12.04 PXE menu, and then Ubuntu released 12.10 Quantal, so now you want to add the 32-bit version of that to your menu. Simply adapt the steps from before to this new release. First, create a directory to store the new release, and pull down and extract the new netboot.tar.gz file:

```
cd /var/lib/tftpboot
sudo mkdir quantal
cd quantal
sudo wget http://us.archive.ubuntu.com/ubuntu/dists/quantal/
 ↪ main/installer-i386/current/images/netboot/netboot.tar.gz
sudo tar xzf netboot.tar.gz
```

Next, copy over the quantal txt.cfg file to your root boot-screens directory, and run a Perl one-liner on it to point it to the right directory:

```
cd /var/lib/tftpboot/boot-screens
sudo cp ../quantal/ubuntu-installer/i386/boot-screens/txt.cfg
```

```
↪ quantal-i386.cfg
sudo perl -pi -e 's|ubuntu-installer|quantal/ubuntu-installer|g'
↪ quantal-i386.cfg
```

Finally, edit /var/lib/tftpboot/boot-screens/menu.cfg again, and add the additional menu entry that points to the quantal-i386.cfg file you created. The additional section you should put below the previous submenus looks like this:

```
menu begin quantal-i386
        menu title Quantal 12.10 i386
        include boot-screens/stdmenu.cfg
        label mainmenu
                menu label ^Back..
                menu exit
        include boot-screens/quantal-i386.cfg
menu end
```

The resulting PXE menu should look something like Figure 4.3. To add the 64-bit release, just adapt the steps from the above Precise 64-bit release to Quantal. Finally, if you want to mix and match Debian releases as well, the steps are just about the same, except you will need to track down the Debian netboot.tar.gz from its project mirrors and substitute precise for Debian project names like squeeze. Also, everywhere you see a search and replace that references ubuntu-installer, you will change that to debian-installer.

Figure 4.3: Now with Three Options

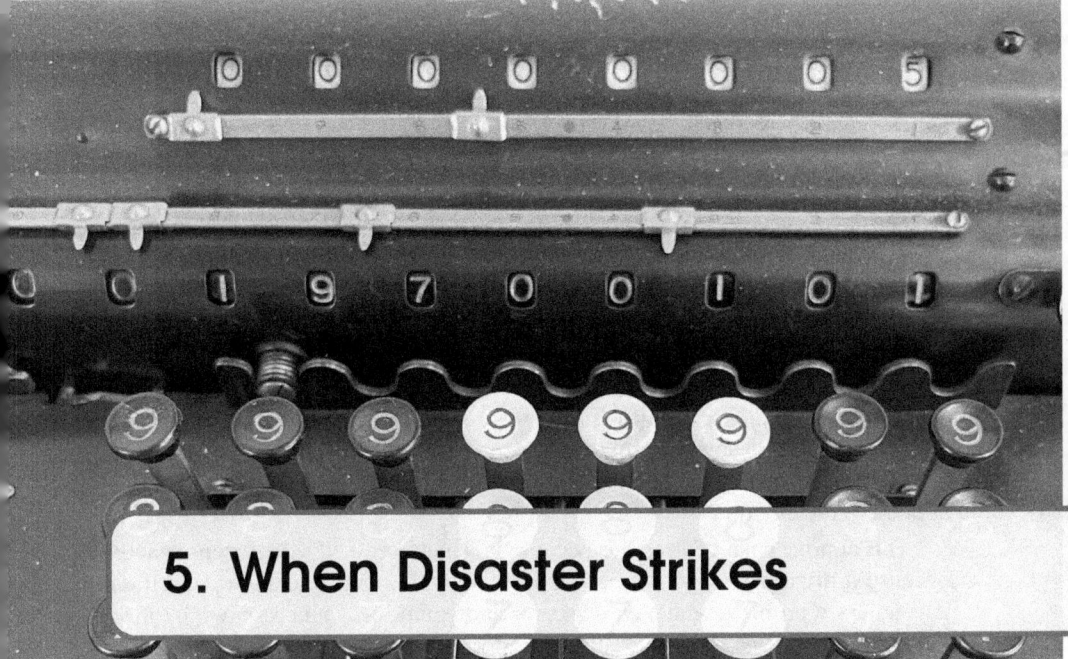

5. When Disaster Strikes

I've learned more about Linux from troubleshooting and fixing disasters, than from any other method. When disaster strikes, whether it's from a mistake you've made, a mistake from your peers, or just a freak occurance, disasters are a great opportunity to learn something new. The key to making a disaster a learning experience, though, is to practice proper troubleshooting technique, work the problem, and resolve it without resorting to rebooting or wiping and reinstalling.

In this chapter I have collected a number of guides on troubleshooting and resolving diasters. First I walk through some troubleshooting fundamentals you can use to diagnose common problems with Linux. Then I discuss how to approach common disasters from disks filling up, hard drive crashes, and deleted files and even master boot records!

5.1 Stop Killing Your Cattle

If you spend enough time at DevOps conferences, you've heard the phrase "pets versus cattle" used to describe server infrastructure. The idea behind this concept is that traditional infrastructure was built by hand without much automation and therefore servers were treated more like special pets–you would do anything you could to keep your pet alive and knew it by name because you hand-crafted its configuration. As a result it would take a lot of effort to create a duplicate server if it ever went down. By contrast, modern DevOps concepts encourage creating "cattle" which means that instead of unique, hand-crafted servers you use automation tools to build your servers so that no individual server is special—they are just farm animals—and therefore if a particular server dies it's no problem because you can respawn an exact copy with your automation tools in no time.

If you want your infrastructure and your team to scale, there is a lot of wisdom in treating servers more like cattle than pets. Unfortunately there's also a downside to this approach. Some administrators, particularly more junior sysadmin, have extended the concept of disposable servers to the point that it has affected their troubleshooting process. Since servers are disposable, and you can spawn a replacement so easily, at the first hint of trouble with a particular server or service, these administrators destroy and replace it in hopes that the replacement won't show the problem. Essentially this is the "reboot the Windows machine" approach IT teams used in the '90s (and Linux admin sneered at) only applied to the cloud.

This approach isn't dangerous because it is ineffective. It's dangerous exactly because it often works. If you have a problem with a machine and reboot it, or if you have a problem with a cloud server and you destroy and respawn it, often the problem does go away. Because the approach appears to work and because it's a lot *easier* than actually performing troubleshooting steps, that success then reinforces rebooting and respawning as the first resort, not the last resort that it should be.

The problem with respawning or rebooting before troubleshooting is that since the problem often goes away after that, you no longer can perform any troubleshooting to track down the root cause. To extend the cattle metaphor, it's like shooting every cow that is a little sluggish or shows signs of a cold, because they might have mad cow disease and not actually testing the cow for the disease. If you aren't careful, you'll find you've let a problem go untreated until it's spread to the rest of your herd. Without knowing the root cause, you can't perform any steps to prevent it in the future, and while the current issue may not have caused a major outage, there's no way to know whether you'll get off so easy the next time it happens. While you may save time by not troubleshooting, that's time you lose from troubleshooting experience. Eventually you will need to flex that troubleshooting muscle and if you haven't exercised it, you may find yourself with a problem you can't solve.

In short, automation is great and it is incredibly important in modern infrastructure to be able to respawn any host quickly and easily. Just don't turn that infrastructure best practice into a troubleshooting worst practice.

5.2 Troubleshooting High Load

This section will be the first in a series of sections dedicated to one of my favorite subjects: troubleshooting. I'm a systems administrator during the day and while I enjoy many aspects of my job, it's hard to beat the adrenaline rush of tracking

5.2 Troubleshooting High Load

down a complex server problem when downtime is being measured in dollars. While it's true that there are about as many different reasons for downtime as there are Linux text editors, and just as many approaches to troubleshooting, over the years I've found that I perform the same sorts of steps to isolate a problem. In this series I'm going to describe some general classes of problems you might find on a Linux system, and then I will discuss how to use common tools, most of which are probably already on your system, to isolate and resolve each class of problem.

For this first section I'm going to start with one of the most common problems you will run into on a Linux system. No, not getting printing to work, I'm talking about a sluggish server that might have high load. Before I talk about how to diagnose and fix high load, though, let's take a step back and talk about what load means on a Linux machine and how to know when it's high.

Uptime and Load

When administrators talk about high load, generally they are talking about the *load average*. When I diagnose why a server is slow, the first command I run when I log into the system is uptime:

```
uptime
 18:30:35 up 365 days,  5:29,  2 users,  load average: 1.37, 10.15, 8.10
```

As you can see, it's my server's uptime birthday today. You can also see that my load average is 1.37, 10.15, 8.10. These numbers represent my average system load over the last 1, 5, and 15 minutes, respectively. Technically speaking, the load average represents the average number of processes that have to wait for CPU time over the last 1, 5, or 15 minutes. For instance, if I have a current load of 0, the system is completely idle. If I have a load of 1, the CPU is busy enough that one process is having to wait for CPU time. If I do have a load of 1 and then spawn another process that would normally tie up a CPU, my load should go to 2. With a load average, the system will give you a good idea of how consistently busy it has been over the past 1, 5, and 10 minutes.

Another important thing to keep in mind when you look at a load average is that it isn't normalized according to the number of CPUs on your system. Generally speaking, a consistent load of 1 means one CPU on the system is tied up. In simplified terms, this means that a single-CPU system with a load of 1 is roughly as busy as a four-CPU system with a load of 4. So in my above example, let's assume that I have a single-CPU system. If I were to login and see the above load average, I'd probably assume that the server had pretty high load (8.10) over the last 15 minutes that spiked around 5 minutes ago (10.15) but recently, at least over the last one minute, the load has dropped significantly. If I saw this I might even assume that the real cause of the load has subsided. On the other hand, if the load averages were 20.68, 5.01, 1.03, I would conclude that the high load had likely started in the last 5 minutes and was getting worse.

How High is High

After you understand what load average means, the next logical question is: "What load average is good and what is bad?" The answer to that is: it depends. You see, there are a lot of different things that can cause load to be high, each of which affects performance differently. One server might have a load of 50 and still be pretty responsive, while another server might have a load of 10 and take forever to log into. I've had servers with load averages in the hundreds that were certainly slow, but didn't crash, and I had one server that consistently had a load of 50 that was still pretty responsive and stayed up for years.

What really matters when you troubleshoot a system with high load is *why* the load is high. When you start to diagnose high load you find that most load seems to fall into three categories: CPU-bound load, load caused by out of memory issues, and I/O-bound load. I will go into each of these categories in detail below and how to use tools like top and iostat to isolate the root cause.

Top

If the first tool I use when I log into a sluggish system is uptime, the second tool I use is top. The great thing about top is that it's available for all major Linux systems, and it provides a lot of useful information in a single screen. top is itself a quite complex tool with many options that could warrant their own section. For this section I'm just going to talk about how to interpret its output to diagnose high load.

To use top, just type top on the command line. By default top will run in interactive mode and update its output every few seconds. Here's sample top output from a terminal:

```
top - 14:08:25 up 38 days,  8:02,  1 user,  load average: 1.70, 1.77, 1.68
Tasks: 107 total,   3 running, 104 sleeping,   0 stopped,   0 zombie
Cpu(s): 11.4%us, 29.6%sy,  0.0%ni, 58.3%id,  .7%wa,  0.0%hi,  0.0%si,  0.0%st
Mem:    1024176k total,   997408k used,    26768k free,    85520k buffers
Swap:   1004052k total,     4360k used,   999692k free,   286040k cached

  PID USER      PR  NI  VIRT  RES  SHR S %CPU %MEM    TIME+  COMMAND
 9463 mysql     16   0  686m 111m 3328 S   53  5.5 569:17.64 mysqld
18749 nagios    16   0  140m 134m 1868 S   12  6.6 1345:01  nagios2db_status
24636 nagios    17   0 34660  10m  712 S    8  0.5 1195:15  nagios
22442 nagios    24   0  6048 2024 1452 S    8  0.1   0:00.04 check_time.pl
```

As you can see, there's a lot of information in only a few lines. The first line mirrors the information you would get from the uptime command and will update every few seconds with the latest load averages. In this case you can see my system is busy, but not what I would call heavily loaded. All the same, this output breaks down well into our different load categories. When I troubleshoot a sluggish system I generally will rule out CPU-bound load, then RAM issues,

5.2 Troubleshooting High Load

then finally I/O issues in that order so let's start with CPU-bound load.

CPU-bound Load

CPU-bound load is load caused when you have too many CPU-intensive processes running at once. Since each process needs CPU resources, they all must wait their turn. To check whether load is CPU-bound, check the CPU line in the top output:

```
Cpu(s):  11.4%us, 29.6%sy,  0.0%ni, 58.3%id,  .7%wa, 0.0%hi, 0.0%si, 0.0%st
```

Each of these percentages are a percentage of the CPU time tied up doing a particular task. Again, you could spend an entire section on all of the output from top so I'll just highlight a few of these values below and how to read them:

us user CPU time. More often than not when you have CPU-bound load, it's due to a process run by a user on the system such as Apache, MySQL, or maybe a shell script. If this percentage is high, then a user process such as these is a likely cause of the load.

sy system CPU time. The system CPU time is the percentage of the CPU tied up by kernel and other system processes. CPU-bound load should either manifest as a high percentage of user or high system CPU time.

id CPU idle time. This is the percentage of the time that the CPU spends idle. The higher the number here the better! In fact if you see really high CPU idle time it's a good indication that any high load is not CPU-bound.

wa I/O wait. The I/O wait value tells you the percentage of time the CPU is spending waiting on I/O (typically disk I/O). If you have high load and this value is high, then it's likely the load is not CPU-bound but is due to either RAM issues or high disk I/O.

Track down CPU-bound load

If you do see a high percentage in the user or system columns, there's a good chance your load is CPU-bound. To track down the root cause, skip down a few lines to where top displays a list of current processes running on the system. By default top will sort these based on the percentage of CPU used with the processes using the most on top:

```
  PID USER      PR  NI  VIRT  RES  SHR S %CPU %MEM    TIME+  COMMAND
 9463 mysql     16   0  686m 111m 3328 S   53  5.5 569:17.64 mysqld
18749 nagios    16   0  140m 134m 1868 S   12  6.6 1345:01   nagios2db\_status
24636 nagios    17   0 34660  10m  712 S    8  0.5 1195:15   nagios
22442 nagios    24   0  6048 2024 1452 S    8  0.1   0:00.04 check\_time.pl
```

The %CPU column will tell you just how much CPU each process is taking up. In this case you can see that MySQL is taking up 53% of my CPU. As you look at this output during CPU-bound load you will probably see one of two things: either you will have a single process tying up 99% of your CPU, or you will see a number of smaller processes all fighting for a percentage of CPU time. In either case it's relatively simple to see the processes that are causing the problem. There's one final note I want to add on CPU-bound load: I've seen systems get incredibly high load simply because a multi-threaded program spawned a huge number of threads on a system without many CPUs. If you spawn 20 threads on a single-CPU system, you might see a high load average even though there are no particular processes that seem to tie up CPU time.

Out of RAM issues

The next cause for high load is a system that has run out of available RAM and has started to go into swap. Since swap space is usually on a hard drive that is much slower than RAM, when you use up available RAM and go into swap, each process slows down dramatically as the disk gets used. Usually this causes a downward spiral as processes that have been swapped run slower, take longer to respond, and cause more processes to stack up until the system either runs out of RAM or slows down to an absolute crawl. What's tricky about swap issues is that since they hit the disk so hard, it's easy to mis-diagnose them as I/O-bound load. After all, if your disk is being used as RAM, any processes that actually want to access files on the disk are going to have to wait in line. So, if I see high I/O wait in the CPU row in top, I check RAM next and rule it out before I troubleshoot any other I/O issues.

When I want to diagnose out of memory issues the first place I look is the next couple of lines in the top output:

```
Mem:   1024176k total,   997408k used,    26768k free,    85520k buffers
Swap:  1004052k total,     4360k used,   999692k free,   286040k cached
```

These lines tell you the total amount of RAM and swap along with how much is used and free, however look carefully as these numbers can be misleading. I've seen many new and even experienced admin who would look at the following output and conclude the system was almost out of RAM since there was only 26768k free. While that does show how much RAM is currently unused, it doesn't tell the full story.

The Linux file cache

See, when you access a file and the Linux kernel loads it into RAM, the kernel doesn't necessarily unload the file when you no longer need it. If there is enough free RAM available, the kernel tries to cache as many files as it can into RAM. That way if you access the file a second time the kernel can retrieve it from RAM instead of the disk and give much better performance. As a system stays running, you will find the free RAM actually will appear to get rather small. If a process needs more RAM, though, the kernel simply uses some of its file cache. In fact, I see a lot of the overclocking crowd that want to improve performance

5.2 Troubleshooting High Load

and create a ramdisk to store their files. What they don't realize is that more often than not if they just let the kernel do the work for them, they'd probably see much better results and make more efficient use of their RAM.

To get a more accurate amount of free RAM you need to combine the values from the free column with the cached column. In my example I would have 26768k + 286040k, or over 300Mb of free RAM. In this case I could safely assume my system was not experiencing an out of RAM issue. Of course, even a system that has very little free RAM may not have gone into swap. That's why you must also check the Swap: line and see if a high proportion of your swap is being used.

Track down high RAM usage

If you do find that you are low on free RAM go back to the same process output from top only this time look in the %MEM column. By default top will sort by the %CPU column so just type M and it will re-sort to show you which processes are using the highest percentage of RAM. In the following output I sorted the same processes by RAM and you can see that the nagios2db_status process is using the most at 6.6%.

```
  PID USER      PR  NI  VIRT  RES  SHR S %CPU %MEM    TIME+  COMMAND
18749 nagios    16   0  140m 134m 1868 S   12  6.6  1345:01  nagios2db_status
 9463 mysql     16   0  686m 111m 3328 S   53  5.5 569:17.64 mysqld
24636 nagios    17   0 34660  10m  712 S    8  0.5  1195:15  nagios
22442 nagios    24   0  6048 2024 1452 S    8  0.1   0:00.04 check_time.pl
```

I/O-bound load

I/O-bound load can be tricky to track down, sometimes. As I mentioned earlier, if your system is swapping it can make the load appear to be I/O-bound. Once you rule out swapping, though, if you do have a high I/O wait the next step is to attempt to track down which disk and partition is getting the bulk of the I/O traffic. To do this you will need a tool like iostat.

The iostat tool, like top, is a complicated and full-featured tool that could fill up its own section. Unlike top, while it should be available for your distribution, it may not be installed on your system by default so you will need to track down which package provides. Under Redhat and Debian-based systems you can get it in the sysstat package. Once it's installed, just run iostat with no arguments to get a good overall view of your disk I/O statistics:

```
Linux 2.6.24-19-server (hostname)        01/31/2009

avg-cpu:      %user   %nice %system %iowait  %steal   %idle
               5.73    0.07    2.03    0.53    0.00   91.64

Device:             tps   Blk_read/s   Blk_wrtn/s   Blk_read   Blk_wrtn
sda                9.82       417.96        27.53   30227262    1990625
sda1               6.55       219.10         7.12   15845129     515216
sda2               0.04         0.74         3.31      53506     239328
```

```
sda3            3.24      198.12      17.09   14328323    1236081
```

Like with top, iostat will give you the CPU percentage output. Below that it will provide you a breakdown of each drive and partition on your system and statistics for each:

tps transactions per second
Blk_read/s blocks read per second
Blk_wrtn/s blocks written per second
Blk_read total blocks read
Blk_wrtn total blocks written

By looking at these different values and comparing them to each other, ideally you will be able to find out first, which partition or partitions is getting the bulk of the I/O traffic, and secondly, whether the majority of that traffic is reads (`Blk_read/s`) or writes (`Blk_wrtn/s`). As I said, tracking down the cause of I/O issues can be tricky but hopefully those values will help you isolate what processes might be causing the load.

For instance, if you have an I/O bound load and you suspect that your remote backup job might be the culprit, compare the read and write statistics. Since you know that a remote backup job is primarily going to read from your disk, if you see that the majority of the disk I/O is writes, you can reasonably assume it's not from the backup job. If on the other hand you do see a heavy amount of read I/O on a particular partition, you might run the lsof command and grep for that backup process and see whether it does in fact have some open file handles on that partition.

As you can see, it is not straightforward to track down I/O issues with iostat. Even with no arguments it can take some time and experience to make sense of the output. That said, iostat does have a number of arguments you can use to get more information about different types of I/O, including modes to get information about NFS shares. I recommend you check out the man page for iostat if you want to know more.

Up until recently, tools like iostat were about the limit systems administrators had in their toolbox for tracking down I/O issues, but due to recent developments in the kernel it has become easier to find out causes of I/O on a per-process level. If you have a relatively new system, check out the iotop tool. Like with iostat it may not be installed by default but as the name implied it essentially acts like top, only for disk I/O. In the below example you can see that an rsync process on this machine is using the most I/O, in this case read I/O.

```
Total DISK READ: 189.52 K/s | Total DISK WRITE: 0.00 B/s
   TID PRIO USER     DISK READ  DISK WRITE  SWAPIN     IO>    COMMAND
  8169 be/4 root     189.52 K/s   0.00 B/s   0.00 %   0.00 %  rsync --server --se
  4243 be/4 kyle       0.00 B/s   3.79 K/s   0.00 %   0.00 %  cli /usr/lib/gnome-
  4244 be/4 kyle       0.00 B/s   3.79 K/s   0.00 %   0.00 %  cli /usr/lib/gnome-
     1 be/4 root       0.00 B/s   0.00 B/s   0.00 %   0.00 %  init
```

Once you track down the culprit

How you deal with these load-causing processes is up to you and depends on a lot of factors. In some cases you might have a script that has gone out of control and is something you can easily kill. In other cases–such as in the case of a database process–it might not be safe to simply kill the process since it could leave corrupted data behind. Plus it could just be that your service is running out of capacity and the real solution is either to add more resources to your current server, or add more servers to share the load. It might even be load from a one-time job that is running on the machine and shouldn't impact load in the future, so you just let the process complete. Since so many different things can cause processes to tie up server resources it's hard to list them all here, but hopefully being able to identify the causes of your high load will get you on the right track the next time you get an alert that a machine is slow.

5.3 Troubleshooting the Local Network

This section is the second in a series dedicated to one of my favorite subjects: troubleshooting. In this section I'm going to describe some general classes of problems you might find on a Linux system, and then I will discuss how to use common tools, most of which are probably already on your system, to isolate and resolve each class of problem.

In the previous section I talked about how to diagnose high load issues on a server, but the fact is that just about every Linux computer is connected to a network, and a large number of the problems you have are based in the network. In this section I'm going to focus on local network troubleshooting and while I will write from the perspective of servers, most of these steps will apply to any Linux machine on a network. Also, since the goal of this section is to show how to become better at troubleshooting, I'm going to list each step from the lowest level on up. In real life I'd probably skip ahead here and there to make the troubleshooting process faster.

Bill is Down

The generic problem I'm going to cover today is how to track down the root cause when one machine can't communicate with another machine on the same network. For this example let's assume I have two servers named bill and shawn. The server shawn is trying to communicate with bill over port 25 (port 25 is used for sending email over SMTP) but wouldn't you know it, bill isn't responding.

Does shawn or bill have a problem?

One of the first things I might do in a scenario like this is find another machine on the same network and try to connect with bill from there. If I can talk to bill from another machine on the same network, then the problem is most likely with shawn or with the network in between shawn and bill. If I have the same problem from another machine on the same network, then it's more likely that the problem is with bill, so I would start troubleshooting from there. Just so I can discuss more troubleshooting steps, let's start troubleshooting from shawn.

One of the most embarrassing things in troubleshooting is to waste an hour only to find out that something wasn't plugged in. So the first step I'm going to perform is to make sure that shawn is plugged in to the network. While I could physically inspect the port on the server, if the server were in a different city I might run a program like ethtool. Ethtool gives you a lot of different diagnostics on your Ethernet devices. By default all you have to do is run ethtool as root and pass the Ethernet device you want to check as an argument. In many cases this will be eth0:

```
sudo ethtool eth0
Settings for eth0:
        Supported ports: [ TP ]
        Supported link modes:   10baseT/Half 10baseT/Full
                                100baseT/Half 100baseT/Full
                                1000baseT/Half 1000baseT/Full
        Supports auto-negotiation: Yes
        Advertised link modes:  10baseT/Half 10baseT/Full
                                100baseT/Half 100baseT/Full
                                1000baseT/Half 1000baseT/Full
        Advertised auto-negotiation: Yes
        Speed: 100Mb/s
        Duplex: Full
        Port: Twisted Pair
        PHYAD: 0
        Transceiver: internal
        Auto-negotiation: on
        Supports Wake-on: pg
        Wake-on: d
        Current message level: 0x000000ff (255)
        Link detected: yes
```

As you can see ethtool gives you all sorts of information including the fact that this machine supports 10 base T, 100 base T, and gigabit networking speeds, but it currently communicates at 100 base T, full duplex. To check for link, just look at the very last line that says "Link detected." As you can see, in my example link is detected, so my cable is plugged in and I can move on.

Before I move past ethtool completely, it's worth mentioning that it does a lot more than just diagnose link problems. A common problem I've found on networks is a host with slower-than-normal network speeds. Often you'll see this crop up after a reboot or a power outage. What often happens is that when the interface connects to the network, it will try to auto-negotiate the fastest speed it can. Sometimes auto-negotiation doesn't work correctly, in which case the interface might fail back to half duplex mode or might even fail back to 10 base T! If you know that your network can support 100 base T at full duplex you can use ethtool to disable auto-negotiation and force full duplex. To do this

5.3 Troubleshooting the Local Network

for eth0 you would type:

```
sudo ethtool -s eth0 autoneg off duplex full
```

Test Local IP Settings

After we have confirmed that shawn is plugged in, the next step is to confirm that eth0 on shawn is configured correctly. To do that I would use the ifconfig command with eth0 as an argument. I should get back all of the network information I need to determine whether eth0 is set up correctly on shawn:

```
ifconfig eth0
eth0      Link encap:Ethernet  HWaddr 00:17:42:c0:ff:ee
          inet addr:10.1.1.9  Bcast:10.1.1.255  Mask:255.255.255.0
          inet6 addr: fe80::217:42ff:fe1f:18be/64 Scope:Link
          UP BROADCAST MULTICAST  MTU:1500  Metric:1
          RX packets:1 errors:0 dropped:0 overruns:0 frame:0
          TX packets:11 errors:0 dropped:0 overruns:0 carrier:0
          collisions:0 txqueuelen:1000
          RX bytes:229 (229.0 B)  TX bytes:2178 (2.1 KB)
```

There is a lot of output in that command, but the first line I would look at is the second line of output. There I can see that eth0's IP address is 10.1.1.9, and that its subnet mask is 255.255.255.0. If the machine were supposed to have a different IP or subnet mask then what I see here, then that could potentially be the cause of the problem. If eth0 didn't have an IP or subnet mask configured at all I might run ifup eth0 to bring the interface up, or I might look into the local network settings (/etc/network/interfaces on a Debian or Ubuntu machine, /etc/sysconfig/network-scripts/ifcfg-eth0 on a Red Hat-based machine) to see if anything is set incorrectly. If I can't seem to get the interface to come up, and this host gets its IP from DHCP, I might have to move my troubleshooting focus to the DHCP server.

Test the Local Subnet

After you have confirmed that the interface is on the network and should be able to communicate, the next step is to test whether you can access another host on the same subnet, specifically the gateway if you have one configured. Why? Well if you can't talk to a host on the same subnet, especially if you can't talk to the gateway, then there's no point in testing communications with hosts outside of your local subnet. First I will use the route command to see what gateway is configured, and then I will use ping to see whether I can access the gateway:

```
sudo route -n
Kernel IP routing table
Destination     Gateway         Genmask         Flags Metric Ref    Use Iface
10.1.1.0        *               255.255.255.0   U     0      0        0 eth0
default         10.1.1.1        0.0.0.0         UG    100    0        0 eth0
```

In this example I have a very basic routing table and the line that begins with the word default defines my default gateway: 10.1.1.1. Be sure to use the -n option with route in this step. Without the -n option, route will try to resolve any IP addresses it lists into hostnames. Besides the fact that route will execute faster with -n, if we have network problems we might not even be able to talk to our DNS server, plus DNS troubleshooting is a topic for another section.

Since I see that the gateway is 10.1.1.1, I would use the ping command to confirm that I can communicate with that gateway:

```
ping -c 5 10.1.1.1
PING 10.1.1.1 (10.1.1.1) 56(84) bytes of data.
64 bytes from 10.1.1.1: icmp_seq=1 ttl=64 time=3.13 ms
64 bytes from 10.1.1.1: icmp_seq=2 ttl=64 time=1.43 ms
64 bytes from 10.1.1.1: icmp_seq=3 ttl=64 time=1.79 ms
64 bytes from 10.1.1.1: icmp_seq=5 ttl=64 time=1.50 ms

--- 10.1.1.1 ping statistics ---
5 packets transmitted, 4 received, 20% packet loss, time 4020ms
rtt min/avg/max/mdev = 1.436/1.966/3.132/0.686 ms
```

This output tells me that my machine can at least talk with the gateway and presumably with the rest of the 10.1.1.x network. Now if I couldn't talk to the gateway, that could mean that my network administrator is being annoying and blocking ICMP packets. If that's the case then I would just choose another machine on the same same subnet (10.1.1.2-10.1.1.254) and try to ping it instead. If I am the network administrator (and therefore not blocking ICMP), or ICMP isn't being blocked for some other reason, then the problem at this phase could be some sort of VLAN issue that you would have to resolve on the network switch itself.

If you run the route command and don't find a default gateway set, you might be tempted to conclude that's the source of the problem. Be careful! That conclusion might be premature. See, if shawn and bill are on the same subnet, I don't need a default gateway configured for those servers to communicate. I'm not going to get into how to calculate subnets in this section, but suffice to say in my example, if shawn has an IP of 10.1.1.9 and a subnet mask of 255.255.255.0, bill could have an IP of 10.1.1.1 through 10.1.1.254 and be on the same subnet. In that case, I might just ping bill directly. Ideally I would have a third host on the same subnet I could also ping. That way if bill doesn't respond, but another host on the same subnet responds, I can narrow in on bill as the likely source of the problem.

Probe bill's ports

If bill is responding to ping, the next step is to test whether port 25 is even open on bill. There are a few different methods to do this but telnet is one of the easiest and is likely to already be installed on your machines. Let's assume bill has an IP of 10.1.1.17, I would type:

5.3 Troubleshooting the Local Network

```
telnet 10.1.1.17 25
Trying 10.1.1.17...
telnet: Unable to connect to remote host: Connection refused
```

If telnet doesn't complain about Connection refused, but instead starts outputting SMTP commands, then congratulations, you don't have a networking problem! On the downside, this means you probably have some sort of SMTP problem, which might be more of a pain to troubleshoot. If telnet complains with Connection refused then either port 25 is down on the remote machine (possibly the SMTP service on bill isn't running or isn't listening on that port), or a firewall is blocking you. This is where a tool like nmap can be handy and is one of the reasons I often use nmap instead of telnet when I want to test whether a port is available.

You see, many firewalls are configured to block ports by dropping packets with no reply. Since normally a server would send a basic reply back to let you know the port is closed, if the packet is dropped instead, nmap will flag it as filtered instead of closed:

```
nmap -p 25 10.1.1.17

Starting Nmap 5.00 ( http://nmap.org ) at 2010-01-04 20:20 PST
Interesting ports on 10.1.1.17:
PORT    STATE    SERVICE
25/tcp  filtered smtp
```

In this case nmap says the port is filtered, which tells me that there is a firewall blocking this port. If these machines were on different subnets, there might be a firewall in between the networks restricting access. Since I know these machines are on the same subnet, I would assume that there is some iptables firewall configured on bill that needs to be checked.

Test bill directly

Let's assume that we think the problem is on bill. After I've performed the same network troubleshooting on bill that I have had from shawn, the next step is to log into bill and test whether port 25 is open and listening for connections. For this we will use the netstat tool. Netstat can be used to output all sorts of information about network connections on the machine. In this case, though, I will just use the -lnp options to list listening ports and the processes that have the ports open, then I will grep for the port I'm interested in, port 25:

```
sudo netstat -lnp | grep :25
tcp      0    0 0.0.0.0:25    0.0.0.0:*    LISTEN    1878/master
```

The column I want to pay the most attention to here is the fourth column that lists what local address is open on port 25. In this case I can see it is set to 0.0.0.0:25 which means that bill is listening to port 25 connections on all available interfaces. If I had set up the mail server to only listen on eth0, this would be set to 10.1.1.17:25. If on the other hand, I saw this was set to 127.0.0.1:25, I might have found the cause of the problem: the mail server was set to only listen to the localhost address (127.0.0.1) and isn't listening for any connections from the outside network. In that case I would reconfigure my mail server so that it listens on eth0. If on the other hand, I got no output from the above command, then I know that my problem is that my server isn't running at all (or isn't set to listen on port 25). Then I'd need to start my mail server and troubleshoot why it stopped running to begin with, or why it isn't listening on the right port.

As you can see, network troubleshooting can lead you in all sorts of interesting directions. Even now I've only scratched the surface. In the next section I'll extend network troubleshooting beyond the local network and touch on how to track down routing and DNS problems from your local networks to the Internet itself.

5.4 Troubleshooting Remote Networks

This section is the third in a series dedicated to one of my favorite subjects: troubleshooting. In this series I'm going to describe some general classes of problems you might find on a Linux system, and then I will discuss how to use common tools, most of which are probably already on your system, to isolate and resolve each class of problem.

In the previous section I introduced some ways to troubleshoot network problems on your local network. Many network problems extend past your local network and either onto other local subnets or onto the Internet itself. In this section I'll provide you with the tools and techniques so that you can answer that immortal question: is the Internet down or is it just me?

The Internet is Down

The scenario we will use to test our troubleshooting skills is one that all of us have run into at one point or another—we try to load a website, perhaps even a reliable site like Google, and it won't come up. Since I already covered local network troubleshooting in my last section I'm going to assume you have already gone through those steps and are ready to proceed past the local network. Even though this example will deal with testing access to the Internet, you can use the same steps to troubleshoot problems accessing any remote network.

Test Your Gateway

For your computer to communicate with any other computer outside of your local network, you must have a gateway (router) configured on your local network and must be able to reach it. Without getting into heavy-duty network theory, a

5.4 Troubleshooting Remote Networks

router connects two or more networks and knows how to route packets between those networks. Your Linux computer has a list of all of the routers it knows about for each network it is a member of and when it should use those routers all stored in its *routing table*. You can use the route command to show your computer's current routing table:

```
route -n
Kernel IP routing table
Destination     Gateway         Genmask         Flags Metric Ref    Use Iface
10.1.1.0        *               255.255.255.0   U     0      0        0 eth0
default         10.1.1.1        0.0.0.0         UG    100    0        0 eth0
```

> **Note:** I should note that the route command has been deprecated in favor of the ip command. In particular `ip route` is used to list the routing table on modern systems.

In the above example I have one gateway defined: 10.1.1.1. It is listed as my default gateway, which is the router it will use whenever it doesn't have any other routers defined for that network. In my case it's also my only router in my routing table. That means that any time my machine wants to communicate with a remote network (in my example anything that's not within 10.1.1.0/255.255.255.0, or 10.1.1.1 - 10.1.1.254) it's going to send the packet to 10.1.1.1 to forward on.

So now that I know my default gateway, I'll use ping to test whether it's available:

```
ping -c 5 10.1.1.1
PING 10.1.1.1 (10.1.1.1) 56(84) bytes of data.
64 bytes from 10.1.1.1: icmp_seq=1 ttl=64 time=3.13 ms
64 bytes from 10.1.1.1: icmp_seq=2 ttl=64 time=1.43 ms
64 bytes from 10.1.1.1: icmp_seq=3 ttl=64 time=1.79 ms
64 bytes from 10.1.1.1: icmp_seq=5 ttl=64 time=1.50 ms

--- 10.1.1.1 ping statistics ---
5 packets transmitted, 4 received, 20% packet loss, time 4020ms
rtt min/avg/max/mdev = 1.436/1.966/3.132/0.686 ms
```

In this example 4 out of 5 ping packets were received so I can be reasonably sure my gateway works. If I couldn't ping the gateway, then either my network admin is blocking ICMP packets (I hate when they do that), my switch port is set to the wrong VLAN, or my gateway is truly down. If the gateway is down, fixing the problem might mean rebooting your DSL or wireless router (if that's how you connect to the Internet) or moving your troubleshooting to whatever device is acting as your gateway.

Test DNS

In my case I was able to ping the gateway so I'm ready to move on to DNS. Since most of us don't browse the web by IP address, we need DNS to resolve the hostnames we type into IP addresses. If DNS isn't working correctly, even if we can technically reach that remote IP address, we will never know what the IP address is.

A basic way to test DNS is via the nslookup command:

```
nslookup www.linuxjournal.com
Server:         10.2.2.2
Address:        10.2.2.2#53

Non-authoritative answer:
Name:   www.linuxjournal.com
Address: 76.74.252.198
```

In this example DNS is functioning correctly as far as we can tell. I say as far as we can tell because I'm assuming that 76.74.252.198 is the correct IP address for www.linuxjournal.com. If it were the wrong address that could very well be the cause of our problem! Our DNS server in this case is 10.2.2.2 but in some environments it could be the same IP address as your gateway.

Even though our DNS server worked, since I want to show how to troubleshoot DNS we need some examples of how it can fail. To illustrate this I will show a few different nslookup commands that have failed:

```
nslookup www.linuxjournal.com
;; connection timed out; no servers could be reached
```

This error tells me that nslookup couldn't communicate with my DNS server. This could be either because I don't have any name servers configured on my system or I just can't reach them. To see whether I have any name servers configured, I would check my /etc/resolv.conf file. This file keeps track of what name servers I should use. In my case it would look like this:

```
search example.net
nameserver 10.2.2.2
```

If your resolv.conf file doesn't have a name server entry, then you have found the problem: you need to add the IP address of your name server here. Since I do have a name server defined in resolv.conf, the next step is to attempt to ping the name server's IP with the same ping command as you used for the gateway above. If you can't ping the name server, then either a firewall is blocking ICMP (those pesky network administrators!) or there's a routing problem between you and the name server. To rule out the latter we will use a tool called traceroute. Traceroute will test the route between you and a remote IP address. To use it, type traceroute followed by the IP address you want to reach. In our case we would use 10.2.2.2:

```
traceroute 10.2.2.2
traceroute to 10.2.2.2 (10.2.2.2), 30 hops max, 40 byte packets
 1  10.1.1.1 (10.1.1.1)  5.432 ms  5.206 ms  5.472 ms
 2  10.2.2.2 (10.2.2.2)  8.039 ms  8.348 ms  8.643 ms
```

In this example I can successfully route to 10.2.2.2. To get there, my packets first go to 10.1.1.1 and then move straight to 10.2.2.2. This tells me that 10.1.1.1 is

5.4 Troubleshooting Remote Networks

likely the gateway for both networks. If there are more routers between you and your remote server you will have more hops in between. On the other hand, if you do have a routing problem your output might look more like the following:

```
traceroute 10.2.2.2
traceroute to 10.2.2.2 (10.2.2.2), 30 hops max, 40 byte packets
 1  10.1.1.1 (10.1.1.1)  5.432 ms  5.206 ms  5.472 ms
 2  * * *
 3  * * *
```

If you start seeing asterisks in the output, you know that the problem likely begins on the last router on the list so you would need to start troubleshooting from that router. Instead, you might see output like this:

```
traceroute 10.1.2.5
traceroute to 10.1.2.5 (10.1.2.5), 30 hops max, 40 byte packets
 1  10.1.1.1 (10.1.1.1)  5.432 ms  5.206 ms  5.472 ms
 1  10.1.1.1 (10.1.1.1)  3006.477 ms !H  3006.779 ms !H  3007.072 ms
```

This means that your ping timed out at the gateway so the remote host could be down, unplugged or otherwise inaccessible so you would need to troubleshoot its connection to the network.

> **Note:** Traceroute relies on ICMP so if ICMP is blocked on your network install a tool called tcptraceroute to perform a similar test over TCP (the syntax is the same, you just type tcptraceroute instead of traceroute).

If you can ping the name server but it isn't responding to you, then you can go back to my previous section and perform all of the troubleshooting steps to test whether the remote port is open and accessible on the remote host. Keep in mind, though, that DNS servers use port 53 on TCP and UDP. Again, if you aren't sure what port a service uses, check the /etc/services file on your system. It lists most of the common services you will use.

Other Name Server Problems

Another common nslookup error you might run into is this:

```
nslookup web1
Server:       10.2.2.2
Address:      10.2.2.2#53

** server can't find web1: NXDOMAIN
```

Here my name server at 10.2.2.2 responded to me but told me it couldn't find the record for server web1. This error could mean that I don't have web1's proper domain name in my DNS search path. If you don't specify a host's fully qualified domain name (for instance web1.mysite.com) but instead use the shorthand form of the hostname, your system will check /etc/resolv.conf for domains in your DNS search path. It will then add those domains one by one to the end of your hostname to see if it resolves. The DNS search path is the line in /etc/resolv.conf that starts with the word *search*:

```
search example.net example2.net
nameserver 10.2.2.2
```

In my case when I search for web1's IP address, my system will first search for web1.example.net and if that has no records it will search for web1.example2.net. If you want to test whether this is the problem, just run nslookup again but with the fully qualified domain name (such as web1.mysite.com). If it resolves then either make sure you always use the fully qualified domain name when you access that server, or add that domain to the search path in /etc/resolv.conf.

If you try nslookup against the fully qualified domain name and you still get the same NXDOMAIN error above then your problem is with the name server itself. Troubleshooting the full range of DNS server problems is a bit beyond what I could reasonably fit in this section, but here are a few steps to get you started. If you know that your DNS server is configured to have the record you are looking for itself, then you will need to examine its zone records to make sure that particular hostname exists. If on the other hand you are searching for a domain you know it doesn't have a record for (say www.linuxjournal.com) then it's possible your DNS server isn't allowing recursive queries from your host or at all. You can test that by trying to resolve some other remote host on the Internet. If it doesn't resolve then it's probably a recursion setting. If it does resolve then the problem might very well be with that remote site's DNS server.

Test General Internet Routing

If after all these tests you find that your DNS servers are working fine, but you still can't access the remote server, the final step is to perform another traceroute like we did above, only directly against the remote server. So for instance, if we wanted to test our route to www.linuxjournal.com the traceroute might look like the following:

```
traceroute www.linuxjournal.com
traceroute to www.linuxjournal.com (76.74.252.198), 30 hops max, 60 byte packets
 1  10.1.1.1 (10.1.1.1)  1.016 ms  2.222 ms  2.308 ms
 2  75-101-46-1.dsl.static.sonic.net (75.101.46.1)  6.916 ms  7.389 ms  8.386 ms
 3  921.gig0-3.gw.sjc.sonic.net (75.101.33.221)  11.265 ms  12.435 ms  13.050 ms
 4  108.ae0.gw.equinix-sj.sonic.net (64.142.0.73)  13.846 ms  15.233 ms  15.390 ms
 5  GIG2-0.sea-dis-2.peer1.net (206.81.80.38)  35.149 ms  36.272 ms  36.944 ms
 6  oc48.so-2-1-0.sea-coloc-dis-1.peer1.net (216.187.89.190)  37.340 ms  27.884 ms  27.266 ms
 7  10ge.ten1-2.sj-mkp16-dis-1.peer1.net (216.187.88.202)  28.421 ms  29.014 ms  29.688 ms
 8  10ge.ten1-2.sj-mkp2-dis-1.peer1.net (216.187.88.134)  30.903 ms  31.015 ms  31.804 ms
 9  10ge.ten1-3.la-600w-cor-1.peer1.net (216.187.88.130)  40.840 ms  41.279 ms  42.069 ms
10  10ge.ten1-1.la-600w-cor-2.peer1.net (216.187.88.146)  42.587 ms  43.710 ms  44.921 ms
11  10ge.ten1-2.dal-eqx-cor-1.peer1.net (216.187.124.122)  81.702 ms  82.959 ms  83.934 ms
12  10ge.ten1-1.dal-eqx-cor-2.peer1.net (216.187.124.134)  74.876 ms  72.454 ms  72.798 ms
13  10ge.ten1-3.sat-8500v-cor-2.peer1.net (216.187.124.178)  80.224 ms  81.872 ms  82.569 ms
14  216.187.124.110 (216.187.124.110)  83.499 ms  84.162 ms  85.048 ms
15  www.linuxjournal.com (76.74.252.198)  85.484 ms  86.461 ms  87.153 ms
```

In this example I'm 15 hops (or routers) away from the www.linuxjournal.com server. This is an example of a successful query, but if you ran the same query and noticed a number of rows of asterisks that never made it to your destination *and* you couldn't ping www.linuxjournal.com directly, the problem could be an Internet routing problem between your and the remote network. Unfortunately it's probably something outside of your control but fortunately these sorts of problems tend to resolve themselves pretty quickly so just keep trying.

If on the other hand your traceroute command was successful but the remote site still didn't work, go back to the steps I discussed in my previous section on how to use telnet and nmap to test whether a remote port is open. It could actually be that the remote server is down (hey it happens to the best of us), or someone has configured a firewall to block you from that remote server.

I hope that this series has kindled (or rekindled) your interest in troubleshooting under Linux. One of the things I love about Linux is how little it hides from you about how it works and how many tools it provides you for troubleshooting when things do go wrong. If this has piqued your interest there are many more troubleshooting avenues for you to explore from DNS servers like I mentioned previously, to troubleshooting just about any type of service.

5.5 Troubleshooting with Telnet

Poor telnet, it used to be the cool kid on the block. It was the program all sysadmin turned to when they needed to connect to a remote server. Telnet just wasn't that good at keeping a secret—all communication went over plain text—so administrators started switching to ssh for encrypted remote shell sessions. Of course along with the switch came a huge stigma against administrators who still used telnet. Eventually telnet became an outcast—the program you used if you were an out-of-touch old-timer who didn't care about security.

I for one think telnet isn't all bad. Sure it can't keep a secret but it still can do a lot of useful things around the server room. Really, telnet just provides you a convenient way to connect to a network port and send commands. Telnet can work well to diagnose problems with one of the many services out there that still accept plain text commands in their protocol. In fact, it's one of my go-to command-line programs when I'm troubleshooting. In this section I'm going to give telnet a second chance and describe how to use it to perform some common troubleshooting tasks.

Test Remote Ports

There are many different ways to test whether a network port is listening on a system including GUI port scanners, nmap, and nc. While all of those can work well, and even I find myself using nmap more often than not, not all machines end up having nmap installed. Just about every system includes telnet, though, including a lot of embedded systems with busybox environments. So if I wanted to test whether the SMTP port (port 25) was listening on a server with the IP 192.168.5.5 I could type:

```
telnet 192.168.5.5 25
Trying 192.168.5.5...
telnet: Unable to connect to remote host: Connection refused
```

In this case the remote port is unavailable, so I would fall back to some other troubleshooting methods to figure out why. If the port were open and available, though, then I could just start typing SMTP commands (more on that later).

As you can see from the above example, the syntax is to type the command telnet, the IP or hostname to connect to, and the remote port (otherwise it will default to port 23–the default port for telnet). So if I wanted to test a web server instead I would connect to the HTTP port (port 80):

```
telnet www.example.net 80
```

Troubleshoot Web Servers

While we are connecting to port 80, we might as well actually throw some HTTP comands at it and test that it works. For starters you want to make sure you are actually connected:

```
telnet www.example.net 80
Trying 192.168.5.5...
Connected to www.example.net.
Escape character is '^]'.
```

Once you are connected, you can pass a basic HTTP GET request to ask for the default index page followed by the host you want to connect to:

```
GET / HTTP/1.1
host:  www.example.net
```

The GET request specifies which page (/) along with what protocol we will use (HTTP/1.1). Since most web servers end up hosting multiple virtual hosts from the same port you can use the host command so the web server knows which virtual host to direct you to. If I wanted to load some other web page I could replace GET / with, say, GET /forum/. It's possible your connection will time out if you don't type it in fast enough–if that happens you can always copy and paste the command instead. After you type your commands, type Enter one final time and you'll get a lot of headers you don't normally see along with the actual HTML content:

```
HTTP/1.1 200 OK
Date: Tue, 10 Jul 2012 04:54:04 GMT
Server: Apache/2.2.14 (Ubuntu)
Last-Modified: Mon, 24 May 2010 21:33:10 GMT
ETag: "38111c-b1-4875dc9938880"
Accept-Ranges: bytes
Content-Length: 177
Vary: Accept-Encoding
Content-Type: text/html
X-Pad: avoid browser bug
```

5.5 Troubleshooting with Telnet

```
<html><body><h1>It works!</h1>
<p>This is the default web page for this server.</p>
<p>The web server software is running but no content
has been added, yet.</p>
</body></html>
```

As you can see from my output this is just the default Apache web server page, but in this case the HTML output is just one part of the equation. Equally useful in this output are all of the headers you get back from the HTTP/1.1 200 OK reply code to the modification dates on the web page, to the Apache server version. After you are done sending commands, just hit Ctrl-] and Enter to get back to a telnet prompt, then type quit to exit telnet.

I usually just use telnet to do some basic HTTP troubleshooting since once you get into the realm of authentication, following redirects, and other more complicated parts of the protocol it's much simpler to use a command-line tool like curl or I guess if you have to, even a regular GUI web browser.

Send an Email

While I just used telnet for basic web server troubleshooting, telnet ends up being my preferred tool for email troubleshooting, mostly because it's just so simple to send a complete email with just a few telnet commands.

The first step is to initiate a telnet connection with the mail server you want to test on port 25:

```
telnet mail.example.net 25
Trying 192.168.5.5...
Connected to mail.example.net.
Escape character is '^]'.
220 mail.example.net ESMTP Postfix
```

Unlike the blank prompt you may get when you connect to an HTTP server, with SMTP you should get an immediate reply back. In this case the reply is telling me I'm connecting to a Postfix server. Once I get that 220 prompt I can start typing SMTP commands, starting with the HELO command that lets me tell the mail server what server is connecting to it:

```
HELO lappy486.example.net
250 mail.example.net
```

The nice thing about the interactive SMTP connection we have here is that if I do somehow typo a command or make a mistake, it should let me know–otherwise I should get a 250 reply. After HELO we use the MAIL FROM: command to list what email address the email should appear to be from. I say appear to be from because you can put just about any email address you want here, which is a good reason not to blindly trust FROM addresses:

```
MAIL FROM: <root@example.net>
250 Ok
```

In the past I used to just type in the email address directly without surrounding it with <>. My personal Postfix servers are fine with this but other mail servers are more strict and will reply with a syntax error if you don't surround the email address with <>. Since this FROM address was accepted we can follow up with RCPT TO: and specify who the email is addressed to:

```
RCPT TO: <postmaster@example.net>
250 Ok
```

The fact that the mail server responded with 250 should mean that it accepted the TO address you specified here. Finally we can type DATA and type the rest of our email, including any extra headers we want to add like Subject, then finish up with a single period on its own line:

```
DATA
354 End data with <CR><LF>.<CR><LF>
Subject:   Give Telnet a Chance 1
Hi,

All we are saying is give telnet a chance.
.
250 Ok: queued as 52A1EE3D117
```

When I'm testing emails with telnet, I usually put a number in the subject line so I can continually increment it with each test. This way if an email doesn't get delivered I can tell which ones went through and which ones didn't.

Once you are done with the DATA section and the email is queued, you can type quit to exit:

```
quit
221 Bye
Connection closed by foreign host.
```

Now that you have some ways to troubleshoot with telnet, hopefully you won't relegate telnet to the junk drawer of your Linux systems. Sure you may not want to use it for remote shells, but now that just about everyone uses SSH anyway, maybe you can break out telnet on your terminal for all of your other plain text network needs without your friends scolding you.

5.6 Collecting Server Metrics with Sar

There's an old saying: "When the cat's away the mice will play." The same is true for servers. It's as if servers wait until you aren't logged in (and usually in the middle of REM sleep) before they have problems. Logs can go a long way to help you isolate problems that happened in the past on a machine, but if the problem is due to high load, logs often don't tell the full story. In the section "Troubleshooting High Load", I discuss how to troubleshoot a system with high load using tools such as uptime and top. Those tools are great as long as the system still has high load when you are logged in, but if the system had high

5.6 Collecting Server Metrics with Sar

load while you were at lunch or asleep, you need some way to pull the same statistics top gives you, only from the past. That is where sar comes in.

Enable sar Logging

sar is a classic Linux tool that is part of the sysstat package and should be available in just about any major distribution with your regular package manager. Once installed, it will be enabled on a Red Hat-based system, but on a Debian-based system (like Ubuntu), you might have to edit /etc/default/sysstat, and make sure that ENABLED is set to true. On a Red Hat-based system, sar will log seven days of statistics by default. If you want to log more than that, you can edit /etc/sysconfig/sysstat and change the HISTORY option.

Once sysstat is configured and enabled, it will collect statistics about your system every ten minutes and store them in a logfile under either /var/log/sysstat or /var/log/sa via a cron job in /etc/cron.d/sysstat. There is also a daily cron job that will run right before midnight and rotate out the day's statistics. By default, the logfiles will be date-stamped with the current day of the month, so the logs will rotate automatically and overwrite the log from a month ago.

CPU Statistics

After your system has had some time to collect statistics, you can use the sar tool to retrieve them. When run with no other arguments, sar displays the current day's CPU statistics:

```
sar
. . .
07:05:01 PM   CPU   %user   %nice   %system   %iowait   %steal   %idle
. . .
08:45:01 PM   all   4.62    0.00    1.82      0.44      0.00     93.12
08:55:01 PM   all   3.80    0.00    1.74      0.47      0.00     93.99
09:05:01 PM   all   5.85    0.00    2.01      0.66      0.00     91.48
09:15:01 PM   all   3.64    0.00    1.75      0.35      0.00     94.26
Average:      all   7.82    0.00    1.82      1.14      0.00     89.21
```

If you are familiar with the command-line tool top, the above CPU statistics should look familiar, as they are the same as you would get in real time from top. You can use these statistics just like you would with top, only in this case, you are able to see the state of the system back in time, along with an overall average at the bottom of the statistics, so you can get a sense of what is normal. sar provides you with all of the same statistics, just at ten-minute intervals in the past.

- **us** user CPU time. More often than not when you have CPU-bound load, it's due to a process run by a user on the system such as Apache, MySQL, or maybe a shell script. If this percentage is high, then a user process such as these is a likely cause of the load.
- **sy** system CPU time. The system CPU time is the percentage of the CPU tied

up by kernel and other system processes. CPU-bound load should either manifest as a high percentage of user or high system CPU time.

id CPU idle time. This is the percentage of the time that the CPU spends idle. The higher the number here the better! In fact if you see really high CPU idle time it's a good indication that any high load is not CPU-bound.

wa I/O wait. The I/O wait value tells you the percentage of time the CPU is spending waiting on I/O (typically disk I/O). If you have high load and this value is high, then it's likely the load is not CPU-bound but is due to either RAM issues or high disk I/O.

RAM Statistics

sar also supports a large number of different options you can use to pull out other statistics. For instance, with the -r option, you can see RAM statistics:

```
sar -r
. . .
07:05:01 PM kbmemfree kbmemused %memused kbbuffers  kbcached kbcommit  %commit
. . .
08:45:01 PM    881280   2652840    75.06    355284   1028636  8336664   183.87
08:55:01 PM    881412   2652708    75.06    355872   1029024  8337908   183.89
09:05:01 PM    879164   2654956    75.12    356480   1029428  8337040   183.87
09:15:01 PM    886724   2647396    74.91    356960   1029592  8332344   183.77
Average:       851787   2682333    75.90    338612   1081838  8341742   183.98
```

Just like with the CPU statistics, here I can see RAM statistics from the past similar to what I could find in top.

Disk Statistics

In the "Troubleshooting High Load" section I reference sysstat as the source for a great disk I/O troubleshooting tool called iostat. Although that provides real-time disk I/O statistics, you also can pass sar the -b option to get disk I/O data from the past:

```
sar -b
. . .
07:05:01 PM      tps      rtps      wtps    bread/s   bwrtn/s
. . .
08:45:01 PM     2.03      0.33      1.70       9.90     31.30
08:55:01 PM     1.93      0.03      1.90       1.04     31.95
09:05:01 PM     2.71      0.02      2.69       0.69     48.67
09:15:01 PM     1.52      0.02      1.50       0.20     27.08
Average:        5.92      3.42      2.50      77.41     49.97
```

I figure these columns need a little explanation:

tps transactions per second.
rtps read transactions per second.
wtps write transactions per second.
bread/s blocks read per second.
bwrtn/s blocks written per second.

sar can return a lot of other statistics beyond what I've mentioned, but if you want to see everything it has to offer, simply pass the -A option, which will return a complete dump of all the statistics it has for the day (or just browse its man page).

Turn Back Time

So by default, sar returns statistics for the current day, but often you'll want to get information a few days in the past. This is especially useful if you want to see whether today's numbers are normal by comparing them to days in the past, or if you are troubleshooting a server that misbehaved over the weekend. For instance, say you noticed a problem on a server today between 5PM and 5:30PM. First, use the -s and -e options to tell sar to display data only between the start (-s) and end (-e) times you specify:

```
sar -s 17:00:00 -e 17:30:00
Linux 2.6.32-29-server (www.example.net)   02/06/2012    _x86_64_
(2 CPU)

05:05:01 PM     CPU    %user    %nice  %system  %iowait   %steal    %idle
05:15:01 PM     all     4.39     0.00     1.83     0.39     0.00    93.39
05:25:01 PM     all     5.76     0.00     2.23     0.41     0.00    91.60
Average:        all     5.08     0.00     2.03     0.40     0.00    92.50
```

To compare that data with the same time period from a different day, just use the -f option and point sar to one of the logfiles under /var/log/sysstat or /var/log/sa that correspond to that day. For instance, to pull statistics from the first of the month:

```
sar -s 17:00:00 -e 17:30:00 -f /var/log/sysstat/sa01
Linux 2.6.32-29-server (www.example.net)   02/01/2012    _x86_64_
(2 CPU)

05:05:01 PM     CPU    %user    %nice  %system  %iowait   %steal    %idle
05:15:01 PM     all     9.85     0.00     3.95     0.56     0.00    85.64
05:25:01 PM     all     5.32     0.00     1.81     0.44     0.00    92.43
Average:        all     7.59     0.00     2.88     0.50     0.00    89.04
```

You also can add all of the normal sar options when pulling from past logfiles, so you could run the same command and add the -r argument to get RAM statistics:

```
sar -s 17:00:00 -e 17:30:00 -f /var/log/sysstat/sa01 -r
Linux 2.6.32-29-server (www.example.net)   02/01/2012    _x86_64_
(2 CPU)

05:05:01 PM kbmemfree kbmemused  %memused kbbuffers  kbcached  kbcommit  %commit
05:15:01 PM    766452   2767668     78.31    361964   1117696   8343936   184.03
05:25:01 PM    813744   2720376     76.97    362524   1118808   8329568   183.71
Average:       790098   2744022     77.64    362244   1118252   8336592   183.87
```

As you can see, sar is a relatively simple but very useful troubleshooting tool. Although plenty of other programs exist that can pull trending data from your servers and graph them (and I use them myself), sar is great in that it doesn't require a network connection, so if your server gets so heavily loaded it doesn't respond over the network anymore, there's still a chance you could get valuable troubleshooting data with sar.

5.7 Dynamic DNS Disaster

Typically when a network is under my control, I like my servers to have static IPs. Whether the IPs are truly static (hard-coded into network configuration files on the host) or I configure a DHCP server to make static assignments, it's far more convenient when you know a server will always have the same IP. Unfortunately, in the default Amazon EC2 environment, you don't have any say over your IP address. When you spawn a server in EC2, their DHCP server hands out a somewhat random IP address. The server will maintain that IP address even through reboots as long as the host isn't shut down. If you halt the machine, the next time it comes up it will likely be on a different piece of hardware and will have a new IP.

Dhclient Overrides

To deal with this unpredictable IP address, over the years I've leaned heavily on dynamic DNS updates within my EC2 environments. When a host starts for the first time and gets configured or any time the IP changes, the host will update internal DNS servers with the new IP. Generally this approach has worked well for me but it has one complication. If I controlled the DHCP server, I would configure it with the IP addresses of my DNS servers. Since Amazon controls DHCP, I have to configure my hosts to override the DNS servers they get from DHCP with mine. I use the ISC DHCP client, so that means adding three lines to the /etc/dhcp/dhclient.conf file on a Debian-based system:

```
supersede domain-name "example.com";
supersede domain-search "dev.example.com", "example.com";
supersede domain-name-servers 10.34.56.78, 10.34.56.79;
```

With those options, once the network has been restarted (or the machine reboots), these settings will end up in my /etc/resolv.conf:

```
domain example.com
search dev.example.com.    example.com
nameserver 10.34.56.78
nameserver 10.34.56.79
```

I've even gone so far as to add a bash script under /etc/dhcp/dhclient-exit-hooks.d/ that fires off after I get a new lease. For fault tolerance I have multiple puppetmasters and if you were to perform a DNS query for the puppet hostname, you would get back multiple IPs. These exit hook scripts perform a DNS query to try to identify the puppetmaster that is closest to it and adds a little-known setting to resolv.conf called sortlist. The sortlist setting tells your resolver that in the case that a query returns multiple IPs, to favor the specific IP or subnets in this line. So for instance, if the puppetmaster I want to use has an IP of 10.72.52.100, I would add the following line to my resolv.conf:

```
sortlist 10.72.52.100/255.255.255.255
```

5.7 Dynamic DNS Disaster

Next time I query the hostname that returns multiple A records, it will always favor this IP first even though it returns multiple IPs. If you use ping you can test this and see that it always pings the host you specify in sortlist, even if a dig or nslookup returns multiple IPs in random order. In the event the first host goes down, if your client has proper support for multiple A records it will fail over to the next host in the list.

Dhclient is Not So Dynamic

This method of wrangling a bit of order into such a dynamic environment as EC2 has worked well for me, overall. That said, it isn't without a few complications. The main challenge with a system like this is that the IPs of my DNS servers themselves might change. No problem you might say. Since I control my dhclient.conf with a configuration management system, I can just push out the new dhclient.conf. The only problem with that approach is that dhclient does not offer any way that I have been able to find, to reload the dhclient.conf configuration file without restarting dhclient itself (which means bouncing the network). See, if you controlled the DHCP server, you could update the DHCP server's DNS settings and it would push out to clients when they ask for their next lease. In my case, a DNS server IP change meant generating a network blip throughout the entire environment.

I discovered this requirement the hard way. I had respawned a DNS server and pushed out the new IP to the dhclient.conf on all of my servers. As a belt-and-suspenders approach, I also made sure that the /etc/resolv.conf file was updated by my configuration management system to show the new IP. The change pushed out and everything looks great so I shut down the DNS server. Shortly after that, disaster struck.

I started noticing that a host would have internal health checks time out, the host became sluggish and unresponsive, and long after my resolv.conf change should have made it to the host, it seemed it was updating the file again. When I examined the resolv.conf on faulty systems, I noticed it had the old IP scheme configured even though the DNS servers with that information were long gone. What I eventually realized was that even though I updated dhclient.conf, the dhclient script itself never grabbed those changes so after a few hours when it renewed its lease, it overwrote resolv.conf with the old DNS IPs it had configured!

The Blip Heard Round the World

I realized that basically every host in this environment was going to renew its lease within the next few hours so the network needed to be bounced on every single host to accept the new dhclient.conf. My team scrambled to stage the change on groups of servers at a time. The real problem was less that dhclient changes required a network blip, but more that the network blip was more like an outage that lasted a few seconds. We have database clusters that don't take kindly to the network being removed. At least, they view it (rightly so) as a failure on the host and immediately trigger failover and recovery of the database cluster. The hosts seemed to be taking way longer than they should to bounce their network, were triggering cluster failovers, and in some cases required some manual intervention to fix things.

Fortunately for us, this issue only affected the development environment, but we needed to respawn DNS servers in production as well and definitely couldn't handle that kind of disruption there. I started researching the problem and after confirming that there was no way to update dhclient.conf without bouncing the network, I turned to why it took so long to restart the network. My dhclient-exit-hook script was the smoking gun. Inside the script I slept for 5 seconds to make sure the network was up, and then performed a dig request. This meant that when restarting the network, the DNS queries configured for the old IPs would time out and cause the host to pause before the network was up. The fix was for me to replace the sleep and dig query with a template containing a simple echo to append my sortlist entry to resolv.conf. My configuration management system would do the DNS query itself and update the template. With the new, faster script in place, I saw that my network restarts barely caused a network blip at all. Once I deployed that new exit hook, I was able to bounce the network on any host without any ill effects. The final proof was when I pushed changes to DNS server IPs in production with no issues.

5.8 Troubleshoot Full Disks

No matter how big your hard drives are, at some point you look at your storage and wonder where all the space went. Your /home directory is probably a good example. If you are like me, you don't always clean up after yourself or organize immediately after you download a file. Sure, I have directories to organize my ISOs, my documents, and my videos, but more often than not my home directory becomes the digital equivalent of a junk drawer with a few tarballs here, an old distribution ISO there, and PDF specs for hardware I no longer own. While some of these files don't really take up space on the disk–it's more a matter of clutter–when I'm running out of storage I'd like to quickly find the files that take up the most space and decide how to deal with them. Below you will find some of my favorite commands to locate space wasting files on my system. Then I will follow up with some common ways to free up some space on a system.

Think Locally

First let's start with file clutter in your main home directory. While all major GUI file managers make it easy to sort a directory by size, since the rest of these

5.8 Troubleshoot Full Disks

tips are from the command line let's cover how to find the largest files in the current directory via the old standby, ls. If you type:

```
ls -1Sh
```

you will get back a list of all of the files in your current directory sorted by size. Of course if you have a lot of files in the directory the files you most want to see are probably somewhere along the top of the list so I typically like to type:

```
ls -1Sh | less
```

to view the list slowly starting at the top, or if I'm in a hurry I type:

```
ls -1Sh | head
```

to just see the top 10 largest files. Now this is pretty basic, but it's worth reviewing since you will use these commands over and over again as you track down space-wasting files. Depending on how you structure your home directory, you probably won't find all of the large files together. It's more likely they are scattered into different subdirectories so you then need to scan through your directory structure recursively, tally up the disk space used in each directory, and then sort the output. Luckily you don't have to resort to ls for this, du does the job quite nicely. For instance, one common use for du that I see referenced a lot is the following:

```
du -sh *
```

This scans through all of your subdirectories you list as arguments (in this case all of the subdirectories within my current directory) and then lists them one by one with "human readable" file sizes (the -h option converts the file sizes from into megabytes, gigabytes, etc. so it's easier to read). Here's some example output from the command:

```
456K    bin
28K     Default-Compiz
16K     hl4070cdwcups-1.0.0-7.i386.deb
344K    hl4070cdwlpr-1.0.0-7.i386.deb
27M     images
60K     LexmarkC750.ppd
850M    mail
```

While you could certainly work with this information it would be much easier if it were sorted, so to do that, replace the -h argument with -k and then pipe the output to sort:

```
du -sk * | sort -n

16      hl4070cdwcups-1.0.0-7.i386.deb
28      Default-Compiz
60      LexmarkC750.ppd
344     hl4070cdwlpr-1.0.0-7.i386.deb
456     bin
```

```
10224    writing
26948    images
869588   mail
```

This works better since I can now see that my local email cache is taking up the bulk of the storage, but now I would need to change to the mail directory and run the command again over and over until I narrow it down to the subdirectory within that had the large files. That's why I normally skip the above commands and go straight for what I affectionately call "the duck command"

```
du -ck | sort -n
. . .
87704     ./.mozilla
87704     ./.mozilla/firefox
119236    ./mail/example.net/sent-mail-2004
119236    ./mail/example.net/sent-mail-2004/cur
869852    ./mail
869852    ./mail/example.net
1064100   .
1064100   total
```

What the -c option does is essentially recurse into each subdirectory like before, only it keeps a running tally of the space used by each subdirectory down the tree, not just the first level of directories. When it reports back its findings as you can see it might list the same top-level directory multiple times. This makes it easy to drill down to the actual directory that consumes the most space which in this example seems to be ./mail/example.net/sent-mail-2004/cur. If I wanted to clean up files there I could cd to that directory and then run the ls commands I used above to see which files used the most space.

Act Globally

The duck command works great to find out where your space is being used in your home directory, but if you are like me your home directory is actually on a different partition from your root. If root is filling up, you can still use the duck command (with a slight tweak) to see which directories consume the most space. You will need root privileges to scan all of the directories in your root file system so either use su or sudo -s (depending on how you get root permissions) before the duck command:

```
cd /
sudo du -ckx | sort -n
. . .
243920    ./usr/lib/openoffice
277600    ./var/cache/apt
296376    ./var/cache
475144    ./var
952096    ./usr/share
1099264   ./usr/lib
2259332   ./usr
2908804   .
2908804   total
```

5.8 Troubleshoot Full Disks 155

The extra -x argument I added tells du to stay on one file system, in this case the root file system. Otherwise if you don't specify -x and you have /home or other directories on different file systems, du will scan through those partitions as well so you will ultimately have to skip them out as you scan through your results. As you can see from this output the /usr directory takes up the bulk of the space on my system with /usr/lib using almost half of the space inside /usr. Also note that /var/cache/apt is listed here—more on how to deal with that below.

Free as in Space

Now that you know where your storage is being used, here are a few common sense ways to manage some of those files and free up some space. If you do Linux programming, build software from source, or regularly download tarballs, you probably have these tarballs lying around along with their extracted directories. One easy way to free up space is to delete either the tarball or the extracted directory. If you build your own kernels, you probably have a number of old kernel source trees in /usr/src that you won't ever use again and could stand to delete.

Another common space waster is old ISO files. Do you really still need that Red Had 7.2 ISO? If so burn an archive copy or two to CD and then delete the image. Along those same lines audio files always end up either with an extra copy in a directory for a mix CD or if you play with video conversion tools like me you have video files in different phases of being transcoded. If you are done with the project, why not delete them and save the space?

On desktops but especially on servers one of the most common places you will find wasted space is in log directories. Logs can definitely be useful but some logs and some levels of debugging are only useful immediately after a bug is found and the rest of the time they can be safely truncated or archived. Take a look in /var/log/ and see how many large uncompressed log files you have. If the file is no longer being used you should gzip it. You would be amazed how far you can compress incredibly large log files if you haven't tried it before. If you aren't sure whether a log file is still being written to, use lsof to check:

```
sudo lsof | grep "/path/to/filename"
```

If you regularly find yourself cleaning up or gzipping the rotated log files in /var/log (they append .0, .1, etc. as they are being rotated), edit /etc/logrotate.conf and enable compression. Usually this requires that you find the commented line labeled "#compress" and uncomment it.

One of the other great places to free up space is in your package manager's local package cache. For instance, in the case of Debian-based systems packages apt downloads are cached in /var/cache/apt/archives. You could go to that directory and manually remove the files, or you could just become root and type

```
sudo apt-get autoclean
```

to remove all of the cached packages you no longer need. If you use a distribution that uses yum, you can use the following two commands to clear out the cached headers and packages from your system:

```
sudo yum clean headers
sudo yum clean packages
```

And for systems that use dnf:

```
sudo dnf clean all
```

Finally, archival can be a good solution to clean up your storage. If you have a local file server or one machine with more storage than the rest, why not make sure all your large files only exist there and then access them over the network? Alternatively burn large files you want to keep but don't immediately need to CD or DVD. Once you are done you'll have plenty of newly-freed space, hopefully to last you until next spring.

5.9 Hard Drive Crashes

Nothing teaches you about Linux like a good disaster. Whether it is a hard drive crash, a wayward rm -rf command, or fdisk mistakes, there are any number of ways your normal day as a Linux user can turn into a nightmare. Now with that nightmare is a great opportunity: I've learned more about how Linux works by accidentally breaking it and then having to fix it again, than I ever have when everything was running smoothly. Believe me when I say that the following series of sections on system recovery is hard-earned knowledge.

Treated well, computer equipment is pretty reliable. While I've experienced failures in just about all major computer parts over the years, the fact is I've had more computers outlast their usefulness than not. That having been said, there's one computer component that you can almost count on to fail on you at some point–the hard drive. You can blame it on the fast-moving parts, the vibration and heat inside a computer system, or even a mistake on a fork lift at the factory, but when your hard drive fails prematurely, no five-year warranty is going to make you feel better about all that lost data that you forgot to back up.

The most important thing you can do to protect yourself from a hard drive crash or really most Linux disasters is backup your data. Backup your data! Not even a good RAID system can protect you from all hard drive failures (plus RAID doesn't protect you if you delete a file accidentally) so if the data is important be sure to back it up. Testing your backups is just as important and backing up in the first place. You have not truly backed anything up if you haven't tested restoring the backup. The methods I will list below for recovering data from a crashed hard drive are much more time-consuming than restoring from a backup so if at all possible, backup your data.

5.9 Hard Drive Crashes

Now that I'm done with my lecture, let's assume that for some reason one of your hard drives crashed and you did not have a backup. All is not necessarily lost. There are many different kinds of hard drive failure. Now in a true hard drive crash, the head of the hard drive will actually crash into the platter as it spins at high speed. I've seen platters after a head crash that are translucent in sections as the head scraped off all of the magnetic coating. If this has happened to you, no command I will list will help you. Your only recourse will be one of the forensics firms out there that specialize in hard drive recovery. Now when most people say their hard drive has crashed they are talking about a less extreme failure. Often what has happened is that the hard drive has developed a number of bad blocks–so many that you cannot mount the file system or in other cases there is some other failure that results in I/O errors when you tried to read from the hard drive. In many of these circumstances you can recover at least some if not most of the data. I've been able to recover data from drives that sounded *horrible* and other people had completely written off, and it only took a few commands and a little patience.

Create a Recovery Image

Hard drive recovery works on the assumption that not all of the data on the drive is bad. Generally speaking if you have bad blocks on a hard drive they are often clustered together. The rest of the data on the drive could be fine if you could only access it. When hard drives start to die they often do it in phases so you want to recover as much data from it as quickly as possible. If a hard drive has I/O errors you can sometimes damage the data further if you run file system checks or other repairs on the device itself. Instead what you want to do is create a complete image of the drive stored on good media and then work with that image.

There are a number of imaging tools available for Linux from the classic dd program to advanced GUI tools, but the problem with most of them is that they are designed to image healthy drives. The problem with unhealthy drives is that when you attempt to read from a bad block you will get an I/O error and most standard imaging tools will fail in some way when they get an error. While you can tell dd to ignore errors it will just happily skip to the next block and write nothing for the block it can't read so you can end up with an image that's smaller than your drive. When you image an unhealthy drive you want a tool designed for the job. For Linux that tool is ddrescue.

5.9.0.1 ddrescue or dd_rescue

To make things a little confusing, there are two similar tools with almost-identical names. dd_rescue (with an underscore) is an older rescue tool that still does the job, but works in a fairly basic manner–it starts at the beginning of the drive and when it encounters errors it retries a number of times and then moves to the next block. Eventually (usually after a few days) it reaches the end of the drive. Often bad blocks are clustered together and in the case all of the bad blocks are near the beginning of the drive, you could waste a lot of time trying to read them instead of recovering all of the good blocks.

The ddrescue tool (no underscore) is part of the GNU project and takes the basic algorithm of dd_rescue further. ddrescue tries to recover all of the good data from the device first and then divides and conquers the remaining bad blocks until it has tried to recover the entire drive. Another added feature of ddrescue is that it can optionally maintain a log file of what it has already recovered so that you can stop the program and then resume later right where you left off. This is useful when you believe ddrescue has recovered the bulk of the good data–you can stop the program and make a copy of the mostly-complete image so you can attempt to repair it and then start ddrescue again to complete the image.

Prepare to Image

The first thing you will need to create an image of your failed drive is another drive of equal or greater size to store the image. If you plan to use the second drive as a replacement, then you will probably want to image directly from one device to the next. However if you just want to mount the image and recover particular files, want to store the image on an already-formatted partition, or want to recover from another computer you will likely create the image as a file. If you do want to image to a file, your job will be simpler if you image one partition from the drive at a time. That way it will be easier to mount and fsck the image later.

The ddrescue program is available either as a package (ddrescue in Debian and Ubuntu) or you can download and install it from the project page. Note that if you are trying to recover the main disk of a system you will clearly need to either recover using a second system, or find a rescue disk that has ddrescue or can install it live.

Run ddrescue

Once ddrescue is installed, it is relatively simple to run. The first argument is the device you want to image. The second argument is the device or file you want to image to. The optional third argument is the path to a log file ddrescue can maintain so that it can resume. So for our example let's say I have a failing hard drive at /dev/sda and have mounted a large partition to store the image at /mnt/recovery/, I would run the following command to rescue the first partition on /dev/sda:

```
sudo ddrescue /dev/sda1 /mnt/recovery/sda1_image.img /mnt/recovery/logfile
Press Ctrl-C to interrupt
Initial status (read from logfile)
```

5.9 Hard Drive Crashes

```
rescued:           0 B,   errsize:     0 B,   errors:            0
Current status
rescued:      349372 kB,   errsize:     0 B,   current rate:  19398 kB/s
   ipos:      349372 kB,   errors:      0,    average rate:  16162 kB/s
   opos:      349372 kB
```

Note that you need to run ddrescue with root privileges. Also notice that I specified /dev/sda1 as the source device since I wanted to image to a file. If I were going to output to another hard drive device (like /dev/sdb) I would have specified /dev/sda instead. If there were more than one partition on this drive I wanted to recover, I would repeat this command for each partition and save each as its own image.

As you can see a great thing about ddrescue is that it gives you constantly updating output so you can gauge your progress as you rescue the partition. In fact in some circumstances I prefer using ddrescue over dd for regular imaging as well just for the progress output. Having constant progress output is additionally useful considering how long it can take to rescue a failing drive. In some circumstances it might even take a few days depending on the size of the drive, so it's good to know how far along you are.

Repair the Image File System

Once you have a complete image of your drive or partition, the next step is to repair the file system. Presumably there were bad blocks and areas that ddrescue could not recover, so the goal here is to attempt to repair enough of the file system so that you can at least mount it. Now if you had imaged to another hard drive, you would run the fsck against individual partitions on the drive. In my case I created an image file so I can run fsck directly against the file:

```
sudo fsck -y /mnt/recovery/sda1_image.img
```

I'm presuming I will run across errors on the file system so I added the -y option so fsck will go ahead and attempt to repair all of the errors without prompting me.

Mount the Image

Once the fsck has completed now I can attempt to mount the file system and recover my important files. In the case you imaged to a complete hard drive and want to try to boot from it, after you fsck each partition you would try to mount them individually and see if you can read from them and then swap the drive into your original computer and try to boot from it. In my example I just want to try to recover some important files from this image so I would mount the image file loopback:

```
sudo mount -o loop /mnt/recovery/sda1_image.img /mnt/image
```

Now I can browse through /mnt/image and hope that my important files weren't among the corrupted blocks.

Method of Last Resort

Unfortunately in some cases a hard drive has far too many errors for fsck to correct. In these cases you might not even be able to mount the file system at all. If this happens you aren't necessarily completely out of luck. Depending on what type of files you want to recover, you may be able to pull the information you need directly from the image. If, for instance, you have a critical term paper or other document you need to retrieve from the machine, just run the strings command on the image and output to a second file:

```
sudo strings /mnt/recovery/sda1_image.img > /mnt/recovery/sda1_strings.txt
```

The sda1_strings.txt file will contain all of the text from the image (which might turn out to be a lot of data) from man page entries to config files to output within program binaries. It's a lot of data to sift through but if you know a keyword in your term paper, you can open up this text file in less and then hit the / key and type your keyword in and see if it can be found. Alternatively you can grep through the strings file for your keyword and the surrounding lines. For instance if you were writing a term paper on dolphins you could run:

```
sudo grep -C 1000 dolphin /mnt/recovery/sda1_strings.txt >
↪ /mnt/recovery/dolphin_paper.txt
```

This would not only pull out any lines containing the word dolphin, it would also pull out the surrounding 1000 lines. Then you can just browse through the dolphin_paper.txt file and remove lines that aren't part of your paper. You might even need to tweak the -C argument in grep so that it grabs even more lines.

In conclusion, when your hard drive starts to make funny noises and won't mount, it isn't necessarily the end of the world. While ddrescue is no replacement for a good, tested backup, it can still save the day when disaster strikes your hard drive. Also note that ddrescue will work on just about any device, so you can use it to attempt recovery on those scratched CD-ROM discs too.

5.10 Recover the Master Boot Record

I have to admit that I've learned more about how Linux works by breaking it and fixing it, than I have any other way. There really is nothing quite like the prospect of losing valuable data, or the idea that your only computer won't boot, to motivate you to learn more about your system. In this section I discuss a surprisingly small part of your computer that plays a surprisingly large role in booting and using it–The Master Boot Record, or MBR for short. I will cover some of my favorite ways to destroy your MBR and a few ways to restore it once you have.

5.10 Recover the Master Boot Record

> **Note:** This section on recovering the Master Boot Record is no longer applicable to many modern computers that have migrated to the GUID Partition Table (GPT) partitioning scheme. However you could adapt it to attempt to backup and recover GPT partitions by researching and adapting the byte sizes and locations of GPT to the below MBR instructions.

Before you can fully understand how to restore the MBR you should have a good idea of what it actually is. The MBR comprises the first 512 bytes of a hard drive. Now that's *bytes*, not megabytes or even kilobytes. In our terabyte age it's hard to really appreciate how small that is, but to give you an idea, you could already fit about three MBRs at this point in this section, if this were plain text.

This 512-byte space is then split up into two smaller sections. The first 446 bytes of the MBR contains the boot code–code like the first stage of grub that allows you to load an operating system. The final 66 bytes contains a 64-byte partition table and a 2 byte signature at the very end. That partition table is full of information about the primary and extended partitions on a disk such as at which cylinder they start, at which cylinder they end, what type of partition they are, and other useful data that you typically don't think much about after a disk is set up, at least until it's gone.

A Routine Lecture on Backups

This is the part of the section where I repeat some of the best disaster recovery device I know–make backups. In this case we are talking about MBR disasters so here are a few ways to backup your MBR. After all, it's 512 bytes, there's no reason why you can't afford to back it up. Heck, it's small enough to tattoo on your arm, except I guarantee once you do you'll end up migrating to a new system or changing the partition layout.

The best tool to back up the MBR is coincidentally the best tool at destroying it (more on that later): dd. In fact, dd is one of those ancient, powerful, and blunt Unix tools that blindly does whatever you tell it to and it's adept at destroying all sorts of valuable data (more precisely, it's adept at following your explicit orders to destroy your valuable data). The following command will back up the MBR on the /dev/sda disk to a file named mbr_backup:

```
sudo dd if=/dev/sda of=mbr_backup bs=512 count=1
```

Basically this tells dd to read from /dev/sda 512 bytes at a time and output the result into mbr_backup, but to only do one 512-byte read. Now you can copy mbr_backup to another system, or print it out and tattoo it on your arm. Later on if you were to wipe out your MBR you could restore it (likely from some sort of rescue disk) with a slight twist on the above command, just swap the input and output sources:

```
sudo dd if=mbr_backup of=/dev/sda bs=512 count=1
```

More Than One Way to Skin an MBR

There are a number of elaborate ways you can destroy some or all of your MBR. Please be careful with this first command. It will actually delete your MBR at the very least, and with a typo could potentially delete the entire disk, so step lightly. Let's start with the most blunt, dd:

```
sudo dd if=/dev/zero of=/dev/sda bs=512 count=1
```

This command will basically blank out your MBR by overwriting it with zeroes. Now unless you are masochistic, or you were like me and used this in a demonstration of MBR recovery tools, you probably wouldn't ever run this command. Most people end up destroying part of their MBR in one of two ways: mistakes with boot loaders and mistakes with fdisk or other partitioning tools.

Mistakes with partitioning tools are probably the most common way people break their MBR, or more specifically, their partition table. It could be that you ran fdisk on sda when you mean to run it on sdb. It could be that you just made a mistake when resizing a partition and after a reboot it won't mount. The important thing to keep in mind is that when you use partitioning tools, they typically only update the partition table on the drive. Even if you resize a drive, unless you tell a partitioning tool to reformat the drive with a fresh file system, the actual data on the drive doesn't change. All that has changed is that 64 bytes at the beginning of the drive that says where the partitions begin and end. So if you make a partitioning mistake, your data is fine. You just have to reconstruct that partition table.

It would figure that the first time I really destroyed my MBR, it was through the second, less common way–mistakes with boot loaders. In my case it was a number of years ago and I was struggling to get an early version of grub installed on a disk. After the standard command line commands didn't work, I had the bright idea that maybe I could use the grub boot floppy image. After all, it was 512 bytes and so was my MBR, right? Well, it sort of worked. GRUB did appear, however what I didn't realize was that in addition to writing grub over the first 446 bytes of my MBR, I also wrote over the last 66 bytes–my partition table. So while GRUB worked it didn't see any partitions on the drive.

Guessing Games Fix a Partition Table

I had at least used Linux long enough that after I made my mistake, I realized that my actual data was still there and that there *must* be some way to restore the partition table. This was when I first came across the wonderful tool called gpart.

5.10 Recover the Master Boot Record

Gpart is short for Guess Partition and that is exactly what it does. When you run the gpart command, it will scan through a disk looking for signs of partitions. If it finds what appears to be the beginning of a Windows FAT32 partition, for instance, it jots it down and continues until eventually it sees what appears to be the end. Once the tool has scanned the entire drive it will output its results to the screen for you to check and edit. It can also optionally write this reconstructed partition table back to the disk.

Gpart has been around for quite some time and is packaged by all of the major distributions, so you should be able to install it with your standard package manager. Don't confuse it with gparted, which is a graphical partitioning tool. Of course if your main system is the one with the problem you will need to find a rescue disk that has it. Knoppix and a number of other rescue-focused disks all include gpart out of the box.

To use gpart, run it with root privileges and give it the disk device to scan as an argument. Here's gpart's output from a scan of my laptop's drive:

```
sudo gpart /dev/sda
```

```
Begin scan...
Possible partition(Linux ext2), size(9773mb), offset(0mb)
Possible partition(Linux swap), size(980mb), offset(9773mb)
Possible partition(SGI XFS filesystem), size(20463mb), offset(10754mb)
End scan.

Checking partitions...
Partition(Linux ext2 filesystem): primary
Partition(Linux swap or Solaris/x86): primary
Partition(Linux ext2 filesystem): primary
Ok.
Guessed primary partition table:
Primary partition(1)
   type: 131(0x83)(Linux ext2 filesystem)
   size: 9773mb #s(20016920) s(63-20016982)
   chs:  (0/1/1)-(1023/254/63)d (0/1/1)-(1245/254/56)r

Primary partition(2)
   type: 130(0x82)(Linux swap or Solaris/x86)
   size: 980mb #s(2008120) s(20016990-22025109)
   chs:  (1023/254/63)-(1023/254/63)d (1246/0/1)-(1370/254/58)r

Primary partition(3)
   type: 131(0x83)(Linux ext2 filesystem)
   size: 20463mb #s(41909120) s(22025115-63934234)
   chs:  (1023/254/63)-(1023/254/63)d (1371/0/1)-(3979/184/8)r

Primary partition(4)
   type: 000(0x00)(unused)
   size: 0mb #s(0) s(0-0)
   chs:  (0/0/0)-(0/0/0)d (0/0/0)-(0/0/0)r
```

To hammer home the point about how easy it is to backup the MBR, now I have an extra backup of my laptop partition table–on this page.

As you can see it correctly identified the two primary partitions (/ and /home) and the swap partition on my laptop and noted that the fourth primary partition was unused. Now after reviewing this if I decided that I wanted gpart to write its data to the drive I would run:

```
sudo gpart -W /dev/sda /dev/sda
```

That isn't a typo, the -W argument tells gpart which disk to write the partition table to, but you still need to tell it which drive to scan. Gpart could potentially scan one drive and write the partition table to another. Once you specify the -W option gpart will give you some warnings to accept but it will also prompt you to edit the results from within gpart itself. Personally I've always found it a bit more difficult to do it that way than it needs to be so I skip the editor, have it write to the disk, and then use a tool like fdisk or cfdisk to examine the drive afterwards and make tweaks if necessary.

Gpart Limitations

Gpart is a great tool and has saved me a number of times, but it does have some limitations. For one, while gpart works very well with primary partitions, it is much more difficult for it to locate extended partitions depending on which tool actually created them. Secondly, take gpart results with a grain of salt. It does its best to reconstruct drives but always give its results a sanity check. For instance I've seen where it has identified the end of a partition one or two megabytes short from the actual end. Typically when we partition drives we put one partition immediately after another so these sorts of errors are pretty easy to find.

Reload the Boot Code

Now if you have only destroyed the partition table, then you should hopefully be restored at this point. If you managed to destroy the boot code as well, then you will need to restore it, too. Most Linux distributions use grub, so with your restored partition table, if you are currently booted into the affected system run:

```
sudo grub-install -recheck /dev/sda
```

Replace /dev/sda with the path to your primary boot device. If you use an Ubuntu system you could optionally use the update-grub tool instead. If you are currently booted into a rescue disk, then you will first need to mount your root partition at say /mnt/sda1 and then use chroot to run grub-install within it:

```
sudo mkdir /mnt/sda1
sudo mount /dev/sda1 /mnt/sda1
sudo chroot /mnt/sda1 /usr/sbin/grub-install -recheck /dev/sda
```

If the chrooted grub-install doesn't work you can typically use your rescue disk's grub-install with the --root-directory option:

```
sudo /usr/sbin/grub-install -recheck -root-directory /mnt/sda1 /dev/sda
```

Well hopefully if you didn't have a profound respect for those 512 bytes at the beginning of your hard drive, you do now. If not, don't worry, the MBR is like many things in life that you don't miss until they are gone. At least in this case, when it's gone, you might be able to bring it back.

5.11 Restoring Deleted Files

There are some commands on the command line so blunt, so potentially devastating, that every time I use them I pause for a moment before I press Enter. Of course as useful as dd is, I don't use it every single day so even though I approach the command with reverence, you might argue it doesn't compare to the true master of data destruction: rm. True, dd can wipe out your hard drive in a few short keystrokes, but nothing really matches the compact destructive power of rm -rf /.

True, most people aren't bitten by that version of the command. Usually it's its more sinister brother, rm -rf ./ run from the wrong directory. The scene plays out something like this:

```
rm -rf ./
*clicking noises from the hard drive*
"Hmm, that's taking longer than I tho...HEY!"
CTRL-C CTRL-C CTRL-C
```

It's too late. By the time you noticed you ran that command in the wrong terminal, half of your home directory is gone. Now when I started out with Linux, I was always told in true Unix form that when you rm a file, it is gone and there is no way you can get it back. Undelete commands were for DOS users anyway—we Linux users knew better, right? Well it turns out we don't. Most Linux users I know have deleted the wrong files at least once in their life. Now the best protection against this is a backup (noticing a common thread in this series?), but if you don't have a backup you aren't completely without hope. Everything you might have been told about the rm command isn't entirely true, and by the end of this section you'll find that Linux does have an undelete of sorts.

Free Space Isn't Free

To understand how to recover a deleted file, it's important to understand what rm does. When rm deletes a file, it essentially adds those blocks to the available free space on that file system. Unless you use a tool like shred, the data in those blocks stays intact until another file overwrites them. Blocks aren't reused in any date order, so some freed blocks might stay on the system for days, weeks, or even years before they are reallocated to a new file while others could be reused almost immediately.

Since a Linux system writes files constantly, time is against you when you accidentally delete a file. The first thing you should do if you delete important files is to unmount that file system. If you can't easily unmount the file system then shut down the system or if the files are extra important you might even pull the plug to ensure no other files are written to disk.

Forensics to the Rescue

It turns out that accident-prone Linux users aren't the only ones who want to recover deleted files. In fact, deleted file recovery is particularly useful for forensics, since an attacker might try to delete files to cover his tracks. Forensics tools work with the file system on a low level as it is, since they try to gather data traditional tools might miss.

To recover deleted files, you will need to install sleuthkit. Most distributions offer it as a package or otherwise you can download the source from the project's website. It may go without saying, but *don't install sleuthkit on the file system you are recovering!* If you need to recover files from the root file system this may mean you have to take the hard drive to a second system or use a rescue disk like Kali that includes sleuthkit.

Once you have sleuthkit installed you will need to get a second disk that is large enough to store any files you want to recover. Unlike some other recovery methods with sleuthkit you don't have to create a complete image of the free space so you won't need nearly as much storage. You can use the df tool to see how much free space you have:

```
df -h
Filesystem          Size  Used Avail Use% Mounted on
/dev/sda1           9.4G  7.0G  2.0G  79% /
/dev/sda3            20G   17G  3.6G  83% /home
```

In this case I have around 2Gb of space on my / partition and 3.6Gb in /home to restore files to. For this example let's assume I have connected the recovery file system to this machine and it has shown up as /dev/sda1. Be sure to not mount this file system, or if your machine automatically mounted it be sure to unmount it before you continue, so you won't accidentally write to it. Since /home has more free space I will recover to it so I create a directory to store the recovered files and then use the sleuthkit fls (forensic ls) command to create a list of all of the deleted files it can find on /dev/sda1:

```
mkdir   /recovery
sudo fls -f ext -d -r -p /dev/sdb1 >  /recovery/deleted_files.txt
```

This command might take some time, depending on how much free space it has to pore through. In the mean time we can discuss what these different arguments mean. The fls man page goes into more detail, but the -f argument specifies what file system fls is scanning (ext is used for ext2 and ext3). If you are unsure what value to use, type `fls -f list` to see a complete list of file systems.

5.11 Restoring Deleted Files

By default fls can list all of the files on a particular file system but when you specify -d, it will only list deleted ones. The -r option turns on recursion so it will traverse all directories it finds, and the -p option will output the full path to each file. Without -p if multiple files have the same name it might be difficult to tell them apart. Finally you list the partition you want fls to scan.

Once fls completes, you can open /recovery/deleted_files.txt to see a complete list of all of the deleted files on the file system. It will look something like:

```
d/d * 944680:    home/kyle/.mutt
r/r * 943542:    home/kyle/.muttrc
r/r * 910452:    home/kyle/may_lj_article.txt
```

The first field tells you whether the file is a directory (d/d) or a regular file (r/r). Next is an inode number for the file and then finally you see the path to the file. Let's say for this example that I want to recover the /home/kyle/may_lj_article.txt file. I would then use the sleuthkit icat tool to recover it. The icat program is a special version of cat that takes inodes as arguments. In this case I would specify the inode 910452:

```
sudo icat -f ext -r -s /dev/sdb1 910452 > /recovery/may_lj_article.txt
```

Like with fls this might take some time to complete. You can read about all of its arguments in the icat man page but here I use -f to specify the file system type like with fls. The -r option tells icat to go into a special recovery mode it uses for deleted files. The -s option will cause icat to output the full contents of any sparse files it finds. Finally I specify the partition to recover from and the inode to recover. Once the command completes I can open /recovery/may_lj_article.txt and see if it was able to restore it.

This method works fine when you only need to recover a few files, but what if you need to recover hundreds? Well if you search online you will find a number of different shell scripts people have written to automatically recover all deleted files from fls output. Below is one I originally found on the Gentoo forums[1] and then improved it a bit:

```
#!/bin/bash

DISK=/dev/sdb1 # disk to scan
RESTOREDIR=/home/kyle/recovery # directory to restore to

mkdir -p "$RESTOREDIR"
cat $1 |
while read line; do
    filetype=`echo "$line" | awk '{print $1}'`
    filenode=`echo "$line" | awk '{print $3}'`
    filenode=${filenode%:}
    filenode=${filenode%(*}
    filename=`echo "$line" | cut -f 2`
```

[1] http://forums.gentoo.org/viewtopic-t-365703.html

```
        echo "$filename"
        if [ $filetype == "d/d" ]; then
            mkdir -p "$RESTOREDIR/$filename"
        else
            mkdir -p "$RESTOREDIR/`dirname $filename`"
            icat -f ext -r -s "$DISK" "$filenode" > "$RESTOREDIR/$filename"
        fi
done
```

Save this script under /usr/local/bin/restore. To use this script, replace the **DISK** and **RESTOREDIR** variables at the top of the script so they match your environment, give it executable permissions, then run it with the fls output you created before as an argument. All of your recovered files will be wherever you set **RESTOREDIR** nested within their parent directories.

```
sudo chmod a+x /usr/local/bin/restore
sudo /usr/local/bin/restore   /recovery/deleted_files.txt
```

Now don't let this get you too comfortable with rm–there's no guarantee a particular file will be complete or even recovered at all. I still say the best policy is to have backups followed by a thoughtful pause before you hit Enter on any recursive rm command.

A. My Favorite Infrastructure

Working at a startup has many pros and cons, but one of the main benefits over a traditional established company is that a startup often gives you an opportunity to build a completely new infrastructure from the ground up. When you work on a new project at an established company, you typically have to account for legacy systems and design choices that were made for you, often before you even got to the company. Yet at a startup you are often presented with a truly blank slate: no pre-existing infrastructure, no existing design choices to factor in.

Brand new, from-scratch infrastructure is a particularly appealing prospect if you are at a Systems Architect level. One of the distinctions between a senior-level systems administrator and architect level is that you have been operating at a senior level long enough that you have managed a number of different high-level projects personally and have seen which approaches work and which approaches don't. When you are this level, it's very exciting to be able to build a brand new infrastructure from scratch according to all of the lessons you've learned from past efforts without having to support any legacy infrastructure.

Over the last decade I've worked at a few different startups where I was asked to develop new infrastructure completely from scratch but with high security, uptime and compliance requirements so there was no pressure to cut corners for speed like you might normally face at a startup. I've not only gotten to realize the joy of designing new infrastructure, I've been able to do it multiple times. Each time I've been able to bring along all of the past designs that worked while leaving behind the bits that didn't all the while updating all of the tools to take advantage of new features. This series of infrastructure designs culminated in what I realize looking back on it, is my favorite infrastructure–the gold standard on which I will judge all future attempts.

In this section I'm going to dig into some of the details of my favorite infrastructure. I will describe some of the constraints around the design and then explore how each part of the infrastructure fits together, why I made the design decisions I did, and how it all worked. I'm not saying that what worked for me will work for you, but hopefully you can take some inspiration from my approach and adapt it for your needs.

Constraints

Whenever you describe a solution you think works well, it's important to preface it with your design constraints. Often when people are looking for infrastructure cues, the first place they look is how "big tech companies" do it. The problem with that approach is that unless you are also a big tech company (and even if you are) your constraints are likely very different from theirs. What works for them with their budget, human resources, and the problems they are trying to solve very likely won't work for you unless you are very much like them.

Also, the larger an organization gets, the more likely they are going to solve problems in-house instead of using off-the-shelf solutions. There is a certain stage in the growth of a tech company, where they have enough developers on staff that when they have a new problem to solve, they will likely use their army of developers to create a custom, proprietary tools just for them instead of using something off the shelf–even if the off-the-shelf solution gets them 90% there. This is a shame because if all of these large tech companies put that effort into improving existing tools and sharing their changes, we would all spend less time reinventing wheels. If you've ever interviewed someone who has spent a long time at a large tech company, you quickly realize that they are really well trained to administer that specific infrastructure, but without those custom tools, many of them have a hard time working anywhere else.

Startup constraints are also very different from large company constraints so it might equally be a mistake to apply solutions that work for a small startup to a large-scale company. Startups typically have very small teams but also need to build infrastructure very quickly. Mistakes that make their way to production often have a low impact on startups. They are most concerned about getting some kind of functioning product out to attract more investment before they run out of money. This means that startups are more likely to favor not only off-the-shelf solutions, but cutting corners.

All that to say, what worked for me under my constraints might not work for you under your constraints. So before I dig into details, you should understand the constraints I was working under:

Constraint 1: Seed Round Financial Startup

This infrastructure was built for a startup that was developing a web application in the financial space. We had limitations both on the amount of time we could spend on building the infrastructure and the size of the team we had available to build it. In many cases there were single-member teams. In previous iterations of building my ideal infrastructure I had a team of at least one other person if not multiple people to help me build out the infrastructure, but here I was on my own.

The combination of a time constraint along with the fact that I was doing this alone meant I was much more likely to pick stable solutions that worked for me in the past using technologies I was deeply familiar with. In particular I put heavy emphasis on automation so I could multiply my efforts. There is a kind of momentum you can build when you use configuration management and orchestration in the right way.

Constraint 2: Non-sysadmin Emergency Escalation

I was largely on my own not just to build the infrastructure, but also when it came to managing emergencies. Normally I try to stick to a rule that limits production access to systems administrators, but in this case that would mean we would have no redundancy in case I was unavailable. This constraint meant that in the event I was unavailable for whatever reason, alerts needed to escalate up to someone who primarily had a developer background with only some Linux server experience. Because of this, I had to make sure that it was relatively straightforward to respond to the most common types of emergencies.

Constraint 3: PCI Compliance

I love the combination of from-scratch infrastructure development you get to do in a startup, with tight security constraints that prevent you from cutting corners. A lot of people in the security space look down a bit on PCI compliance, because so many companies think of it as a box to check and hire firms known for checking that box with minimal fuss. However, there are a lot of good practices within PCI-DSS if you treat them as a minimum security bar to manage honestly, instead of a maximum security bar to skirt by. We had a hard dependency on PCI compliance and so meeting and exceeding that policy had some of the greatest impact on the design.

Constraint 4: Custom Rails Web Applications

The development team had a strong background in Rails and so most of the in-house software development was for custom middleware applications based on a standard database-backed Rails application stack. There are a number of different approaches for packaging and distributing this kind of application and so this also factored into the design.

Constraint 5: Minimal Vendor Lock-in

It's somewhat common for venture capital-backed startups to receive credits from cloud providers to help them get started. It not only helps startups manage costs while they are trying to figure out their infrastructure, if the startup manages to use cloud-specific features it has the side benefit of making it harder for the startup to move to a different provider down the road once they have larger cloud bills.

Our startup had credits with more than one cloud provider and so we wanted the option to switch over to another provider in case we were cash-strapped when we ran out of credits. This meant that our infrastructure must be designed for portability and use as few cloud-specific features as possible. The cloud-specific features we did use needed to be abstracted away and easily identified so we could port them to another provider more easily later.

Architecture

PCI policy pays a lot of attention to systems that manage sensitive cardholder data. These systems are labeled as "in scope" which means they must comply with PCI-DSS standards. This scope extends to systems that interact with these sensitive systems and there is a strong emphasis on compartmentation–separating and isolating the systems that are in scope from the rest of the systems so you can put tight controls on their network access including which administrators can access them and how.

Our architecture started with a strict separation between development and production environments. In a traditional data center this might be accomplished by using separate physical network and server equipment (or using abstractions to virtualize this separation). In the case of cloud providers one of the easiest, safest, and most portable ways to do this is by using completely separate accounts for each environment. In this way there's no risk that a misconfiguration would expose production to development and it has a side benefit of making it easy to calculate how much each environment is costing you per month.

When it came to the actual server architecture, we divided servers into individual roles and gave them generic role-based names. We then took advantage of the Virtual Private Cloud feature in Amazon Web Services to isolate each of these roles into its own subnet, so we could isolate each type of server from others and tightly control access between them.

By default, Virtual Private Cloud servers are either in the DMZ and have public IP addresses, or they only have internal addresses. We opted to put as few servers as possible in the DMZ and so most servers in the environment only had a private IP address. We intentionally did not set up a gateway server that routed all of these servers' traffic to the Internet–their isolation from the Internet was a feature!

Of course, some internal servers did need some Internet access. For those servers it was only to talk to a small number of external web services. We set up a series of HTTP proxies in the DMZ that handled different use cases and had strict whitelists in place. That way we could restrict Internet access from outside the host itself to just the sites it needed while also not having to worry about collecting lists of IP blocks for a particular service (particularly challenging these days since everyone uses cloud servers).

Fault Tolerance

Cloud services are often unreliable but it was critical that our services could scale and survive an outage on any one particular server. We started by using a minimum of three servers for every service, because fault tolerance systems designed for two systems tend to fall into a traditional primary/failover architecture that doesn't scale well past two. A design that could account for three servers could probably also accommodate four or six or more.

Cloud systems rely on virtualization to get the most out of bare metal, and so any servers you use aren't real physical machines, but instead some kind of virtual machine running alongside others on physical hardware. This presents a problem for fault tolerance: what happens if all of your redundant virtual machines end up on the same physical machine and that machine goes down?

To address this concern, some cloud vendors separate a particular site into multiple standalone data centers, each with its own hardware, power, and network that are independent from the others. In the case of Amazon these are called Availability Zones and it's considered a best practice to spread your redundant servers across Availability Zones. We decided to set up three Availability Zones and divided our redundant servers across them.

In our case we wanted to spread the servers out consistently and automatically so we divided our servers into threes based on the number at the end of their hostname. The software we used to spawn instances would look at the number in the hostname, apply a modulo three to it, and then use that to decide which Availability Zone a host would go to. Hosts like web1, web4 and web7 would be on one group; web2, web5 and web8 in another; and web3, web6 and web9 in a third zone.

When you have multiple servers, you also need some way for machines to fail over to a different server if one goes down. Some cloud providers offer in-house load balancing but because we needed portability we didn't want to rely on any cloud-specific features. While we could have added custom load balancing logic to our applications, instead we went with a more generic approach using the lightweight and fast haproxy service.

One approach to using haproxy would be to set up a load balancing server running haproxy and have applications talk to it on various ports. This would behave a lot like some of the cloud-provided load balancing services (or a load balancing appliance in a traditional data center). Of course if you use that approach you have another problem: what happens when the load balancer fails? For true fault tolerance you would need to set up multiple load balancers and then configure the hosts with their own load balancing logic so they could fail over to the redundant load balancer in the case of a fault, or otherwise rely on a traditional primary/secondary load balancer failover with a floating IP that would get assigned to whichever load balancer was active.

This traditional approach didn't work for us because we realized that there might be cases where one entire Availability Zone might be segregated from the rest of the network. We also didn't want to add additional failover logic to account for a load balancer outage. Instead, we realized that because haproxy was so lightweight (especially compared to the regular applications on the servers) we could just embed an haproxy instance on *every* server that needed to talk to another service redundantly. That haproxy instance would be aware of any downstream service that local server needed to talk to and present ports on localhost that represented each downstream service.

Here's how this worked in practice: if webappA needed to talk to middlewareB, it would just connect to localhost port 8001. Haproxy would take care of health checks for downstream services and if a service went down it would automatically connect to another. In that circumstance, webappA might see that its connection dropped, and would just need to reconnect. This meant that the only fault tolerance logic our applications needed was the ability to detect when a connection dropped and retry.

We also organized the haproxy configuration so that each host favored talking to a host within its own Availability Zone. Hosts in other zones were designated as "backup" hosts in haproxy so it would only use those hosts if the primary host was down. This helped optimize network traffic as it stayed within the Availability Zone it started with under normal circumstances. It also made analyzing traffic flows through the network much easier as we could assume that traffic that entered through frontend2 would get directed to middleware2 which would access database2. Since we made sure that traffic entering our network was distributed across our front-end servers, we could be assured that load was relatively evenly distributed, yet individual connections would tend to stick on the same set of servers throughout a particular request.

Finally, we needed to factor disaster recovery into our plans. To do this we created a complete disaster recovery environment in a completely separate geographic region than production that otherwise mimicked the servers and configuration in production. Based on our recovery timelines we could get away with syncing our databases every few hours and because these environments were independent of each other, we could test our disaster recovery procedure without impacting production.

Configuration Management

One of the most important things to get right in this infrastructure was the configuration management. Since I was building and maintaining everything largely by myself and had some tight timelines, the very first thing I focused on was a strong foundation of configuration management using Puppet. I had a lot of experience with Puppet over the years from before it was the mature and robust product it is today. Today though, I could take advantage of all of the high quality modules the Puppet community had written for common tasks to get a head start—why reinvent a Nginx configuration when the main Puppetlabs module worked did everything I needed already? One of the keys to this approach was making sure that we started with a basic vanilla image with no custom configuration on it and set it so that all configuration changes that turned a vanilla server into, say, a middleware app server was done through Puppet.

Another critical reason why I chose Puppet was precisely for the reason many people avoid it: the fact that the Puppetmaster can sign Puppet clients using TLS certificates. Many people hit a big roadblock when they try to set up Puppetmasters to sign clients and opt for a masterless setup instead. In my use case I would have been missing a great opportunity. I had a hard requirement that all communication over the cloud network be protected using TLS, and by having a Puppetmaster that signed hosts, I would get a trusted local Certificate Authority (the Puppetmaster) and have valid local and signed certificates on every host in my network for free!

Many people open themselves up to vulnerabilities when they enable autosigning on Puppet clients, yet having to manually sign new Puppet clients, particularly in a cloud instance, can be cumbersome. I took advantage of a feature within Puppet that lets you add custom valid headers into the Certificate Signing Request (CSR) the Puppet client would generate. I used a particular x509 header that was designed to embed a pre-shared key into the CSR. Then I used Puppet's ability to specify a custom autosigning script. This script then gets passed the client CSR and decides whether to sign it or not. In my script we inspected the CSR for the client's name and the pre-shared key. If they matched the values in the copy of that hostname/pre-shared key pair on the Puppetmaster, we signed it; otherwise we didn't.

This method worked because we spawned new hosts from the Puppetmaster itself. When spawning the host, the spawning script would generate a random value and store it in the Puppet client's configuration as a pre-shared key. It would also store a copy of that value in a local file named after the client hostname for the Puppetmaster autosign script to read. Since each pre-shared key was unique and used only for a particular host, once it was used we deleted that file.

To make configuring TLS on each server simple, I added a simple in-house Puppet module that let me copy the local Puppet client certificate and local

Certificate Authority certificate wherever I needed it for a particular service whether it was Nginx, haproxy, a local webapp or Postgres. Then I could enable TLS for all of my internal services knowing that they all had valid certificates they could use to trust each other.

I used the standard role/profile pattern to organize my Puppet modules and made sure that whenever I had a Puppet configuration that was based on AWS-specific features, I split that off into an AWS-specific module. That way if I needed to migrate to another cloud platform, I could easily identify which modules I'd need to rewrite.

All Puppet changes were stored in Git with the master branch acting as the production configuration and with additional branches for the other environments. In the development environment the Puppetmaster would automatically apply any changes that got pushed, but since that Git repository was hosted out of the development environment, we had a standing rule that no one should be able to directly change production from development. To enforce this rule, changes to the master branch would get synched to production Puppetmasters but never automatically applied–a sysadmin would need to login to production and explicitly push the change using our orchestration tool.

Orchestration

Puppet is great when you want to make sure that a certain set of servers all have the same changes as long as you don't want to apply changes in a particular order. Unfortunately there are a lot of changes you want to make to a system that follow a particular order. In particular when you perform software updates, you generally don't want them to arrive across your servers in a random order over thirty minutes. If there is a problem with the update you want the ability to stop the update process and in some environments roll back to the previous version. When people try to use Puppet for something it's not meant to do, they often get frustrated and blame Puppet when really they should be using Puppet for configuration management, but some other tool for orchestration.

In the era when I was building this environment, Mcollective was the most popular orchestration tool to pair with Puppet. Unlike some orchestration tools which are much closer to the SSH for loop scripts everyone used a few decades ago, Mcollective has a strong security model where the sysadmin is restricted to a limited set of commands within modules they have enabled ahead of time. Every command runs in parallel across the environment and so it's very fast to push changes whether it's to one host or every host.

The Mcollective client doesn't have SSH access to hosts–instead it signs each command it issues and pushes it to a job queue. Each server checks that queue for commands intended for it and validates the signature before it executes it. In this way, compromising the host the Mcollective client runs on doesn't give you remote SSH root access to the rest of the environment–it only gives you access to the restricted set of commands you have enabled.

We used our bastion host as command central for Mcollective and the goal was to remove the need for sysadmin to have to log into individual servers to an absolute minimum. To start, we wanted to make sure that all of the common sysadmin tasks could be performed using Mcollective on the bastion host. Mcollective already contains modules that let you query the hosts on your network that match particular patterns and pull down facts about them such as what version a particular software package is.

The great thing about Mcollective commands is that it lets you build a library of individual modules for particular purposes that you can then chain together in scripts for common workflows. I've written in the past[1] [2] about how you can use Mcollective to write effective orchestration scripts and this was an environment where it really shined.

Let's take one of the most common sysadmin tasks: updating software. Because Mcollective already had modules in place to query and update packages using the native package manager, we packaged all of our in-house tools as Debian packages as well and put them in internal package repositories. To update an in-house middleware package, a sysadmin would normally perform the following series of steps by hand:

- Get a list of servers that run that software
- Start with the first server in the list
- Set a maintenance mode in monitoring for that server
- Tell any load balancers to move traffic away from the server
- Stop the service
- Update the software
- Confirm the software is at the correct version
- Start the service
- Test the service
- Tell any load balancers to move traffic back to the server
- End the maintenance mode
- Repeat for the rest of the hosts

All I did was to take each of the above steps and make sure there was a corresponding Mcollective command for it. Most of the steps already had built-in Mcollective plugins for them, but in a few cases, such as for the load balancers, I wrote a simple Mcollective plugin for haproxy that would control the load balancers. Remember, many of the servers in the environment had their own embedded haproxy instance, but because Mcollective runs in parallel, I could tell them all to redirect traffic at the same time.

Once each of these steps could be done with Mcollective, the next step was to combine them all into a single generic script to deploy an application. I

---

[1] https://www.linuxjournal.com/content/orchestration-mcollective
[2] https://www.linuxjournal.com/content/orchestration-mcollective-part-ii

also added appropriate checks at each of the stages so that in the event of an error, the script would stop and exit with a descriptive error. In the development environment we automatically pushed out updates once they passed all of their tests, so I also made sure that our continuous integration server (we used Jenkins) used this same script to deploy our app updates for dev. That way I could be sure that the script was being tested all the time and could stage improvements there first.

Having a single script that would automate all of these steps for a single app was great, but the reality is that a modern Service Oriented Architecture has many of these little apps. You rarely deploy one at a time, and instead you have a production release that might contain five or more apps, each with their own versions. After doing this by hand a few times I realized there was room to automate this as well.

The first step in automating production releases was to provide a production manifest my script could use to tell it what to do. A production manifest lists all of the different software a particular release will have and which versions you will use. In well-organized companies this sort of thing will get tracked in your ticketing system so you can have proper approval and visibility into what software went to production when–this is especially handy if you have a problem later on because you can more easily answer the question "what changed?"

I decided to make the right approach the easy approach and use our actual production manifest ticket as input for the script. That meant that if you wanted an automated production release, the first step was to create a properly-formatted ticket with an appropriate title and containing a bulleted list of each piece of software you want to deploy and which version you intend on deploying in the order you want them to be deployed. You would then log into production (thereby proving you were authorized to perform production changes), and run the production deploy script which would take as input the specific ticket number it should read. It would perform the following steps:

- Parse the ticket and prompt the sysadmin with the list of packages it will deploy as a sanity check and don't proceed until the sysadmin says yes
- Post a message in group chat alerting the team that a production release is starting, using the ticket title as a description
- Update the local package repository mirrors so they have the latest version of the software
- For each app:
    - Notify group chat that the app is being updated
    - Run the app deployment automation script
    - Notify group chat that the app updated successfully
- Once all apps have been updated successfully, notify group chat
- Email the log of all updates to a sysadmin alias and also as a comment to the ticket

Like with the individual app deploy script, if there were any errors we would immediately abort the script and send alerts with full logs to email, chat, and in the ticket itself so we could investigate what went wrong. We would perform deployments first in a hot disaster recovery environment located in a separate region, and if it succeeded, in production as well. Once the script successfully worked in production, the script was smart enough to close the ticket. In the end, performing a production deployment whether you wanted to update one app or ten involved the following steps:
- Create a properly-formatted ticket
- Login to the disaster recovery environment and run the production deploy script
- Login to the production environment and run the production deploy script

The automation made the process so easy, that production deploys were relatively painless while still following all of our best practices. This meant when I went on vacation or were otherwise unavailable, even though I was the only sysadmin on the team, my boss with a strong development background could easily take over production deployments. The consistent logging and notifications also made it so that everyone was on the same page, and we had a nice audit trail for every software change in production.

I also automated the disaster recovery procedure. You've only really backed something up if you've tested recovery. I set as a goal to test our disaster recovery procedure quarterly, although in practice I actually did it monthly because it was useful to have fresh data in the disaster recovery environment so we could better catch any data-driven bugs in our software updates before they hit production. Compared to many environments this is a much more frequent test, but I was able to do it because I wrote Mcollective modules that would restore the disaster recovery databases from backup and then wrapped the whole thing in a master script that turned it all into a single command that would log the results into a ticket so I could keep track of each time I restored the environment.

Security

We had very tight security requirements for our environment that started (but didn't end) with PCI-DSS compliance. This meant that all network communication between services was encrypted using TLS (and the handy internal certificate authority Puppet provided), and all sensitive data was stored on disks that were encrypted at rest. It also meant that each server generally performed only one role.

Most of the environment was isolated from the Internet, and we went further to define ingress and egress firewall rules both on each host and enforced them in Amazon's security groups. We started with a "deny by default" approach and only opened up ports between services when they were absolutely necessary. As also employed the "principle of least privilege" so only a few employees had production access and we developers did not have access to the bastion host.

Each environment had its own VPN so to access anything but public-facing services you started by connecting to a VPN that was protected with two-factor authentication. From there you could access the web interfaces for our log aggregation server and other monitoring and trending dashboards. To login to any particular server, you first had to SSH into a bastion host, which only accepted SSH keys and also required its own two-factor authentication. It was the only host that was allowed access to the SSH ports on other machines, but generally we used orchestration scripts whenever possible so we didn't have to go further than the bastion host to administer production.

Each host had its own Host-based Intrusion Detection System (HIDS) using ossec which not only would alert on suspicious activity on a server, it would also parse through logs looking for suspicious activity. We also used OpenVAS to perform routine network vulnerability scans across the environment.

To manage secrets, we used Puppet's hiera-eyaml module which allows you to store a hierarchy of key:value pairs in encrypted form. Each environment's Puppetmaster had its own GPG key it could use to decrypt these secrets so we could push development or production secrets to the same Git repository, but because these files were encrypted for different recipients, development Puppetmasters couldn't view production secrets and production Puppetmasters couldn't view development secrets. The nice thing about hiera is that it allowed you to combine plain text and encrypted configuration files and very carefully define which secrets would be available to which class of hosts. The clients would never be able to access secrets unless the Puppetmaster allowed them.

Data that was sent between production and the disaster recovery environment was GPG-encrypted with a key in the disaster recovery environment and also used an encrypted transport between the environments. The disaster recovery test script did all the heavy lifting required to decrypt backups and apply them so the administrator didn't have to deal with them. All of these keys were stored in Puppet's hiera-eyaml module so we didn't have to worry about losing them in the event a host went down.

Conclusion

While I covered a lot of ground in this infrastructure write-up, I still only covered a lot of the higher-level details. For instance, deploying a fault tolerant, scalable Postgres database could be an section all by itself. I also didn't talk much about the extensive documentation I wrote that, much like my articles in Linux Journal, walked the reader through how to use all of these tools we built.

As I mentioned in the beginning of the section, this is only an example of an infrastructure design that I found worked well for me with my constraints. Your constraints might be different and might lead to a different design. The goal with this section is just to provide you with one approach that I found worked well so you might be inspired to adapt it to your own needs.

Index

A

Alerts 19
    emergency contacts 30
    escalations 23
    holidays 25
    on-call rotation 24
    paging 21
apt command
    alternative to apt-get 56
at command
    compared to cron 41
    example usage 41
Automation 9

B

Backups
    migrate data to new drive .. 98

C

Command alternatives
    apt-get and apt 56
command alternatives
    ifconfig and ip 57
    netstat and ss 57
    nslookup and dig 56
    telnet and nc 57
cpio command
    to migrate data 99

D

dd command
    backup MBR 161
    progress bar 57
ddrescue command 157
dhclient command
    dynamic DNS 150
dig command
    alternative to nslookup 56
    get TXT records 52
DNS
    authoritative configuration . 70
    recursive configuration 69
    recursive vs. caching 68

TXT records 51
du command
    troubleshoot disk space . . . 153

E

Email server
    configure postfix 75
ethtool command
    troubleshooting ethernet . . 133
expect command 97

F

Filesystem Hierarchy Standard . . 36
find command
    to migrate data 99
flock command 59
fls command
    list deleted files 166
fsck command
    repair disk image 159

G

glusterfs
    client configuration 81
    nginx cluster 82
    server configuration 79
gpart command
    restore partition table 162
grub-install command
    restore boot code 164

I

icat command
    recover inodes 167
ifconfig command
    test local network 135
iftop command 46

IMAP
    authentication command . . . 96
    query mailboxes 96
iostat command
    troubleshooting load 131
ip command
    alternative to ifconfig 57
iptables command
    port forwarding 66

K

KVM troubleshooting 86

L

ls command
    troubleshoot disk space . . . 152

M

Master Boot Record
    definition 161
    recovering 160
motd file 49
mount command
    image file 159

N

nc command
    alternative to telnet 57
Nginx
    cluster with glusterfs 82
nmap command
    troubleshoot open ports . . . 137
nslookup command
    troubleshoot DNS 139

P

Patch management 17

INDEX

ping command
    troubleshoot hosts 139
postfix
    configure 75
    configure secondary MX ... 92
    relay_domains option 93

R

rm command
    how it works 165
route command
    troubleshoot gateway 138
    troubleshooting routing ... 135
rsync command
    sync live VMs 89

S

sar command 146
    CPU statistics 147
    disk statistics 148
    RAM statistics 148
    retrieve past data 149
sleuthkit 166
sort command
    files by size 44
    numbers 43
    removing duplicates 45
ss command
    alternative to netstat 57
strings command
    file recovery 160
Sysadmin titles 3

T

tcptraceroute command
    traceroute alternative 141
Telecommuting 33
telnet command
    for troubleshooting 143
    send email 145
    troubleshoot HTTP 144
    troubleshoot open ports ... 136
Ticketing 13
    managing and organizing .. 16
top command
    troubleshooting load 128
traceroute command
    test DNS routing 140
    test internet routing 142
Troubleshooting
    CPU load 129
    deleted files 165
    DNS 139
    DNS using traceroute 140
    full disks 152
    hard drive crashes 156
    high load 126
    Internet routing 142
    IO-bound load 131
    KVM 86
    local network 133
    Master Boot Record 160
    out of RAM 130
    ping command 139
    remote networks 138
    routing 135
    test gateway 138
    test open ports 136
    using ethtool 133
    using ifconfig 135
    using iostat 131
    using telnet 143
    using top 128

U

uniq command
    create tally 46

Acknowledgements

Many thanks to the Linux Journal team for all of their hard work on the magazine over the years. Special thanks to Jill who first invited me to write for Linux Journal after a meeting at Linux World Expo and who edited all of my articles for years, and to Carlie, who has encouraged and supported my writing both in and out of Linux Journal, including encouraging me to make this book.

www.ingramcontent.com/pod-product-compliance
Lightning Source LLC
Chambersburg PA
CBHW060843170526
45158CB00001B/224